International
Library of the
Philosophy of
Education

**Knowledge
and the
curriculum**

International
Library of the
Philosophy of
Education

General Editor

R. S. Peters

Professor of Philosophy of Education
Institute of Education
University of London

Knowledge and the curriculum

A collection of philosophical papers

Paul H. Hirst

Professor of Education
University of Cambridge

Routledge & Kegan Paul

London and Boston

First published in 1974
by Routledge & Kegan Paul Ltd
Broadway House, 68–74 Carter Lane,
London EC4V 5EL and
9 Park Street,
Boston, Mass. 02108, USA
Set in Monotype Baskerville
and printed in Great Britain by
Ebenezer Baylis and Son Ltd,
The Trinity Press, Worcester, and London
ISBN 0 7100 7929 X (C)
ISBN 0 7100 7930 3 (P)
Library of Congress Catalog Card No. 74-79359

Contents

General editor's note

There is a growing interest in philosophy of education amongst students of philosophy as well as amongst those who are more specifically and practically concerned with educational problems. Philosophers, of course, from the time of Plato onwards, have taken an interest in education and have dealt with education in the context of wider concerns about knowledge and the good life. But it is only quite recently in this country that philosophy of education has come to be conceived of as a specific branch of philosophy like the philosophy of science or political philosophy.

To call philosophy of education a specific branch of philosophy is not, however, to suggest that it is a distinct branch in the sense that it could exist apart from established branches of philosophy such as epistemology, ethics, and philosophy of mind. It would be more appropriate to conceive of it as drawing on established branches of philosophy and bringing them together in ways which are relevant to educational issues. In this respect the analogy with political philosophy would be a good one. Thus use can often be made of work that already exists in philosophy. In tackling, for instance, issues such as the rights of parents and children, punishment in schools, and the authority of the teacher, it is possible to draw on and develop work already done by philosophers on 'rights', 'punishment', and 'authority'. In other cases, however, no systematic work exists in the relevant branches of philosophy—e.g. on concepts such as 'education', 'teaching', 'learning', 'indoctrination'. So philosophers of education have had to break new ground—in these cases in the philosophy of mind. Work on educational issues can also bring to life and throw new light on long-standing problems in philosophy. Concentration, for instance, on the particular predicament of children can throw new light on problems of punishment and responsibility. G.E. Moore's old worries about what sorts of things are good in themselves can be brought to life by urgent questions about the justification of the curriculum in schools.

There is a danger in philosophy of education, as in any other applied field, of polarisation to one of two extremes. The work could be practically relevant but philosophically feeble, or it could be philosophically sophisticated but remote from practical problems.

The aim of the new International Library of the Philosophy of Education is to build up a body of fundamental work in this area which is both practically relevant and philosophically competent. For unless it achieves both types of objective it will fail to satisfy those for whom it is intended and fall short of the conception of philosophy of education which the International Library is meant to embody.

The writings of Paul Hirst, especially his 'Liberal education and the nature of knowledge', have been one of the most formative influences in the development of philosophy of education during the past ten years. There is a sense in which anyone working in the field has to take up some stand with regard to the 'forms of knowledge'.

There is, of course, little that is philosophically original in Hirst's general thesis that such distinct forms of knowledge exist. Indeed it is almost a stock-in-trade of the idealist tradition. Modern examples are Michael Oakeshott's *Experience and Its Modes*, John MacMurray's *Interpreting the Universe*, and R.G. Collingwood's *Speculum Mentis*. Historically speaking such works attempt to place the emergence of history, psychology, and the biological sciences on a map of knowledge, which has become much more complicated than that for which Kant tried to provide a rationale in his three critiques. This general thesis has support, too, from Wittgenstein's thesis about distinct 'language games'. Paul Hirst first came in contact with the thesis through Louis Arnaud Reid who 'discovered' him. Reid himself wrote a book called *Ways of Knowledge and Experience*.

What is distinctive about Paul Hirst's handling of the forms of knowledge is first his application of this general thesis in epistemology to problems of the school curriculum. Whitehead once said that philosophy never really recovered from the shock of Plato. My guess is that curriculum theory will never recover from the shock of Hirst. Second, there is Paul Hirst's great lucidity and intellectual power. He writes philosophy, like Spinoza, more mathematico.

Hirst himself would be the first to admit the number of fundamental unanswered epistemological questions to which his thesis gives rise. There is, for instance, the question of the type of concepts used to differentiate the forms. Is this a modern restatement of Kant's categories? Is the meaning criterion inseparable from the truth criterion? How widely is 'truth' to be understood? There are then fundamental ethical questions. First there is Herbert Spencer's question about which form of knowledge is most worth. Second, more justification is required than Hirst offers for introducing everyone into every form of knowledge. There is finally a justification required for the pursuit of knowledge itself. In a way, however, it is the incompleteness of Paul Hirst's work in relation to such fundamental questions that constitutes one of its main values to the philosophy of education. It should provide enough work for another generation.

In this book Paul Hirst has, for the first time, put together the various articles in which his views have been articulated. They should prove to be one of the most seminal points in the philosophy of education which it is the privilege of the International Library to publish.

R.S.P.

Preface

This collection of papers brings together in one volume a number of inter-related, yet wide ranging, articles that have up to now been available only in other collections or in various journals, some of them not readily accessible. It also contains three papers not previously published and two papers reconstructed, with additions, from material available elsewhere. As almost all the papers were written for isolated presentation, they are to a large extent self-contained. The price paid for this is that there is inevitably some overlap in content. To prevent undue duplication, the first two papers have been specially constructed for this collection drawing very heavily on four already published articles. Many of the ideas developed in the rest of this volume are to be found in embryo in the paper 'Liberal education and the nature of knowledge'. The full philosophical and educational ramifications of these ideas are, however, immense and quite beyond the scope of one volume of essays. This particular group of papers is thus presented not as a comprehensive and systematic survey of these ramifications, but rather as a series of reflections on certain philosophical issues, mostly first outlined in that one paper, which seem to me of considerable educational importance.

I am indebted to the many colleagues and students, both past and present, with whom I have discussed the ideas in these papers. To Professor Louis Arnaud Reid and Professor Richard Peters I owe a particular debt for the encouragement and intellectual stimulus they have always provided, not to mention their directly helpful comments on many philosophical and educational matters. My thanks are also due to my secretary, Miss Valerie Horler, for her patient deciphering of my handwriting and the preparation of the manuscript for the publishers.

P.H.H.

Acknowledgments

I am grateful to the editors and publishers who have granted permission for the reprinting of material previously published in their books and journals.

Chapters 1 and 2: material reprinted from 'The logic of the curriculum', *Journal of Curriculum Studies*, vol. 1 no. 2, 1969, 'The contribution of philosophy to the study of the curriculum', in J.F. Kerr (ed.), *Changing the Curriculum*, University of London Press, 1968, 'The curriculum', in *The Educational Implications of Social and Economic Change*, Part II, Schools Council Working Paper no. 12, HMSO, 1967, 'Towards a logic of curriculum development', in P.H. Taylor and J. Walton (eds), *The Curriculum: Research, Innovation and Change*, Ward Lock Educational, 1974. Chapter 3: reprinted from R.D. Archambault (ed.), *Philosophical Analysis and Education*, Routledge & Kegan Paul, 1965. Chapter 5: reprinted from *Proceedings of the Philosophy of Education Society of Great Britain*, vol. I, 1966. Chapter 6: material reprinted from 'Forms of knowledge—a reply to Elizabeth Hindess', in *Proceedings of the Philosophy of Education Society of Great Britain*, vol. VII, no. 2, 1973. Chapter 7: reprinted from *Journal of Curriculum Studies*, vol. 3, no. 1, 1971. Chapter 8: reprinted from R.S. Peters (ed.), *The Concept of Education*, Routledge & Kegan Paul, 1967. Chapter 10: reprinted from *Cambridge Journal of Education*, vol. 3, no. 3, 1973. Chapter 11: reprinted from *Education for Teaching*, no. 67, May 1965. Chapter 12: reprinted from *British Journal of Educational Studies*, vol. XIV, no. 1, 1965.

Philosophy and curriculum planning I

It is abundantly clear nowadays that ultimately the crucially important questions of the curriculum are complex practical questions which no mere philosopher of education has a right to answer. Anyone who today advocates curriculum changes on purely philosophical grounds without considering the psychological and sociological factors that are relevant is simply irresponsible. For rational curriculum planning, we must, for instance, have sound empirical evidence on how children learn, we must know the demand in our society for people with specialist knowledge. On these technicalities, no mere philosopher is competent to pronounce. But if a philosopher cannot hope to give any definitive answers, this does not mean that he has nothing to say on curriculum matters, or that what he has to say is of only peripheral importance. Indeed, some of the most basic doubts and questionings about the curriculum from which we now suffer would seem to be in part philosophical in character, and philosophers have at least some centrally important things to say on them.

I

Philosophy, I shall take it, is above all concerned with clarification of the concepts and propositions through which our experience and activities are intelligible. It is interested in answering questions about the meaning of terms and expressions, about the logical relations and the presuppositions these terms and expressions involve. As I shall regard it, philosophy is not a speculative super-science that tries to answer questions about some ultimate reality; it is not the pursuit of moral knowledge; it is not the great integrator of all human understanding into a unified view of man, God and the Universe; it is not a science—as is, for instance, psychology or sociology—concerned to understand what is the case in terms of experiment and observation. It is rather a distinctive type of higher order pursuit, primarily an analytical pursuit, with the ambition of understanding the concepts used in all other forms of lower-order knowledge and awareness. Philosophy, as I see it, is a second-order area of knowledge, concerned above all with the necessary features of our primary forms of understanding and awareness in the sciences, in morals, in history and the like. Philosophical questions are not about, say, particular facts or moral judgments, but about what we mean by facts, what we mean by moral judgments, how these fundamental elements in our understanding relate to each other, and so on.

Philosophers, therefore, come into their own not when people begin to question about particular facts or about particular moral judgments, but when they come to ask questions about these fundamental units in our understanding. They come into their own not when people begin to ask for particular facts about our present secondary school curriculum, about its effectiveness in providing the general knowledge people need in our society, or how best to interest pupils in what we wish to teach; they come into their own when we turn from questions of empirical investigation to ask what is the nature of the things we wish pupils to achieve, what we mean by the acquisition of knowledge and what we mean by capturing pupils' interests. It is when people recognise that in planning the curriculum we are working with unclear and confused notions, that logical issues come to the fore. Just as in a time of moral upheaval, when a reformulation of the moral code is necessary, people may well begin to ask not simply what actions are right and wrong but rather what is meant by right and wrong anyway, and how any justification of moral claims is possible, so today when well established curricular practices are being re-assessed, it may be necessary for us to get a better logical grip on some of the fundamental concepts we are using. That, in the questionings that are now going on, there are signs of serious philosophical confusion in our ideas about the curriculum, I do not doubt, and it is with these alone that I am here concerned. Let me repeat, however, philosophical clarification will not of itself answer our practical problems, even if it cannot but help in promoting more rational solutions of them.

If we are to be concerned with problems in curriculum planning, it is surely important to be clear at the start what precisely a curriculum is. The term curriculum is, of course, used very variedly, but I shall take it to mean a programme of activities designed so that pupils will attain by learning certain specifiable ends or objectives. I do not wish to imply by this that a curriculum must be a programme or sequence of activites that is not to be changed in any respect by the pupils, that it must be completely determined by teachers. Nor do I wish to imply that curriculum activites are teachers' activities as distinct from the activities of pupils. I am concerned, of course, with both. Activities on the part of the child are essential if there is to be any significant learning at all, and activities on the part of the teacher are necessary to produce the learning with which the curriculum is concerned.

What I want to bring out, in making this very brief statement as to how I understand the term curriculum, are the three elements that seem to be implied in the very notion of a curriculum and which are therefore essential features in rational curriculum planning.

First there can be no curriculum without objectives. Unless there is some point to planning the activities, some intended, learnable outcome, however vague this might be, there is no such thing as a curriculum. But if a curriculum is a plan of activities aimed at achieving objectives, it is a plan involving two other elements, a content to be used and methods to be employed to bring about learning. By content is usually meant the particular plays of Shakespeare that are studied, the particular elements of history considered—say, the foreign policy of Great Britain in 1914—the particular social or moral problems that are discussed, and the like. And by methods, we usually mean the types of activities pursued by teachers and pupils together in discussions, group work, surveys, demonstrations, film and TV viewing, and so on. Although we can distinguish the content of the curriculum and the methods employed, this distinction is at times rather artificial, for the content used sometimes depends closely on the sort of methods employed and vice versa. Yet for my present purposes it is important to keep these two elements clearly distinguished, for changes in the one do not necessarily demand a revolution in the other. Clearly, granted certain objectives and methods, one can in many cases change the content that is used to achieve these. If one is after certain forms of aesthetic appreciation, one can use Play A rather than Play B, Poem C rather than Poem D. Equally, given certain objectives and a specific content, one can vary the actual methods employed. One can then, to some extent, consider content and method independently, given a set of objectives, even if it is too simple to regard them in stark isolation.

II

From this simple characterisation, it would seem to follow that for curriculum planning to be rational, it must start with clear and specific objectives, and then, and only then, address itself to discovering the plan of means, the content and methods in terms of which these objectives are to be obtained. It is on this view a logical nonsense to pretend that a series of activities form a curriculum, or a part of a curriculum, if they are not designed to obtain specifiable objectives. The use of free activity periods by the inexperienced and

B

unthoughtful forms an obvious case in point here. There is no reason whatever to suppose that free activity will necessarily promote any desired learning, even if it occurs in a suitably well equipped environment. It is, I think, therefore pure deception to regard such activity as part of a curriculum if it is not structured to obtain certain specified objectives. If one redefines what is meant by a curriculum to include this sort of random pursuit, that is to win only a verbal battle. It remains logically the case that these activities are not designed to achieve any desired ends, and whether any such ends are achieved is in fact purely fortuitous. It seems to me just nonsense to pretend that these pursuits really form part of what is generally known as a curriculum.

For any particular curriculum, deciding what the objectives are to be involves making value judgments of immense complexity and importance. But we must get clear precisely *what* it is we think is of value, characterising it with the greatest possible precision. We may, for instance, wish to pass on our notions of justice, but we shall have to work out in great detail what these notions are before we have any adequate curriculum objectives. In particular we need to know how general terms like this apply in specific situations. If it is not clear what the objectives of the enterprise are, then from a rational point of view the whole pursuit is being vitiated from the start. And a very great deal of curriculum experiment has been vitiated on just these grounds.

With no clear statement of objectives set out to guide them, teachers only too easily take the statement of the mere content of the curriculum or syllabus as a statement of the objectives to be pursued. In this way the teacher pares down what is to be achieved to the acquisition of a body of information and the ability to perform a number of stated operations. Of course the content stated is intended to be gone through and much to be learnt in the process. But if Boyle's Law, Pythagoras's Theorem and *King Lear* are taken as labels of objectives, the result will often be the mere mastery of propositions. Taken as labels for a content to be used, they may be employed as the means of developing understanding, judgment, imagination and many other complex qualities. In a stable context or tradition, where the objectives of the curriculum can be assumed to be fully understood by all teachers, then everything may be well if teachers are given no more than a suggested content for their courses. But under the present circumstances, no such accepted tradition exists any more. We are all too frequently guilty of allowing the established content of syllabuses and curricula to set our objectives for us. We can then evade the difficult matter of deciding what precisely our aim ought to be, we can reduce the tasks of teaching and learning to their most manageable forms and easily appear to be pretty efficient at the job. Of course what is learnt by pupils in courses of this sort is not only unobjectionable, it may be very valuable in many ways. But that is no adequate justification. Curriculum planning is not just a question of whether what is learnt is worthwhile, it is a question of whether or not what we wish to be learnt is in fact being learnt.

If the traditional school curriculum and syllabuses assume an established background of objectives they equally assume an established background of appropriate teaching methods, for these are similarly unspecified. Maybe many of the teaching methods used are excellent, but if the statement of content is taken as setting out what is to be learnt, there is a strong temptation to assume that traditional chalk and talk are pretty well all that is needed. If strings of propositions are to be mastered, and a number of formal skills acquired, what better way is there than the clear, precise, formal presentation of them and plenty of disciplined practice? In this way not only are the objectives pared down, the methods used are undesirably restricted as well.

But the old style curriculum or syllabus does at least have this value, that in stating the content of a course, it gives at least a strong hint of some of the objectives the teacher is to pursue. If, however, the curriculum is set out merely in terms of projects and activities, even an indirect specification of the objectives may be lacking. It matters vitally in a project on the neighbourhood, for instance, what the objectives of the exercise are. If the objectives themselves are not stated, it is not clear how one can justify these activities having a place in the curriculum. Perhaps this approach, setting out the curriculum or syllabus in terms of projects, does prevent teachers being misled by traditional curricular formulations as far as methods are concerned, but it seems to me that it may all too readily lead to little significant learning of the kind it is the school's function assiduously to pursue. In a time of upheaval and radical change, it seems to me that too much freedom for the teacher is not necessarily a good thing.

A further confusion of questions about objectives and questions about content and methods arises over the issue of the 'subject' structure of the curriculum. I regard it as a basic philosophical truth about the nature of knowledge that, whether we like it or not, all knowledge is differentiated into a limited number of logically distinct forms or disciplines.[1] If this is a philosophical truth, then it cannot be ignored. It means that the objectives of knowledge and understanding we are concerned with in most curricula have an implicit organisation, there are distinctions and inter-relations

5

between the objectives which must necessarily be recognised. The distinct conceptual structures within knowledge are part of what has to be mastered in acquiring knowledge. But it does not follow that, because these structures are to be found in the objectives we may be after, they must explicitly map out the content of every curriculum planned for these ends. The content must be planned and structured to achieve objectives that have their own inter-relations. To proceed from saying that there is a given structure in the knowledge we wish to be mastered to saying that this must be the structure of the curriculum, is to be guilty of a simple logical fallacy. Means must not be taken for the characteristics of the ends. I see no reason why a curriculum should not be fully 'topic-organised' provided it is understood that the development of understanding involves the mastery of conceptual structures which are not reflected in the topic-organisation.

There is, I think, a similar confusion between objectives and methods where the progressive curriculum is concerned. We may wish, as an objective, to enable pupils to solve at least some of the many practical problems they are going to face in life. The ability to solve these problems is an objective. It does not follow from this that the curriculum should be directly geared in its *methods* to problem-solving. To assume this is to confuse an objective with a method. We wish to plan the curriculum in content and methods so that pupils will as a result be able to solve practical and theoretical problems. We must therefore set about discovering what pupils need to know in terms of matters of sheer fact, what different methods must be used to solve different types of questions, whether the expertise for one kind is important in another, and so on. All this needs to be disentangled before we can tell how best to educate pupils to cope with their problems. There is no guarantee whatever that the best way is to organise the whole curriculum round problem-saving. Of course there will be elements of problem-solving in the curriculum, but one must not over-emphasise one objective at the expense of others and rush into thinking that appropriate methods can be determined as simply as this logical confusion implies.

Just as some particular objectives must not be allowed to determine teaching methods directly, so also elements of teaching methods must not be glorified into objectives. One example of this must suffice. It is manifestly the case that adequate teaching in many areas must involve pupils in a great deal of first-hand and practical experience. From this it does not follow that all experience is, as such, an appropriate curriculum objective. And further, practical experience is only one element needed in teaching. Of itself it may frequently prove valueless as a teaching method. Unqualified em-

6

phasis on experience as an objective is grossly misleading, as indeed is such emphasis on its significance as a method.

If we are to prevent confusions and inadequacies of the kind I have instanced, then the only way is, I think, to stick to the principle I suggested earlier. We must first formulate our objectives clearly, in realistic and operational terms, and then, in the light of these, move on to the questions of content and method. We must resist the temptation to rush in with new ideas about content and methods with only the haziest notions of what we are trying to achieve, piously hoping that something worthwhile will result in the end. We would be much better off harnessing our energies into finding more successful means for reaching those objectives we are clear about, whilst we thrash out new objectives in more controversial areas. Let us be revolutionary about means when we know what we are after, and when we do not know what we are after let us refrain from ill-considered practices until we have got our intentions straight.

III

In characterising a curriculum as necessarily having objectives, the planning of the means to which constitutes the central problem of curriculum development, I might be accused of a piece of mere prescriptive definition or dogmatic legislation which has conveniently ruled out of the discussion many of the more provocative and exciting ideas that have recently come into educational debate. This legislation as to how I am using the term curriculum is however quite deliberate. What I am seeking to do, is to take what seems to me to be the traditional use of this term in the school context, drawing out its essentially means–ends character. In forcing this character into the open, it is possible to use it not only as a norm to point out weaknesses in traditional curriculum planning but also to use it to show where contemporary developments diverge from this conception. Whether or not these contemporary developments are regarded as lapses from an ideal standard of planning or as important new approaches is a debatable matter. In so far as the situation that provoked the traditional concept continues to exist, and that approach is thoroughly justifiable, the term's traditional use will continue to be important. In so far as that situation has changed, and the approach the term has implied now lacks justification, the evolution of a new concept is to be welcomed.

Granted this situation, it seems to me a matter of some consequence that though the social context of curriculum planning is undergoing much change and our notions of the *particular* objectives we are after in education are changing also, the *general character* of the centrally important achievements has changed little if at all. Indeed it is far from clear that they could change radically in *character*. What is more, the general conditions that are necessary for such central achievements would seem to remain largely unchanged. In our schools we remain to a large extent concerned with pupils acquiring certain forms of thought, developing intellectual abilities and particular character traits. Maybe the precise forms of thought or character traits pursued now differ in important respects from those pursued fifty years ago. But they remain the same kinds of achievement, and kinds of achievement that can only be reached under particular conditions. Pupils still have to take on board concepts, beliefs, practices, sentiments, etc. What is more, these achievements are in no sense mere natural products. Nor are they simple acquisitions. They are all matters of learning, and learning that is not merely being conditioned, learning that involves understanding. Nor is this learning a mere reproduction of the beliefs, practices and sentiments of others, but an engagement with the beliefs, practices and sentiments of others so that one comes to think, believe, feel and imagine for oneself. These objectives are attained only by people coming to use the sophisticated categories, concepts and procedures that are already available in human society so that one can in some minor way contribute to the life of that human society oneself. What is more, these categories, concepts and procedures are by and large articulated only in our language as it is used for a vast variety of purposes in a vast variety of natural and social circumstances. They can be learnt therefore only in the appropriate contexts where the appropriate language is used. The limits of the context and limits of the language used must set the limits as to what can possibly be learnt. If one adds that only the most elementary achievements are articulated in the situations encountered in everyday social life and that the more sophisticated forms are part of extremely complex rule-governed structures of thought and practice, the need for curriculum planning of the traditional kind seems inescapable.

Until our society can provide the necessary conditions for learning in its daily life, until, that is, we have an educative society in a way that is still almost inconceivable let alone practically achievable, pupils will only learn the *kinds* of things we still seem to want, if their learning is deliberately planned. And that planning, because of the essentially social character of objectives, must surely involve planning activities not merely of learning but of teaching. Only by instructing, conversing, correcting, indicating and so on can pupils by practising, listening, discussing, experimenting, come to understand, think, act and feel for themselves at levels quite beyond those of their prior personal interests and the demands of daily life. It is by the develop-

8

ment of disciplined attention, accuracy, patience and other qualities
that new interests and new forms of attainment are opened up to
pupils. Without teaching planned and conducted by those who
themselves possess these achievements it is hardly conceivable that
pupils should reach these goals. Unless therefore new kinds of
objectives are to be sought in education curriculum planning of the
kind outlined would seem to be necessary in any forseeable future.[2]

In saying this, however, it is perhaps important to insist that the
activities of teaching and learning should not be narrowly construed.
It has, for instance, become common in certain circles to contrast the
process of socialisation with that of teaching. In certain contexts
however such a contrast is mistaken, for in socialisation, children
learn social rules, habits, skills, etc., and in so far as such learning is
deliberately planned and manipulated, teaching is a part of the
process. As here conceived, the activities of teaching are activities
deliberately aimed at bringing about learning. No conditions beyond
those implied by that description are being laid down.[3] It follows
from this however that the social organisation of a school and the
pattern of its general life both in and out of class need to be seen as
the vehicles of learning they truly are, and so important vehicles of
teaching within the framework of the school's curriculum in its
wider sense.

I have manifestly tied the notion of the curriculum as I am concerned with it to the notion of teaching, where teaching is a matter of
activities intended to bring about learning. In its turn, this traditional
notion of a curriculum is I think part of what has, up to now at any
rate, been understood by the term 'school'. Being institutions
devoted to teaching, and therefore to learning, schools have had
curricula or planned means for pupils to reach the desired ends.
With an increased knowledge of the social factors that influence
learning and the need for increasing provision in our society for the
general welfare of both adults and youngsters, there has however
now developed a very much wider concept of a school. Alongside the
day to day business of teaching it is now not uncommon to find
housed many of the activities of a community centre. Such multi-
purpose institutions do indeed have much to commend them. It is
important, however, that the different character of the activities
being brought together be not blurred so that the explicit teaching
function of the school gets submerged or lost. Education can be much
enriched in centres of this kind, but if important objectives of the
character outlined earlier are not to be forsaken, curriculum
planning for these ends must remain a major priority and the
planning of teaching and learning not confused with the planning of
club activities and other desirable provisions. If 'de-schooling' is to

9

mean the abolition of planned curricula rather than a shift to new institutions where better curriculum planning is effected, many of the very objectives which de-schoolers themselves say they want will be unattainable.

The concept of the curriculum here outlined is considered liberal enough to accommodate a radical reconstruction and reformulation of the objectives of education and also to cover the introduction of new methods of teaching and learning. It is not at all thought to cover all activities that can and often do result in learning, for much learning goes on outside all curriculum considerations. What is being asserted, however, is that the character of many educational objectives is such that it is only by teaching that they can be achieved and that, in our society, demands curriculum planning of the traditional sort.

IV

In opposition to this approach to the curriculum, it could be protested that the whole treatment is thoroughly artificial, that it is an expression of rationalism run riot, and that no curriculum ever has been, or ever could be, planned in this way. Ought we not rather to recognise that the curricula we have are the result of historical developments, the products of social forces such as vocational needs and the legitimation of certain areas of knowledge by social élites? In its extreme 'historicist' form, this approach views curriculum development as entirely the product of determinist forces of some sort, all that planners and developers can ever do being either so much flotsam on the curriculum sea or the vehicle through which determinism works. This is not the place to rehearse the arguments of Karl Popper and others against different forms of historicism and social determinism, a doctrine not only open to many philosophical objections but one that can lead all too readily to the impossible but dangerous game of attempting to predict the next stage of social evolution. In general, curriculum planners have not seen themselves as involved in this kind of pursuit though there is an occasional hint of this sort in some of the fascinating new work in the sociology of knowledge and the sociology of the curriculum.

In rejecting a historicist view, I am not however wanting to deny that much curriculum practice has simply 'grown' out of its social context and continues so to develop without much overt planning. But that does not imply that curricula cannot be effectively changed by rational planning. True, curriculum planning can be frustrated by social forces beyond the planners' control. But if not everything is under conscious control, that is no ground for assuming that nothing is. Indeed, there is much evidence to suggest that many things are, and that with further knowledge more will be. It must be recognised however that, in practice, it is quite impossible for us to start with a blank sheet progressively working towards a totally rationally planned curriculum. To begin with, no adequate and comprehensive categorisation of objectives is available. Nor could we begin to argue conclusively what objectives any given set of pupils should pursue. We have a grossly inadequate knowledge of the effectiveness of different teaching methods, and indeed the variables involved in this whole procedure are at present quite beyond our over-all control. Yet these factors in no way cast doubt on the logic of rational curriculum planning. Nor must the logic of the business be confused with an account of how, as a matter of fact, past and present curricula have come into being. No amount of explanation of how it is we have come to have our present curricula can of itself justify what we do. The point is that if we are to be able to justify what we do, we must proceed by examining first the objectives of the enterprise and then the means for reaching these. In moving to such a defensible position however, we cannot start from scratch, not only because that is practically impossible in our society, but also because, as already indicated, we do not have the intellectual mastery it presupposes. What is more, new objectives and means arise primarily within the context of present practices and cannot be imaginatively constructed outside these. What we must do therefore is to make our curriculum planning progressively more rational by 'piecemeal engineering'. It is by the perpetual rational questioning and criticism of what we now do, that better practice can be achieved. The challenge to formulate the objectives of our present enterprises and to justify both these and the means we use to pursue them is the way to progress.

A somewhat different objection to this rational approach is that the specification of objectives and planning to achieve these artificialises the situation in another way for it fails to take into account all the unique complex of factors that are inescapable in every individual situation. No one group of teachers has the abilities and qualities of another, pupils in different schools have different backgrounds and needs, the facilities of institutions vary and so on. Abstract planning remote from the particularities of a situation is therefore likely to be unrealistic and unprofitable. What is necessary is that instead of imposing general abstract planning on a particular situation, we begin from a detailed practical knowledge of the unique situation concerned, using all the relevant theoretical abstract knowledge we have to make the curriculum to be used in that context more consistent, more effective, etc. If Michael Oakeshott and others are right, theoretical knowledge alone cannot, logically cannot, be adequate for the rational development of any social affairs. This must always come from within the conduct of the practical affairs themselves as otherwise the unique factors of each situation will render it abortive. Such factors, however, in no way invalidate what is here being outlined. The demand for the specification of objectives in no way implies that the selection of objectives judged appropriate for every situation will be the same. That selection needs to be made in the light of the particular context. Equally, the means planned to achieve these must depend on local circumstances.

Perhaps more serious is yet another objection, that by the nature of the case at least some of the most important objectives of education, particularly in the area of the arts, cannot be specified as they are to be pupils' unique and novel achievements and responses. If what is wanted is something unique, how could it be specified or planned for? Clearly each individual result cannot be pre-specified, but equally clearly teachers must, even in the arts, have in mind a limited range of objectives of a specifiable character. The objective may be any achievement with certain features, but if there is teaching going on at all there are objectives to the enterprise. It is simply not true that teaching creative writing or poetic appreciation has no specifiable objectives. The nature of that specification of course depends entirely on what the objectives are, no one formula being suitable for all achievements. But variations of characterisation in no way undermine the claim that there always are objectives in teaching activities. A variant on this objection is the view that what we often want is that pupils come to act in ways governed by general principles rather than that they act in specific ways. Just so, but then the objectives are principled forms of action. The insistence on the specification of objectives in no way restricts objectives to particular actions, indeed objectives can be immensely varied in character.

Most fundamental of all, however, is perhaps the objection that the achievements of education are misconceived if thought of in this specifiable way. They are rather the outcomes, whatever those may be, of certain processes and activities that are educational, and it is for these we must plan, not the achievements themselves. The trouble here is to know how the processes and activities are to be characterised and then judged as educational, without the characterisation and assessment of what they bring about. And if that is necessary we are in fact back to a set of objectives once more. One senses in this and some of the earlier objections, a reticence to accept the outlined features of planning because it throws the ultimate decisions onto the planners and their value judgments. But then if educators evade these decisions or try to thrust them onto their pupils, surely all they do is opt out of their job as educators. If one takes on the responsibility of education, it seems to me one takes on the job of teaching to achieve a set of objectives and to do that rationally is to be involved in curriculum planning.[4]

V

One further, more technical objection to curriculum planning of this kind must be mentioned. The whole approach has been seen as the planning of means to ends. But is that model appropriate? Might not some of the previous objections really be attempts at questioning this framework rather than details within it? Can we even in principle settle the objectives of the enterprise and then look round for the most efficient means of reaching these? Are we not in education concerned with achievements and processes that are more complexly connected than those usually considered under the labels 'ends' and 'means'? Is one not just setting up an engineering or production model when an analogy with a process of growth or artistic creation might be more appropriate? After all are these not also processes or activities with end achievements of a distinctive character? The reply is surely that one is not concerned with an engineering model any more than with one of growth or artistic creation. Indeed the search for a model in this way is, I think, thoroughly misleading. True, in engineering, growth and aesthetic creation there are outcomes of various kinds of processes; but what is involved in each process is dependent on the character of the outcome and in each case it is radically different. The learning achievements with which the curriculum is concerned are not at all like engineering products, plants or works of art. They are what they are and the character of curriculum planning must stem from that, not an analogy or model. Of course if the objectives are mis-characterised in strictly behavioural terms, curriculum planning might well get close to planning a production line. But the answer to that is not to look for another model, but to look at the character of curriculum planning in its own right.

But then might we not reject the terminology of 'means' and 'ends' altogether? If it is narrowly interpreted this indeed might be wise. Certainly in many human situations the ends we seek and the means we can take to reach them are independently describable. Their relationship is then simply contingent and a matter of empirical investigation. If, being in London, I wish to be in Liverpool ten days from now, I can get there by land, sea or air, in a variety of vehicles by a variety of routes. No one means to the end is logically necessary, and which is the best means depends on numerous facts about me and my circumstances. In other situations, however, the ends men seek do sometimes logically necessitate certain prior achievements as at least part of all possible means. The more complex concepts of science and mathematics for instance can only be understood if certain simpler concepts from which the former are constructed are already intelligible. In this case, the mastery of the simpler concepts is logically necessary to the mastery of the more complex ones and is therefore necessarily part of the means to the latter. Here there is one form of logical relationship between the ends and the means. Just what different forms of such logical relationship there can be, is by no means clear, but that there are such relationships is surely not disputable, and in the learning with which curriculum planning is concerned they are much in evidence.[5] It is not that the ends being sought frequently lay down one unique means to their being acquired, but rather that the nature of the ends sets limits to the means that can be used. Another important aspect of the means involved in curriculum planning is that frequently they involve achievements which are themselves valuable as ends in their own right. In education it is frequently the case that if more distant ends are not reached what is achieved *en route* is itself sufficient to justify the attempt.

If, therefore, curriculum planning is to be understood as a means–ends matter, it must be interpreted to cover both logical and empirical relationships. If this is done, I see little reason to doubt its suitability. What it does, is assert unmistakably the need for a clarification of what we want achieved and that alone makes it a useful framework in terms of which to examine the contemporary flood of curriculum developments.

VI

In this paper, I have been primarily concerned with the nature of curriculum planning. Clarifying and defending the account given has been largely a philosophical matter, if not a very sophisticated one. In the process, other philosophical questions of considerable importance within curriculum planning have arisen. In particular, there is much more to be said about the nature of the objectives and, what is more, about their logical inter-relations. There is much too that needs elucidation about teaching and the activities it involves. The majority of the papers collected in this volume are concerned with issues at a general level in these two areas, especially with matters that bear on the balance and organisation of curricula. In the more detailed matters of planning in particular areas of objectives, the philosophy of particular subjects, such as mathematics, the sciences, history, aesthetics and religion, and also certain particular areas of philosophy of mind, has much to contribute. Such issues are in general beyond the scope of this volume, though one very controversial paper on the nature of the arts is included. Two papers are also included on aspects of moral education, partly because they illustrate how philosophical problems arise in considering a particular area of objectives, and partly because the all pervading character of moral education raises special problems for curriculum planning as a whole. All these essays are primarily concerned with epistemological questions which until recently have received much too scant attention in educational circles. Very little indeed is said about the justification of curriculum decisions. What has been attempted is rather a contribution to a clearer understanding of what is at stake in some of these decisions—a clarification of certain of the considerations that are necessarily involved in rational planning.

Notes

1 See Chapter 3, 'Liberal education and the nature of knowledge'.
2 In the two preceding paragraphs I am much indebted to a paper by Michael Oakeshott, 'Education: the engagement and its frustration', *Proceedings of the Philosophy of Education Society of Great Britain*, vol. V, no. 1, January 1971.
3 See Chapter 7, 'What is teaching?'.
4 This, and a number of other criticisms here discussed, are expressed in L. Stenhouse, 'Some limitations of the use of objectives in curriculum research and planning', in *Pedagogica Europa*, 1971. For a fuller treatment of these issues, see P.H. Hirst, 'Towards a logic of curriculum development' in P.H. Taylor and J. Walton (ed), *Proceedings of the Standing Conference on Curriculum Development*, vol. 1, 1973.
5 Much the most penetrating discussion to date of the means–ends relationship in curriculum planning is to be found in H. Sockett, 'Curriculum aims and objectives: taking a means to an end', *Proceedings of the Philosophy of Education Society of Great Britain*, vol. VI, no. 1, January 1972.

2   The nature and structure of curriculum objectives

If curriculum planning is a matter of planning means to specified ends, and an educational curriculum therefore serves educational ends, the clearer we are about those ends and their nature the more adequate the planning can be. Something has already been said about their character in discussing the logic of curriculum planning, but further elucidation is called for if even the most general problems we face in contemporary planning are to be rationally approached. Not long ago educationists talked about 'aims' rather than 'objectives' and this shift to a more technical term alone indicates a growing awareness that more detailed description of the achievements we are after is desirable. If what it is we want to achieve is first indicated in expressions of great generality, these need to be unpacked into much more specific terms or little positive guidance is provided for educational practice. To be of value we must eventually analyse these ends down to particular achievements we wish pupils to reach, detailed enough for us to be able to judge how to promote these and not other achievements with which they could be confused, and detailed enough for us to be able to judge when pupils have and have not reached them. By curriculum objectives, I shall mean the achievements we want, specified to this degree. In common parlance and educational debate, both 'aims' and 'objectives' can have varying degrees of specificity and nothing is gained by attempting to legislate particular uses for these terms. Indeed, it seems to me necessary on different occasions to discuss educational ends at different levels depending on the character of the issues at stake. When we get down to the job of drawing up curricula for implementation in school, however, the greater the degree of specificity the better, and in speaking of curriculum objectives I shall have in mind as tight a description of what is to be learnt as is available.

There is however one way of characterising educational ends which is unsatisfactory not merely because it is general, but because it can be used to evade the detailed specification of what is being aimed at and even to suggest that specification is unnecessary or undesirable. It has begun to be extremely common to speak of the curriculum as being concerned with promoting pupils' 'growth', satisfying their 'needs' or following their 'interests'. These terms are global in their intentions, and their content is totally unspecified. 'Growth' and 'need' can be used as educational objectives because they presuppose a set of in-built norms, in-built standards, and so indicate, however vaguely, something that is thought to be desirable. But talking about the pursuit of growth and the satisfaction of needs must not blind us to the need to formulate in detail what objectives constitute growth and what precisely it is that pupils need. The notion of growth itself, once taken out of its biological context, contains no clear indications as to what is to be aimed at. Take Dewey's old example: is pursuing burglary, and developing a high art in this, 'growth'? Well, obviously in an educational sense, no. But why not exactly? What developments, what objectives, do constitute growth? The term itself picks out no clear answer; we have to determine quite independently what content it shall have. If one turns to a term like 'needs', then one can certainly talk about basic needs which people may have of a biological or a psychological kind. But do these really spell out curriculum objectives for us? In what sense do children need arithmetic or need to solve practical problems? In what sense do they need to understand the science taught to them? Only in a highly conventionalised social sense. The norm or value that makes us think of these as needs is a social norm, not a 'natural' one. Saying what children need is only a cloaked way of saying what we judge they ought to have. Let us then remove the cloak and its suggestions that in nature alone we can find what children ought to have in terms of their growth and their needs. And let us accept the fact that we must plan and specify ourselves which educational objectives we are after.

The idea that educational objectives can be spelt out in terms of interests can, I think, also be analysed away. The interests of children—if one takes the felt interests that they have—will never, in many cases, produce the educational objectives we want. What is more important is the frequent assumption that interests, like needs, are naturally given and are not the product of social factors. But interests can be created, and it is surely a basic function of education to create interests in what is worthwhile. Once more we must realise that a global term cannot be the source of specific educational objectives. It just hides the fact that people are writing in their own judgments as to what objectives should be chosen. Such terms cannot give us specific educational objectives which can function as aims in the educational enterprise at a working level, for to be meaningful they all presuppose a particular content of the very kind we are seeking.[1]

But what does the demand for the detailed specification of objectives involve? What categories are we to use? What is the nature of these objectives and what inter-relations do they have?

B.S. Bloom and his colleagues have in recent years produced two instalments of a now celebrated classification of objectives.[2] They divide the area into three domains: the cognitive, the affective, and the psycho-motor. In the cognitive domain they list first such objectives as a knowledge of specifics—meaning by this, a knowledge of particular items of information, of terminology, of conventions, of classifications, of methodologies, of principles and generalisations, of theories. They then classify intellectual abilities and skills, dividing these into such groups as the abilities and skills connected with comprehension, translation, application, the analysis and breaking down into elements of communications that we receive, synthesising communications and evaluating them.

In the same way there is an attempt to classify objectives in the affective domain. First there are objectives connected with attending to phenomena, from awareness of controlled selection. There follow groupings of dispositions to respond, from mere acquiescence to enjoyment. Similarly in matters of valuing, organising and the formation of a whole complex of values.

This attempt at setting out a framework of categories in which we can clearly distinguish educational objectives has enormous value. To begin with, it brings out the tremendous diversity of the kinds of objectives we are after in education. We are not simply after people learning facts, not simply after their learning skills, not simply after their learning values or attitudes or habits. We are after all these things and more, and within any of these categories, with very diverse skills, attitudes and dispositions. Certainly to list objectives in these categories, provided we formulate them in great detail, is an extremely important exercise if only as an antidote to our concentrating on the usual limited range of objectives of which we are most directly conscious when we think about school work. But the classification is also concerned with specifying objectives in terms of intended changes in the behaviour of students. Set out in these terms, it is then possible to see whether or not students do in fact achieve these objectives intended as a result of the education they receive.

But in spite of these advantages, the taxonomy is limited in its value. Though it can help us in listing objectives, it provokes rather than answers questions about the nature and structure of objectives. What is involved in knowing facts, solving problems, applying knowledge and so on? Even in general terms what kinds of achievements are they and how does one achievement relate to another? What for instance is involved in teaching a child a simple fact, such as that in 1973 Heath was Prime Minister. If a child is to understand this fact, this item of knowledge, then to begin with he must understand what a Prime Minister is. He must also be able to identify

Edward Heath. What is more, if he is to learn this as a fact he must know that it is true, and he must have some idea of what difference it makes that Edward Heath and not someone else was the Prime Minister. I would suggest therefore that it is quite impossible to learn facts, to know them as facts, without acquiring the basic concepts and the criteria for truth involved. Now that is to suggest that the notion of a fact is not a logically primitive educational objective. It presupposes certain other more fundamental objectives so that without the pursuit of these, possibly in the same context, one cannot teach facts. One might, of course, teach words, but that is not the point. In commenting on this I have given the beginnings of a simple analysis of what is meant by a fact. We usually think of facts, in our everyday context, as just lying about the world, somehow being registered by us as on sensitive plates. But of course the facts are always what we know to be the case, and, without certain concepts, we would fail to be aware of certain facts, even about a room in which we may be sitting. The notion of a fact needs therefore to be spelt out with great care if we are to know what is involved in teaching facts. And one can go further, of course. I have said that one cannot have facts without concepts. But what is a concept? Is this a logically primitive element?

Or take another range of objectives altogether. What is an intellectual skill, for example adding up in arithmetic, being able to count? What is the ability to deduce that we wish children to acquire? Unless we know what we mean by deduction, or by counting, it seems to me that we may be using methods in our education which are not seriously, in a considered way, directed to the objectives. Deduction is a very good example here. Is to deduce something to have a piece of mental machinery ticking over in a certain way? Is a person who can deduce from A and B that C is the case, somebody who has got a piece of psychological machinery 'tuned' to work effectively? Is the person who cannot deduce one who suffers from having a 'rusty' piece of machinery instead? We usually think of deduction as a psychological process, but is it a sequence of events in the mind? Are there any actual psychological processes which are in fact necessary to deducing? The prime example of deduction is perhaps a mathematical theorem, so how do mathematicians work out theorems? Do they go down a ladder of reasoning, working strictly in a given order? Generally speaking, no mathematician does that. Frequently he starts from the bottom and works backwards, he shoots up a blind alley in the middle and fails to get anywhere, or thinks of a useful analogy. What the sequence of his thought is does not in fact matter, for his processes of thought are not the deduction; the deduction is the pattern of the end achievement that he establishes.

C

To teach children to deduce is not to teach them to think along particular psychological channels, it is to teach them, whatever channels or psychological processes they use, to produce certain patterns of statements in the end. If one sees deducing as achieving certain public performances rather than as achieving an inner sequence of thought, one's objectives in this enterprise are of a quite different nature.

Or again, take something like the ability to solve problems. What is meant by this phrase? Obviously one begins by asking what problems: moral problems, scientific problems, mathematical problems? Clearly these are very different in nature. Can we assume that the ability to solve mathematical problems is the same as the ability to solve problems in morals? What is more, even to understand a scientific problem, as distinct from a moral problem, presupposes a great deal of scientific knowledge. It is only when one has done a lot of science that one can recognise scientific problems for what they are. And similarly, it is only when one has done a great deal of thinking about moral matters that one recognises moral problems as different in kind from those of science, needing to be solved in a quite different manner. The notion, therefore, of developing an ability to solve problems is radically suspect in a way that cannot be revealed simply by a classification of objectives. And further, one can only pursue the solving of particular types of problems if at the same time one is prepared to teach a very great deal of fact, a very large number of principles, of criteria and tests for truth. All of these must be employed in recognising a problem for what it is, let alone solving it. One cannot therefore pursue the end of problem-solving for one type of problem in isolation from pursuing other objectives; and one cannot, in pursuing the ability to solve scientific problems, assume one is thereby pursuing the ability to solve moral problems or historical problems as well. There are many terms of this sort for objectives, but listing them without a grasp of their character helps little.

From what has been said, curriculum planning seems to lack some overall structure within which possible objectives can be seen in their logical relationships to each other and this would not seem likely to be forthcoming unless we can get clear at least the general character of objectives. One doctrinaire answer to all questions about their nature has troubled work in this area for many years and it is perhaps as well to comment on it right away. Under the influence of behaviourist psychology, it has repeatedly been said that all significant objectives are changes of behaviour. In its extreme forms this thesis claims either that a statement of an objective is a statement of the observable behavioural changes that are being sought, or that the behavioural changes such an objective implies are all that is relevant in curriculum planning. From this point of view, to pursue the development of a pupil's understanding and appreciation of a poem is to pursue his responding in certain ways to particular stimuli. To teach a child a certain fact is to teach him a new pattern of speech and action. To this account, there are many objections. One immediate objection is that one can doubt if it is in fact possible to specify the pattern of speech and action that goes with knowledge of a fact. Is not that infinitely variable, depending entirely on the circumstances? More fundamentally important, however, this view either legislates a meaning for such terms as say 'understanding' and 'appreciation' which is simply false, or it confuses understanding and appreciation with observable evidence for them. Achieving understanding does not necessarily result in a person's doing or saying anything of any kind, no matter what the stimuli. And to achieve certain outward and visible signs as the objectives in one's teaching is all too frequently consistent with failing to achieve the state of mind desired.

Most of the central objectives we are interested in in education are not themselves reducible to observable states, and to imagine they are, whatever the basis of that claim, is to lose the heart of the business. What is certainly true is that the observable correlates are the only evidence we have that objectives which label states of mind have been achieved, but states of mind should never be confused with the evidence for them. That this is the case can be most obviously seen if we consider states such as that of being in pain. To be in pain is certainly not to be equated with emitting shrieks and groans and to change a person's behaviour so that he makes no such noises does not itself modify his state of mind at all. Confusing what Wittgenstein called the criteria for a state of mind with that state is simply to succumb to a logical confusion.

What we need in curriculum planning is as specific and detailed a characterisation of objectives as possible, using as logically simple terms as are available. But these terms must reflect the proper character of the objectives and not distort them. States of mind are not analysable into observable states without committing category mistakes of some consequence. Of course we do want to know the observable criteria for the states of mind we are after. Not so that these can be aimed at in themselves, however, but so that we are able to assess responsibly when the objectives have been achieved. Assessment and evaluation rely on observable evidence, but these evidences are not the object of the teaching enterprise.

If objectives are not all behavioural in this doctrinaire sense, though certainly some may be of this character, can we give a more accurate account of the general nature of at least the central objectives? From a cursory survey of the objectives mentioned by Bloom and from what has already been said, it would seem that they are above all developments of a person and primarily developments of the characteristics of a rational mind. This is not to say that education is concerned only with intellectual development, as if, for example, emotional development was to be ignored, and knowledge and belief taken to be the only manifestations of mind. Nor is it even to say that education is concerned only with mental development in its widest sense. Rather it is to say that all those forms of development with which education is concerned are related to the pupil's progress in rational understanding. This means that physical education, for instance, is pursued in accordance with a rational appraisal of the place and value of physical activities in human life which we wish the pupil to acquire, that the activities themselves are viewed as those of a developing rational being, not merely an animal, and that they therefore constitute part of the life of a rational person. But to characterise the objectives of education in relation to the development of rationality, is certainly to put at the very centre of what is pursued those forms of knowledge and belief in which we make sense of our experience. It is necessarily by means of knowledge, if not by knowledge alone, that fancy gives place to a recognition of fact, that irrational wishes give place to reasonable wants, and that emotional reactions give place to justifiable actions. Thus, although all the possible or justifiable objectives of education are not themselves explicitly developments of mind, it is, I suggest, by their connection with such specific developments that other objectives have their place and their justification in education at all. In seeking to clarify further the nature and structure of objectives I shall therefore confine myself to considering what is involved in the achievement of those most central objectives of all, the acquisition of knowledge and rational beliefs, without which the development of rationality in any wider sense is logically impossible.

What then is involved in the acquisition of knowledge? Certainly it involves learning many different concepts, using these in a growing awareness of facts, truths and norms of many kinds, mastering many logical operations and principles, applying the criteria of different types of judgment and so on. What an exhaustive list of elements would be, I would not like to say, but what matters for my purpose at the moment is not a complete classification of them in independent categories, so much as a recognition of the kind of achievements that these are. They are, in fact, neither more nor less than the achievements basic to the development of mind itself.

Unfortunately our concept of mind is so persistently bedevilled by myths, largely of an empiricist nature, that we all too easily misconceive entirely what is going on in learning to understand and in acquiring knowledge. We have an almost ineradicable conviction that the mind is to be thought of as a room or box into which, via the senses, ideas or images come as ready-made copies of objects or events or facts in the external world. Further, these ideas come into the mind as quite distinct elements of awareness, rather as furniture might be put into a room. The ideas are there in the room, but they are in no sense essentially part of the room. In addition we tend to regard the mind as a kind of machine, designed to carry out certain processes of rational thought on the ideas which the senses convey, thereby building new ideas from what is given, by processes of abstraction, deduction and the like. Thus there is produced new furniture to be housed and stored, within the mind, ready for use when required. Some of us have less effective machinery than others when it comes to reasoning, and practice and exercise are needed to get the best out of what each of us is given. But essentially the processes of rational thought are regarded as natural activities of the mind. On this kind of picture, the acquiring of knowledge and understanding as the objective of education, involves two major tasks: furnishing the mind with the right ideas, and getting the machine working properly.

Now there are many reasons why this kind of account of mind must be totally rejected, three of which are particularly relevant here. First the account does not begin to do justice to what we know about the development of understanding, even at the level of sense-perception. What we see or understand about any situation is not a simple given. It is dependent on those concepts and categories, those basic units of intelligibility, which the mind brings to the situation. The possibility of discriminating elements in our experience at all necessitates having concepts. To see things is not just to register things for what they are, it is for them to be picked out or articulated in our consciousness. Only by the use of certain concepts is the mind able to discriminate. What the development of understanding involves is, in fact, a progressive differentiation of our experience through the acquisition of new concepts under which it is intelligible. The mind is therefore not a passive recipient of ideas which bring understanding from the external world. It is rather that we achieve understanding through the use of categorial and conceptual apparatus. Having such an apparatus of concepts is a necessary part of what it means to have a mind. Thus the development of a mind involves the achievement of an array of concepts and on this all intelligibility depends. The provision of experience in itself is quite inadequate for

23

developing even the simplest body of concepts, and without these nothing more complex can possibly be achieved.[3]

In the second place, the view I am criticising regards knowledge as something which the mind may or may not possess. Knowledge is not in any sense constitutive of mind. To acquire new knowlege is simply as it were to acquire different furniture or new furniture for a room. To have scientific knowledge as distinct from historical knowledge, is for the furniture to be of one kind rather than another. For the mind itself, nothing turns on this, the room itself remains unchanged; it simply lacks the other type of furniture. In essence minds do not differ in any way by having different knowledge. The real differences between minds are simply in what is naturally given. To acquire one form of knowledge rather than another in no way affects the fundamental characteristics of the mind. Yet surely this will not do. To be without any knowledge at all is to be without mind in any significant sense. Nor is it just that the mind needs some content to work on, as if otherwise its characteristics could not be expressed. The acquisition of knowledge is itself a development of mind and new knowledge means a new development of mind in some sense. Knowledge is not a free-floating possession. It is a characteristic of minds themselves. Thus to fail to acquire knowledge of a certain fundamental kind, is to fail to achieve rational mind in that significant respect. Not all knowledge is of equal importance in the development of rationality, of course, yet the fundamental relationship between knowledge and the development of mind is of central educational significance. Nor must we regard knowledge as unrelated to the development of other aspects of mind, an outlook encouraged by the view I am opposing. It is in large measure by acquiring new knowledge that we begin to reconceive our activities and that we come to feel differently about them.

In the third place we must, as I suggested earlier when discussing the nature of deduction, reject the notion that the mind naturally carries out certain mental activities according to the canons of valid reasoning, as if logical principles were laws of psychological functioning. The question of the development of the rational mind is surely not a question of the strengthening or habitualising of certain patterns of mental functioning. It is rather a question of developing a recognition that one's beliefs and one's arguments, the outcomes of thought, must satisfy important public tests. Tests of rationality are tests to be applied to the *achievements* of one's thought as formulated in propositions, not tests for thought *processes* themselves. To say one has reasoned something out is not to describe a particular sequence of mental occurrences, it is to say that one has achieved in the end a relationship between propositions which satisfies the public criteria

24

necessary for giving reasons. What is more, these standards that define the achievements of reason, are certainly not natural possessions of mind. They have to be learnt, usually by dint of considerable hard work. The development of rationalty is, therefore, not dependent on the exercising of particular mental processes, but it is dependent on one's coming to recognise that there are tests of validity for one's arguments and tests of truth for one's beliefs.

But if the fundamental objectives of education are developments of the rational mind, what formal relationships are there between the various objectives, the concepts, facts, norms, principles, and so on? In spite of an immediate tendency to think of these items of knowledge as detached and isolated from each other, a little reflection quickly suggests this is not the case. It is because the concepts are used in a particular way that any proposition is meaningful. The concepts on which our knowledge is built form distinctive networks of relationships. If we transgress the rules of the relationships which the concepts meaningfully permit, we necessarily produce nonsense. If we talk about magnetic fields being angry, actions being coloured, beauty having weight, or stones being right or wrong we have simply produced conceptual confusions. But not only do we convey meaning by the use of networks of interrelated concepts, meaningful propositions are judged true or false, valid or invalid, by criteria appropriate to the types of propositions. A moral judgment is not validated in the same way as a mathematical theorem, nor a historical explanation in the same way as a theological proposition. There are thus within knowledge a number of distinct types of rational judgment. From considerations of this kind it can be seen that the acquisition of knowledge in any area involves the mastery of an interrelated group of concepts, of operations with these, of particular criteria of truth or validity associated with these concepts, as well as more general criteria of reasoning common to all areas of knowledge. Indeed, the objectives of education we have been considering are closely related together as elements of distinguishable cognitive structures, each unique in crucial respects.

Looked at this way, the development of mind has been marked by the progressive differentiation in human consciousness of some seven or eight distinguishable cognitive structures, each of which involves the making of a distinctive form of reasoned judgment and is, therefore, a unique expression of man's rationality. This is to say that all knowledge and understanding is logically locatable within a number of domains, within, I suggest, mathematics, the physical sciences, knowledge of persons, literature and the fine arts, morals, religion and philosophy. These would seem to me to be the logically distinct areas, though this division might well be disputed. It is not, of course, that these forms of knowledge are totally separate from each other. That is not what I am saying. Manifestly there are overlaps in the concepts used in the different forms, and there are overlaps in the patterns of valid reasoning. But in respect of the distinctive rational judgments concerned, each structure involves elements which are irreducible to any of the others, singly or in combination. Moral judgments and scientific judgments are different in logical character, needing distinct forms of justification, and that in spite of the fact that these may at times use some of the same concepts and some of the same criteria for reasoning. The objectives with which education is most centrally concerned are thus not isolated ends but elements within integrated developing structures of understanding. Certainly all the concepts, truths, norms, principles, criteria, all the developments of mind we are interested in, have their appropriate place in relation to these structures, and even those elements which are common to different areas have significance only within these structures.[4]

If what I have said is valid, then the domain of knowledge can be seen to have important structural features, and nothing could be further from the truth than to suggest that that domain is an unintelligible chaos. Knowledge has not disintegrated, it has become more clearly differentiated. It is not even that the traditional medieval map of knowledge has become totally unacceptable, for many of the logical distinctions there made are perfectly valid.[5] It is simply that the picture is more complicated than was once the case, or thought to be the case, and that the development of knowledge necessitates some new lines in the picture. We may no longer have a hierarchy of knowledge based on realist metaphysics, but we are not without the important logical distinctions that make it possible for us to see some intelligible pattern of knowledge. We may no longer have a clear grasp of the unity of knowledge, as if it all formed, in the end, one coherent network of harmonious elements. Yet unifying theories are part of the pursuit of the sub-divisions within the areas I have mentioned and there is every reason to hope that we can become much clearer on the relationships between the logically distinct forms that I have distinguished.

Yet what then of the modern transgressions of the old frontiers? Is it not the case that besides the progressive differentiation of, say, the sciences or historical studies, there are new disciplines or forms of knowledge emerging? Maybe this is so. I see no *a priori* reason whatever why new forms of knowledge should not arise. But there is, I think, little positive reason to think that this is in fact what is happening. What there are in abundance now, are new inter-disciplinary areas of study in which different forms of knowledge are focused on some particular interest, and because of the relations between the forms, what is understood in each discipline is thereby deepened. Such new areas of study do not constitute new areas on a map of knowledge based on the logical distinctions I have mentioned. They are essentially composite, second-order constructions, not to be confused with the primary forms of knowledge which I have distinguished on logical grounds. In terms of these primary forms of knowledge, the new areas seem to be exhaustively analysable.

From the preceding paragraphs it is no doubt apparent that to my mind understanding the nature of curriculum objectives is first and foremost a matter of understanding what is involved in the acquisition of knowledge. Other objectives would seem to be intelligible in character only in relation to the acquisition of knowledge. The forms of character development and skills that are frequently sought, for instance, are what they are in part because of the cognitive elements they necessarily involve. Having a critical attitude, or a preparedness to accept social change, is dependent on possessing much relevant knowledge without reference to which neither quality of mind can be adequately described or acquired. It would seem likely then that our analysis of the nature of educational objectives will in general reveal their being tied to and dependent on cognitive objectives and that their over-all structure of logical inter-relations will show them to rest on the logical structure of knowledge.

It is a logical mapping of objectives that curriculum planning needs, not a categorisation of them that fails to display their logical relations. Only with this is it plain just what has to be learnt, what must necessarily be grasped, in achieving any particular objective we may care to select.

The elucidation of this logical structure is a vast philosophical undertaking and one indeed which in different ways philosophers have always been engaged on. Its difficulties are immense and the agreed conclusions modest. At present curriculum planning must work with the very partial and scattered achievements of episte-mology and philosophy of mind using these where appropriate. The significance of philosophical considerations of this nature should not however be underestimated, for they can constitute powerful argu-ments in determining educational practice. That this is so can be seen from certain implications of the two main philosophical claims that have been voiced earlier.

If the acquisition of knowledge is the logically basic form of the development of a rational mind, and if the domain of knowledge consists of a limited number of different autonomous forms, the importance within the curriculum of the pursuit of knowledge is seen to be considerable and the significance of restricting the curriculum to certain areas of knowledge carries inescapable results for the pupils. On the first of these points, a curriculum which underplays objectives of a cognitive nature is limiting the pupils' development not only in those cognitive respects but in all other ways that presuppose those cognitive achievements. It seems to me to follow that we must firmly reject the anti-intellectualism of certain contemporary movements in education. No matter what the ability of the child may be, the heart of all his development as a rational being is, I am saying, intellectual, and we must never lose sight of these ends on which so much else, nearly everything else, depends. This means that we must get away completely from the idea that linguistic and abstract forms of thought are not for some people. If one is to develop any degree of understanding in any area of knowledge, then it is logically necessary to master the use of the appropriate symbolism. Mastery of that symbolism is not an extra to understanding but the very medium in which these forms of understanding can be acquired. I am, of course, here including the symbolism of music and the fine arts. The use of symbolism is basic to the development of mind, each area of understanding necessarily demanding a grasp of the appropriate symbols. We must therefore get away from what can be called a retreat into the arts and practical activities, as being more suitable for the less intellectually able. There is a central place in education for the arts and the practical, and that goes for all pupils. But the educational significance of these is limited, and any retreat from the demands of the many forms of language that are so central to human development is to set barriers to that development for many children.

How we can best teach such abstract, intellectual elements to the majority of pupils, let alone the less able, is not obvious. There are ways of easing the difficulties. But there are good ways of doing this and bad ways, and we need to distinguish between them. It is all too easy, with the best intentions in the world, to cease to teach such elements to the less able pupil in any significant sense at all. By not really bothering whether or not they have got hold of the concepts and can use them, by being content with memorised statements, by allowing pure repetition of operations, by omitting anything which demands even the briefest unrehearsed argument or justification, we simply evade all the problems and totally fail to develop any significant understanding. However we accommodate ourselves to the less able, it must not be by losing essential concepts, by losing genuine operations with them, by being uncritical of invalid reasoning, and so on. The necessary elements of knowledge are necessary elements and we cannot evade the implications of that simple tautology, try as we may. Yet there are things we can do. We can reduce the complexities by seeing that the conceptual relations we include are those absolutely essential for our purpose. Every unnecessary element that might befog an explanation can be omitted. We can cut down the extent of sustained argument by carefully analysing the stages that are demanded. We can use every opportunity to emphasise the central core of what is being done, rather than go in for extension and exploration of the ideas and their more complex applications. At least this is how we can set about things in the first place, and in our best teaching we do this already.

But if the cognitive objectives of the curriculum are important, the range of such objectives must not be forgotten. If the concepts and logical structure of one form of knowledge are necessarily valueless as vehicles for knowledge and understanding in another domain, to narrow the range of a child's curriculum to exclude certain forms is to leave the pupil unhelped in certain whole dimensions of thought and mental development. The business of 'subject-mindedness', paraded so outrageously in the Crowther Report as a natural phenomenon,[6] is not to be wondered at if knowledge is fundamentally differentiated. For our 'specialisation' we necessarily must pay the price.

Philosophical claims can at times provide powerful arguments in curriculum planning. And whether we like it or not our planning reflects certain philosophical beliefs. The question is simply how justifiable these are. The philosophical claims voiced here are to say the least debatable, but their significance surely is not. What we need above all in curriculum planning is a much more profound grasp of the nature of the objectives of the exercise and their logical inter-relations. If we can get the ends clearer maybe we can plan more effective means.

Notes

1 For a fuller discussion of the role of 'growth', 'needs' and 'interests' in educational planning, see R.F. Dearden, *The Philosophy of Primary Education*, Routledge & Kegan Paul, 1968.

2 B.S. Bloom, *et al.*, *Taxonomy of Educational Objectives*, McKay Co., Inc., New York, 1956.

3 R.S. Peters, *Ethics and Education*, Allen & Unwin, 1966, ch. 2; also W. Kneale, *On Having a Mind*, Cambridge University Press, 1962.

4 For a further discussion of the distinctions between different forms of knowledge see Chapter 3, 'Liberal education and the nature of knowledge.' See also S. Elam (ed.), *Education and the Structure of Knowledge*, Rand McNally, Chicago, 1964.

5 J. Maritain, *The Degrees of Knowledge*, Geoffrey Bles, 1959, Pt 1.

6 '*15 to 18*' a Report of the Central Advisory Council for Education, vol. 1, ch. 25, HMSO, 1959. See also A.D.C. Peterson, 'The myth of subjectmindedness', *Universities Quarterly*, June 1960.

3   Liberal education and the nature of knowledge

The phrase 'liberal education' has today become something of a slogan which takes on different meanings according to its immediate context. It usually labels a form of education of which the author approves, but beyond that its meaning is often entirely negatively derived. Whatever else a liberal education is, it is *not* a vocational education, *not* an exclusively scientific education, or *not* a specialist education in any sense. The frequency with which the term is employed in this way certainly highlights the inadequacies of these other concepts and the need for a wider and, in the long run, more worthwhile form of education. But as long as the concept is merely negative in what it intimates, it has little more than debating value. Only when it is given explicit positive content can it be of use in the serious business of educational planning. It is my contention in this chapter that whatever vagaries there have been in the use of the term, it is the appropriate label for a positive concept, that of an education based fairly and squarely on the nature of knowledge itself, a concept central to the discussion of education at any level.

The Greek notion of liberal education

The fully developed Greek notion of liberal education was rooted in a number of related philosophical doctrines; first about the significance of knowledge for the mind, and secondly about the relationship between knowledge and reality. In the first category there was the doctrine that it is the peculiar and distinctive activity of the mind, because of its very nature, to pursue knowledge. The achievement of knowledge satisfies and fulfils the mind which thereby attains its own appropriate end. The pursuit of knowledge is thus the pursuit of the good of the mind and, therefore, an essential element in the good life. In addition, it was held that the achievement of knowledge is not only the attainment of the good of the mind itself, but also the chief means whereby the good life as a whole is to be found. Man is more than pure mind, yet mind is his essential distinguishing characteristic, and it is in terms of knowledge that his whole life is rightly directed.

That knowledge is equal to its task was guaranteed by the second group of doctrines. These asserted that the mind, in the right use of reason, comes to know the essential nature of things and can apprehend what is ultimately real and immutable. Consequently, man no longer needs to live in terms of deceptive appearances and doubtful opinions and beliefs. All his experiences, life and thought can be given shape and perspective by what is finally true, by knowledge that corresponds to what is ultimately real. Further, the particular way in which reason is here represented as attaining knowledge, results in a view of the whole of man's understanding as hierarchically structured in various levels. From the knowledge of mere particulars to that of pure being, all knowledge has its place in a comprehensive and harmonious scheme, the pattern of which is formed as knowledge is developed in apprehending reality in its many different manifestations.

From these doctrines there emerged the idea of liberal education as a process concerned simply and directly with the pursuit of knowledge. But the doctrines give to this general idea particular meaning and significance; for they lead to a clear definition of its scope and content, and to a clear justification for education in these terms. The definition is clear, because education is determined objectively in range, in structure and in content by the forms of knowledge itself and their harmonious, hierarchical interrelations. There is here no thought of defining education in terms of knowledge and skills that may be useful, or in terms of moral virtues and qualities of mind that may be considered desirable. The definition is stated strictly in terms of man's knowledge of what is the case. The development of the mind to which it leads, be it in skills, virtues or other characteristics, is thought to be necessarily its greatest good.

The justification that the doctrines lend to this concept of education is threefold. First, such an education is based on what is true and not on uncertain opinions and beliefs or temporary values. It therefore has a finality which no other form of education has. Secondly, knowledge itself being a distinctive human virtue, liberal education has a value for the person as the fulfilment of the mind, a value which has nothing to do with utilitarian or vocational considerations. Thirdly, because of the significance of knowledge in the determination of the good life as a whole, liberal education is essential to man's understanding of how he ought to live, both individually and socially.

Here, then, the Greeks attained the concept of an education that was 'liberal' not simply because it was the education of free men rather than slaves, but also because they saw it as freeing the mind to function according to its true nature, freeing reason from error and illusion and freeing man's conduct from wrong. And ever since

Greek times this idea of education has had its place. Sometimes it has been modified or extended in detail to accommodate within its scheme new forms of knowledge: for instance Christian doctrines and the various branches of modern science. Sometimes the concept has been misinterpreted: as in Renaissance humanism when classical learning was equated with liberal education. Sometimes it has been strongly opposed on philosophical grounds: as by Dewey and the pragmatists. Yet at crucial points in the history of education the concept has constantly reappeared. It is hard to understand why this should be so.

Education, being a deliberate, purposeful activity directed to the development of individuals, necessarily involves considerations of value. Where are these values to be found? What is to be their content? How are they to be justified? They can be, and often are, values that reflect the interests of a minority group in the society. They may be religious, political or utilitarian in character. They are always open to debate and detailed criticism, and are always in need of particular justification. Is there not perhaps a more ultimate basis for the values that should determine education, some more objective ground? That final ground has, ever since the Greeks, been repeatedly located in man's conception of the diverse forms of knowledge he has achieved. And there has thus arisen the demand for an education whose definition and justification are based on the nature and significance of knowledge itself, and not on the predilections of pupils, the demands of society, or the whims of politicians. Precisely this demand was behind the development by the Greeks of an education in the seven liberal arts, an introduction to and a pursuit of the forms of knowledge as they were then conceived. It was precisely this demand that prompted Newman and Arnold in the nineteenth century to call for an education that aimed at the cultivation and development of the mind in the full range of man's understanding. It is the same demand that today motivates such classical realists as Maritain and R.M. Hutchins.

A typical modern statement: the Harvard Report

It may well be asked, however, whether those who do not hold the doctrines of metaphysical and epistemological realism can legitimately subscribe to a concept of education of this kind. Historically it seems to have had positive force only when presented in this particular philosophical framework. But historical association must be distinguished from logical connection and it is not by any means obvious that all the characteristic features of the concept are dependent on such philosophical realism. If the doctrines about mind, knowledge and reality mentioned at the beginning of this paper are regarded as at best too speculative a basis for educational planning, as well they may be, the possibility of an education defined and justified entirely in terms of the scope and character of knowledge needs re-examination. The significance of the concept originally came directly from the place the basic doctrines give to knowledge in a unified picture of the mind and its relation to reality. Knowledge is achieved when the mind attains its own satisfaction or good by corresponding to objective reality. A liberal education in the pursuit of knowledge is, therefore, seeking the development of the mind according to what is quite external to it, the structure and pattern of reality. But if once there is any serious questioning of this relationship between mind, knowledge and reality, the whole harmonious structure is liable to disintegrate. First there arise inevitably problems of definition. A liberal education defined in terms of knowledge alone is acceptable as long as knowledge is thought to be necessarily developing the mind in desirable ways, and hence promoting the good life. But if doubt is cast on these functions of knowledge, must not liberal education be redefined stating explicitly the qualities of mind and the moral virtues to which it is directed? And if knowledge is no longer seen as the understanding of reality but merely as the understanding of experience, what is to replace the harmonious, hierarchical scheme of knowledge that gave pattern and order to the education? Secondly there are equally serious problems of justification. For if knowledge is no longer thought to be rooted in some reality, or if its significance for the mind and the good life is questioned, what can be the justification for an education defined in terms of knowledge alone?

Difficulties of both kinds, but particularly those of definition, can be seen in the well-known Harvard Committee Report: *General Education in a Free Society*.[1] (In the Committee's terminology the aims of a 'liberal' and a 'general' education are identical.) Though certain of the doctrines that originally supported the concept of a liberal education are implicit in this work, the classical view of the significance of knowledge for the mind is considerably weakened, and the belief that in metaphysics man has knowledge of ultimate reality is ignored, if not rejected. The result is an ambiguous and unsatisfactory treatment of the problem of definition and a limited and debatable treatment of the question of justification. Some examination of the Report on both these scores, particularly the former, will serve to show that adequate definition and justification are not only not dependent on the classical doctrines, but can in fact be based directly on an explication of the concepts of 'mind' and 'knowledge' and their relationships.

The Report attempts the definition of a liberal education in two distinct ways: in terms of the qualities of mind it ought to produce and the forms of knowledge with which it ought to be concerned. What the precise relationship is between these two is not clear. It is asserted that they are 'images of each other', yet that there is no escape from 'describing general education at one time looking to the good man in society and at another time as dictated by the nature of knowledge itself'.[2] Which of the forms of description is to be given pride of place soon emerges, however. First, three areas of knowledge are distinguished, primarily by their distinctive methods: the natural sciences, the humanities and social studies. But it is made plain that 'the cultivation of certain aptitudes and attitudes of mind' is being aimed at, the elements of knowledge being the means for developing these. Liberal education is therefore best understood in terms of the characteristics of mind to which it leads. 'By characteristics we mean aims so important as to prescribe how general education should be carried out and which abilities ought to be sought above all others in every part of it. These abilities in our opinion are: to think effectively, to communicate thought, to make relevant judgments, to discriminate among values'.[3] The meaning of each of these four is elaborated at some length. Amongst the many things detailed of 'effective thinking' it is first said to be logical thinking of a kind that is applicable to such practical matters as deciding who to vote for and what wife to choose: it is the ability to extract universal truths from particular cases and to infer particulars from general laws: it is the ability to analyse a problem and to recombine the elements by the use of imagination. This thinking goes further than mere logic, however. It includes the relational thinking of everyday life, the ability to think at a level appropriate to a problem whatever its character. It includes too the imaginative thinking of the poet, the inventor, and the revolutionary. 'Communication', though 'obviously inseparable from effective thinking', is said to involve another group of skills, those of speaking and listening, writing and reading. It includes certain moral qualities such as candour, it covers certain vital aspects of social and political life and even the high art of conversation. 'The making of relevant value judgments' involves 'the ability of the student to bring to bear the whole range of ideas upon the area of experience', it is the art of effectively relating theory to practice, abstractions to facts, thought to action. Finally there is 'discrimination among values'. This includes the distinction of various kinds of value and their relative importance, an awareness of the values of character like fair play and self-control, intellectual values like the love of truth and aesthetic values like good taste, and, in addition, a commitment to such values in the conduct of life.[4]

34

As to how exactly these abilities come to be those developed by the three types of knowledge, little is said. It is noted that 'the three phases of effective thinking, logical, relational, and imaginative, correspond roughly to the three divisions of learning, the natural sciences, the social studies, and the humanities, respectively'.[5] The difficult connection between education in the making of value judgments and the formation of moral character is noted. Otherwise the remarks are of a general nature, emphasising that these abilities must be consciously developed in all studies and generalised as far as possible.

This double, if one-sided, characterisation of liberal education seems to me unsatisfactory and seriously misleading if what is said of the four abilities is examined more closely. In the first place, the notion that a liberal education can be directly characterised in terms of mental abilities and independently of fully specifying the forms of knowledge involved, is I think false. It is the result of a mis-understanding of the way in which mental abilities are in fact distinguishable. From what is said of 'effective thinking', it is perfectly plain that the phrase is being used as a label for mental activity which results in an achievement of some sort, an achieve-ment that is, at least in principle, both publicly describable and publicly testable—the solving of a mathematical problem, respon-sibly deciding who to vote for, satisfactorily analysing a work of art. Indeed there can be effective thinking only when the outcome of mental activity can be recognised and judged by those who have the appropriate skills and knowledge, for otherwise the phrase has no significant application. Thus although the phrase labels a form of mental activity, and such mental processes may well be directly accessible only to the person whose processes they are, its description and evaluation must be in public terms occurring in public language. Terms which, like 'effective thinking', describe activities involving achievements of some sort, must have public criteria to mark them. But in that case, none of the four abilities can in fact be delineated except by means of their detailed public features. Such characteri-sation is in fact forced on the Committee when they come to amplify what they mean. But their approach is simply illustrative, as if the abilities are directly intelligible in themselves, and the items and features of knowledge they give merely examples of areas where the abilities can be seen. If the public terms and criteria are logically necessary to specifying what the abilities are, however, then no adequate account of liberal education in terms of these can be given without a full account in terms of the public features of the forms of knowledge with which it is concerned. Indeed the latter is logically prior and the former secondary and derivative.

D

In the second place, the use of broad, general terms for these abilities serves in fact to unify misleading quite disparate achievements. For the public criteria whereby the exercise of any one of these abilities is to be judged are not all of a piece. Those that under the banner of 'effective thinking' are appropriate in, say, aesthetic appreciation are, apart from certain very general considerations, inappropriate in, say, mathematical thinking. In each case the criteria are peculiar to the particular area of knowledge concerned. Similarly, for instance, 'communication' in the sciences has only certain very basic features in common with 'communication' in poetic terms. It is only when the abilities are fully divided out, as it were, into the various domains and we see what they refer to in public terms that it is at all clear what is involved in developing them. To talk of developing 'effective thinking' is like talking of developing 'successful games playing'. Plainly that unifying label is thoroughly misleading when what constitutes playing cricket has practically nothing in common with what constitutes playing tiddly-winks. The implications of the term are not at all appreciated until what is wanted is given detailed specification. It is vitally important to realise the very real objective differences that there are in forms of knowledge, and therefore in our understanding of mental processes that are related to these. Maybe this unfortunate desire to use unifying concepts is a relic of the time when all forms of knowledge were thought to be similar, if not identical in logical structure and it was thought that the 'laws of logic' reflected the precise psychological operations involved in valid thinking. Be that as it may, the general terms used in the Report are liable both to blur essential distinctions and to direct the attention of educational planners into unprofitable descriptions of what they are after.

Thirdly, in spite of any protestations to the contrary, the impression is created by this terminology that it is possible to develop general unitary abilities of the stated kind. The extent to which this is true is a matter for empirical investigation into the transfer of training. Nevertheless such abilities must necessarily by characterised in terms of the public features of knowledge, and whatever general abilities there may be, the particular criteria for their application in diverse fields are vital to their significance for liberal education. But to think in these terms is to be in danger of looking for transfer of skills where none is discernible. We must not assume that skill at tiddly-winks will get us very far at cricket, or that if the skills have much in common, as in say squash and tennis, then rules for one activity will do as the rules for the other.

Failure to appreciate these points leads all too readily to programmes of education for which quite unwarranted claims are made. It is sometimes said, for instance, that the study of one major science can in itself provide the elements of a liberal education—that it can lead to the development of such abilities as effective thinking, communication, the making of relevant judgments, and even to some extent, discrimination among values. But this facile view is seen to be quite untenable if it is once understood how these abilities are defined, and how any one form of knowledge is related to them. Much more plausible and much more common is the attempt to relate directly the study of particular subjects to the development of particular unitary abilities. The Harvard Committee do this with subdivisions of 'effective thinking' when they suggest that, roughly speaking, logical thinking is developed by the sciences, relational thinking by social studies, and imaginative thinking by the humanities. This, of course, could be said to be true by definition if logical thinking were taken to be just that kind of thinking that is developed by the study of the sciences. But such a straight and limited connection is not at all what is indicated in the Report. The forms of thinking there are much more generalised. It follows then that logical, relational and imaginative thinking must be independently defined. Because of the vagueness of the terms it might appear that this would be simple enough. But in fact this very vagueness makes the task almost impossible, for any one of the three terms might, with considerable justice, be applied to almost any example of thinking. (And the appropriateness of using such a term as 'imaginative' to describe a distinct type of thinking rather than its manner or style is very debatable.) Even if these forms of thinking can be satisfactorily defined, it remains to be shown that each one of them demands the exercise of one distinct but general ability and that this ability can be developed by study in one particular area of human learning. Generally speaking there is little such evidence. What there is on transfer of training suggests that it occurs only where there is marked logical similarity in the elements studied.[6]

Finally the characterisation of a liberal education in these terms is misleading owing to the tendency for the concept to be broadened so that it is concerned not only with the development of the mind that results from the pursuit of knowledge, but also with other aspects of personal development, particularly emotional and moral, that may or may not be judged desirable. This tendency can be clearly seen in the Report's comments on the abilities of communication, making relevant judgments and discriminating among values. Stretching the edges of the concept in these ways leads to a much wider, more generalised notion of education. It then ceases to be one defined directly in terms of the pursuit of knowledge as liberal education originally was, and thus cannot be justified by justifying that pursuit. But this is surely to give up the concept in favour of another one that needs independent justification. The analysis of such a concept is beyond our present concern.

A re-assertion and a reinterpretation

On logical grounds, then, it would seem that a consistent concept of liberal education must be worked out fully in terms of the forms of knowledge. By these is meant, of course, not collections of information, but the complex ways of understanding experience which man has achieved, which are publicly specifiable and which are gained through learning. An education in these terms does indeed develop its related abilities and qualities of mind, for the mind will be characterised to a greater or lesser degree by the features of the understanding it seeks. Each form of knowledge, if it is to be acquired beyond a general and superficial level, involves the development of creative imagination, judgment, thinking, communicative skills, etc., in ways that are peculiar to itself as a way of understanding experience. To list these elements, picking them out, as it were, across the forms of knowledge of which they are part and in each of which they have a different stamp, draws attention to many features that a liberal education must of course include. But it draws attention to them at the expense of the differences among them as they occur in the different areas. And of itself such listing contributes nothing to the basic determination of what a liberal education is. To be told that it is the development of effective thinking is of no value until this is explicated in terms of the forms of knowledge which give it meaning: for example in terms of the solving of problems in Euclidean geometry or coming to understand the poems of John Donne. To be told instead that it is concerned with certain specified forms of knowledge, the essential characteristics of which are then detailed explicitly as far as possible, is to be given a clear understanding of the concept and one which is unambiguous as to the forms of thinking, judgment, imagination and communication it involves.

In his Gulbenkian Foundation Report *Arts and Science Sides in the Sixth Form*, Mr A.D.C. Peterson comes considerably nearer than the Harvard Committee to the definition of a liberal education (once more termed here a 'general education') by proceeding in just this fashion. Being concerned that this should not be worked out in terms of information, he shies away from any direct use of the term 'knowledge' and defines the concept modestly as one that 'develops the intellect in as many as possible of the main modes of thinking'.[7] These are then listed as the logical, the empirical, the moral and the aesthetic. The phrase 'modes of thinking', it is true, refers directly to forms of mental activity, and Mr Peterson's alternatives for it, 'modes of human experience', 'categories of mental experience' and (elsewhere) 'types of judgment', all look in the same direction. Yet the 'modes' are not different aspects of mind that cut across the forms that human knowledge takes, as the Harvard Report's 'abilities' are. They are, rather, four parallel forms of mental development. To complete this treatment so that there is no ambiguity, however, it must be made clear in a way that Mr Peterson does not make it clear, that the four forms can only be distinguished, in the last analysis, in terms of the public features that demarcate the areas of knowledge on which they stand. Logical, empirical, moral and aesthetic forms of understanding are distinguishable from each other only by their distinctive concepts and expressions and their criteria for distinguishing the true from the false, the good from the bad. If Mr Peterson's 'modes' are strictly explicated on the basis of these features of knowledge, then his concept of education becomes one concerned with the development of the mind as that is determined by certain forms of knowledge. This is to be in sight of a modern equivalent of the traditional conception of liberal education.

But the reassertion of this concept implies that there is once more the acceptance of some kind of 'harmony' between knowledge and the mind. This is, however, not now being maintained on metaphysical grounds. What is being suggested, rather, is that the 'harmony' is a matter of the logical relationship between the concept of 'mind' and the concept of 'knowledge', from which it follows that the achievement of knowledge is necessarily the development of mind—that is, the self-conscious rational mind of man—in its most fundamental aspect.

Whatever else is implied in the phrase, to have 'a rational mind' certainly implies experience structured under some form of conceptual scheme. The various manifestations of consciousness, in, for instance, different sense perceptions, different emotions, or different elements of intellectual understanding, are intelligible only by virtue of the conceptual apparatus by which they are articulated. Further, whatever private forms of awareness there may be, it is by means of symbols, particularly in language, that conceptual articulation becomes objectified, for the symbols give public embodiment to the concepts. The result of this is that men are able to come to understand both the external world and their own private states of mind in common ways, sharing the same conceptual schemata by learning to use symbols in the same manner. The objectification of understanding is possible because commonly accepted criteria for using the terms are recognised even if these are never explicitly expressed. But further, as the symbols derived from experience can be used to examine subsequent experience, assertions are possible which are testable as true or false, valid or invalid. There are thus also public criteria whereby certain forms of expression are assessable against experience. Whether the 'objects' concerned are themselves private to the individual like mental processes, or publicly accessible like temperature readings, there are here tests for the assertions which are themselves publicly agreed and accepted.

It is by the use of such tests that we have come to have the whole domain of knowledge. The formulating and testing of symbolic expressions has enabled man to probe his experience for ever more complex relations and for finer and finer distinctions, these being fixed and held for public sharing in the symbolic systems that have been evolved. But it is important to realise that this progressive attainment of a cognitive framework with public criteria has significance not merely for knowledge itself, for it is by its terms that the life of man in every particular is patterned and ordered. Without its structure all other forms of consciousness, including, for example, emotional experiences, or mental attitudes and beliefs, would seem to be unintelligible. For the analysis of them reveals that they lack independent intelligible structure of themselves. Essentially private though they may be in many or all of their aspects, their characteristic forms are explicable only by means of the publicly rooted conceptual organisations we have achieved. They can be understood only by means of the objective features with which they are associated, round which they come to be organised and built. The forms of knowledge are thus the basic articulations whereby the whole of experience has become intelligible to man, they are the fundamental achievement of mind.

Knowledge, however, must never be thought of merely as vast bodies of tested symbolic expressions. These are only the public aspects of the ways in which human experience has come to have shape. They are significant because they are themselves the objective elements round which the development of mind has taken place. To acquire knowledge is to become aware of experience as structured, organised and made meaningful in some quite specific way, and the varieties of human knowledge constitute the highly developed forms in which man has found this possible. To acquire knowledge is to learn to see, to experience the world in a way otherwise unknown, and thereby come to have a mind in a fuller sense. It is not that the mind is some kind of organ or muscle with its own inbuilt forms of operation, which if somehow developed, naturally lead to different kinds of knowledge. It is not that the mind has predetermined patterns of functioning. Nor is it that the mind is an entity which suitably directed by knowledge comes to take on the pattern of, is conformed to, some external reality. It is rather that to have a mind basically involves coming to have experience articulated by means of various conceptual schemata. It is only because man has over millennia objectified and progressively developed these that he has achieved the forms of human knowledge, and the possibility of the development of mind as we know it is open to us today.

A liberal education is, then, one that, determined in scope and content by knowledge itself, is thereby concerned with the development of mind. The concept is thus once more clearly and objectively defined in precisely the same way as the original concept. It is however no longer supported by epistemological and metaphysical doctrines that result in a hierarchical organisation of the various forms of knowledge. The detailed working out of the education will therefore be markedly different in certain respects. The distinctions between the various forms of knowledge which will principally govern the scheme of education will now be based entirely on analyses of their particular conceptual, logical and methodological features. The comprehensive character of the education will of course remain, since this is essentially part of the definition of the concept, but any question of the harmonious organisation of its various elements will depend on the relationships between them that are revealed by these analyses.

But if the concept is reasserted in these terms, what now of the question of its justification? The justification of a liberal education as supported by the doctrines of classical realism was based on the ultimacy of knowledge as ordered and determined by reality, and the significance of knowledge for the mind and for the good life. Having weakened these doctrines, the Harvard Committee's justification of their concept ignores the question of the relationship between knowledge and reality, and there is a specific rejection of the view that knowledge is in itself the good of the mind. They assert, however, the supreme significance of knowledge in the determination of all human activity, and supplement this, as is certainly necessary because of the extended nature of their concept, by general considerations of the desirability of their suggestions. When once more the concept is strictly confined so as to be determined by the forms of knowledge, the return to a justification of it without reference to what is generally thought desirable on social or similar grounds becomes possible. And such justification for the concept is essential if the education it delineates is to have the ultimate significance that, as was earlier suggested, is part of its *raison d'être*. This justification must now however stem from what has already been said of the nature of knowledge as no metaphysical doctrine of the connection between knowledge and reality is any longer being invoked.

If the achievement of knowledge is necessarily the development of mind in its most basic sense, then it can be readily seen that to ask for a justification for the pursuit of knowledge is not at all the same thing as to ask for the justification for, say, teaching all children a foreign language or making them orderly and punctual in their behaviour. It is in fact a peculiar question asking for justification for any development of the rational mind at all. To ask for the justification of any form of activity is significant only if one is in fact committed already to seeking rational knowledge. To ask for a justification of the pursuit of rational knowledge itself therefore pre-supposes some form of commitment to what one is seeking to justify. Justification is possible only if what is being justified is both intelligible under publicly rooted concepts and is assessable according to accepted criteria. It assumes a commitment to these two principles. But these very principles are in fact fundamental to the pursuit of knowledge in all its forms, be it, for instance, empirical knowledge or understanding in the arts. The forms of knowledge are in a sense simply the working out of these general principles in particular ways. To give justification of any kind of knowledge therefore involves using the principles in one specific form to assess their use in another. Any particular activity can be examined for its rational character, for its adherence to these principles, and thus justified on the assumption of them. Indeed in so far as activities are rational this will be possible. It is commitment to them that characterises any rational activity as such. But the principles themselves have no such assessable status, for justification outside the use of the principles is not logically possible. This does not mean that rational pursuits in the end lack justification, for they could equally well be said to have their justification written into them. Nor is any form of viciously circular justification involved by assuming in the procedure what is being looked for. The situation is that we have here reached the ultimate point where the question of justification ceases to be significantly applicable. The apparent circularity is the result of the inter-relation between the concepts of rational justification and the pursuit of knowledge.

Perhaps the finality of these principles can be brought out further by noting a negative form of the same argument. From this point of view, to question the pursuit of any kind of rational knowledge is in the end self-defeating, for the questioning itself depends on accepting the very principles whose use is finally being called in question.

It is because it is based on these ultimate principles that character-ise knowledge itself and not merely on lower level forms of justifi-cation that a liberal education is in a very real sense the ultimate form of education. In spite of the absence of any metaphysical doctrine about reality this idea of liberal education has a significance parallel to that of the original Greek concept. It is an education concerned directly with the development of the mind in rational knowledge, whatever form that freely takes. This parallels the original concept in that according to the doctrine of function liberal education was the freeing of the mind to achieve its own good in knowledge. In each case it is a form of education knowing no limits other than those necessarily imposed by the nature of rational knowledge and thereby itself developing in man the final court of appeal in all human affairs.

As here reformulated the concept has, again like the original, objectivity, though this is no longer backed by metaphysical realism. For it is a necessary feature of knowledge as such that there be public criteria whereby the true is distinguishable from the false, the good from the bad, the right from the wrong. It is the existence of these criteria which gives objectivity to knowledge; and this in its turn gives objectivity to the concept of liberal education. A parallel to another form of justification thus remains, and the concept continues to warrant its label as that of an education that frees the mind from error and illusion. Further, as the determination of the good life is now considered to be itself the pursuit of a particular form of rational knowledge, that in which what ought to be done is justified by the giving of reasons, this is seen as a necessary part of a liberal education. And as all other forms of knowledge contribute in their way to moral understanding, the concept as a whole is once more given a kind of justification in its importance for the moral life. But this justification, like that of objectivity, no longer has the distinct significance which it once had, for it is again simply a necessary consequence of what the pursuit of knowledge entails. Nevertheless, liberal education remains basic to the freeing of human conduct from wrong.

Certain basic philosophical considerations

Having attempted a reinstatement of the concept without its original philosophical backing, what of the implications of this for the practical conduct of education? In working these out it is necessary first to try to distinguish the various forms of knowledge and then to relate them in some way to the organisation of the school or college curriculum. The first of these is a strictly philosophical task. The second is a matter of practical planning that involves many considerations other than the purely philosophical, and to this I will return when certain broad distinctions between forms of knowledge have been outlined.

As stated earlier, by a form of knowledge is meant a distinct way in which our experience becomes structured round the use of accepted public symbols. The symbols thus having public meaning, their use is in some way testable against experience and there is the progressive development of series of tested symbolic expressions. In this way experience has been probed further and further by extending and elaborating the use of the symbols and by means of these it has become possible for the personal experience of individuals to become more fully structured, more fully understood. The various forms of knowledge can be seen in low level developments within the common area of our knowledge of the everyday world. From this there branch out the developed forms which, taking certain elements in our common knowledge as a basis, have grown in distinctive ways. In the developed forms of knowledge the following related distinguishing features can be seen:

(1)   They each involve certain central concepts that are peculiar in character to the form. For example, those of gravity, acceleration, hydrogen, and photo-synthesis characteristic of the sciences; number, integral and matrix in mathematics; God, sin and predestination in religion; ought, good and wrong in moral knowledge.

(2)   In a given form of knowledge these and other concepts that denote, if perhaps in a very complex way, certain aspects of experience, form a network of possible relationships in which experience can be understood. As a result the form has a distinctive logical structure. For example, the terms and statements of mechanics can be meaningfully related in certain strictly limited ways only, and the same is true of historical explanation.

(3)   The form, by virtue of its particular terms and logic, has expressions or statements (possibly answering a distinctive type of question) that in some way or other, however indirect it may be, are testable against experience. This is the case in scientific knowledge, moral knowledge, and in the arts, though in the arts no questions are explicit and the criteria for the tests are only partially expressible in words. Each form, then, has distinctive expressions that are testable against experience in accordance with particular criteria that are peculiar to the form.

(4)   The forms have developed particular techniques and skills for exploring experience and testing their distinctive expressions, for instance the techniques of the sciences and those of the various literary arts. The result has been the amassing of all the symbolically expressed knowledge that we now have in the arts and the sciences.

Though the various forms of knowledge are distinguishable in these ways it must not be assumed that all there is to them can be

44

made clear and explicit by these means. All knowledge involves the use of symbols and the making of judgments in ways that cannot be expressed in words and can only be learnt in a tradition. The art of scientific investigation and the development of appropriate experimental tests, the forming of an historical explanation and the assessment of its truth, the appreciation of a poem: all of these activities are high arts that are not in themselves communicable simply by words. Acquiring knowledge of any form is therefore to a greater or lesser extent something that cannot be done simply by solitary study of the symbolic expressions of knowledge, it must be learnt from a master on the job. No doubt it is because the forms require particular training of this kind in distinct worlds of discourse, because they necessitate the development of high critical standards according to complex criteria, because they involve our coming to look at experience in particular ways, that we refer to them as disciplines. They are indeed disciplines that form the mind.

Yet the dividing lines that can be drawn between different disciplines by means of the four suggested distinguishing marks are neither clear enough nor sufficient for demarcating the whole world of modern knowledge as we know it. The central feature to which they point is that the major forms of knowledge, or disciplines, can each be distinguished by their dependence on some particular kind of test against experience for their distinctive expressions. On this ground alone however certain broad divisions are apparent. The sciences depend crucially on empirical experimental and observational tests, mathematics depends on deductive demonstrations from certain sets of axioms. Similarly moral knowledge and the arts involve distinct forms of critical tests though in these cases both what the tests are and the ways in which they are applied are only partially statable. (Some would in fact dispute the status of the arts as a form of knowledge for this very reason.) Because of their particular logical features it seems to me necessary to distinguish also as separate disciplines both historical and religious knowledge, and there is perhaps an equally good case, because of the nature of their central concepts, for regarding the human sciences separately from the physical sciences. But within these areas further distinctions must be made. These are usually the result of the groupings of knowledge round a number of related concepts, or round particular skills or techniques. The various sciences and the various arts can be demarcated within the larger units of which they are in varying degrees representative in their structure, by these means.

But three other important classifications of knowledge must in addition be recognised. First there are those organisations which are not themselves disciplines or subdivisions of any discipline. They

are formed by building together round specific objects, or phenomena, or practical pursuits, knowledge that is characteristically
rooted elsewhere in more than one discipline. It is not just that these
organisations make use of several forms of knowledge, for after all
the sciences use mathematics, the arts use historical knowledge and
so on. Many of the disciplines borrow from each other. But these
organisations are not concerned, as the disciplines are, to validate
any one logically distinct form of expression. They are not concerned with developing a particular structuring of experience. They
are held together simply by their subject matter, drawing on all
forms of knowledge that can contribute to them. Geography, as the
study of man in relation to his environment, is an example of a
theoretical study of this kind, engineering an example of a practical
nature. I see no reason why such organisations of knowledge, which
I shall refer to as 'fields', should not be endlessly constructed
according to particular theoretical or practical interests. Second,
whilst moral knowledge is a distinct form, concerned with answering
questions as to what ought to be done in practical affairs, no
specialised subdivisions of this have been developed. In practical
affairs, moral questions, because of their character, naturally arise
alongside questions of fact and technique, so that there have been
formed 'fields' of practical knowledge that include distinct moral
elements within them, rather than the subdivisions of a particular
discipline. Political, legal and educational theory are perhaps the
clearest examples of fields where moral knowledge of a developed
kind is to be found. Thirdly, there are certain second order forms of
knowledge which are dependent for their existence on the other
primary areas. On the one hand there are the essentially scientific
studies of language and symbolism as in grammar and philology. On
the other hand there are the logical and philosophical studies of
meaning and justification. These would seem to constitute a distinct
discipline by virtue of their particular concepts and criteria of
judgment.

In summary, then, it is suggested that the forms of knowledge as
we have them can be classified as follows:

I Distinct disciplines or forms of knowledge (subdivisible):
mathematics, physical sciences, human sciences, history, religion,
literature and the fine arts, philosophy.

II Fields of knowledge: theoretical, practical (these may or may
not include elements of moral knowledge).

It is the distinct disciplines that basically constitute the range of
unique ways we have of understanding experience if to these is added
the category of moral knowledge.

The planning and practical conduct of liberal education

Turning now to the bearing of this discussion on the planning and conduct of a liberal education, certain very general comments about its characteristic features can be made though detailed treatment would involve psychological and other considerations that are quite beyond the scope of this chapter.

In the first place, as liberal education is concerned with the comprehensive development of the mind in acquiring knowledge, it is aimed at achieving an understanding of experience in many different ways. This means the acquisition by critical training and discipline not only of facts but also of complex conceptual schemes and of the arts and techniques of different types of reasoning and judgment. Syllabuses and curricula cannot therefore be constructed simply in terms of information and isolated skills. They must be constructed so as to introduce pupils as far as possible into the interrelated aspects of each of the basic forms of knowledge, each of the several disciplines. And they must be constructed to cover at least in some measure the range of knowledge as a whole.

In a programme of liberal education that is based directly on the study of the specific disciplines, examples of each of the different areas must of course be chosen. Selection of this kind is not however simply an inevitable practical consequence of the vast growth of knowledge. It is equally in keeping with what a liberal education is aiming at. Though its aim is comprehensive it is not after the acquisition of encyclopaedic information. Nor is it after the specialist knowledge of the person fully trained in all the particular details of a branch of knowledge. Such a specialist can not only accurately employ the concepts, logic and criteria of a domain but also knows the skills and techniques involved in the pursuit of knowledge quite beyond the immediate areas of common human experience. Nor is liberal education concerned with the technician's knowledge of the detailed application of the disciplines in practical and theoretical fields. What is being sought is, first, sufficient immersion in the concepts, logic and criteria of the discipline for a person to come to know the distinctive way in which it 'works' by pursuing these in particular cases; and then sufficient generalisation of these over the whole range of the discipline so that his experience begins to be widely structured in this distinctive manner. It is this coming to look at things in a certain way that is being aimed at, not the ability to work out in minute particulars all the details that can be in fact discerned. It is the ability to recognise empirical assertions or aesthetic judgments for what they are, and to know the kind of considerations on which their validity will depend, that matters.

47

Beyond this an outline of the major achievements in each area provides some grasp of the range and scope of experience that has thus become intelligible. Perhaps this kind of understanding is in fact most readily distinguishable in the literary arts as critical appreciation in contrast to the achievement of the creative writer or the literary hack. But the distinction is surely applicable to other forms of knowledge as well.

This is not to assert that 'critical' appreciation in any form of knowledge can be adequately achieved without some development of the understanding of the specialist or technician. Nor is it to imply that this understanding in the sciences, the arts or moral issues can be had without participation in many relevant creative and practical pursuits. The extent to which this is true will vary from discipline to discipline and is in fact in need of much investigation, particularly because of its importance for moral and aesthetic education. But it is to say that the aim of the study of a discipline in liberal education is not that of its study in a specialist or technical course. The first is concerned with developing a person's ways of understanding experience, the others are concerned with mastering the details of knowledge, how it is established, and the use of it in other enterprises, particularly those of a practical nature. It is of course perfectly possible for a course in physics, for example, to be devoted to a double purpose if it is deliberately so designed. It may provide both a specialist knowledge of the subject and at the same time a genuine introduction to the form of scientific knowledge. But the two purposes are quite distinct and there is no reason to suppose that by aiming at one the other can automatically be achieved as well. Yet it would seem to be true that some specialist study within a discipline, if it is at all typical of the discipline, is necessary to understanding the form of knowledge in any developed sense. The study of a discipline as part of liberal education, however, contributes practically nothing directly to any specialist study of it, though it does serve to put the specialism into a much wider context.

A liberal education approached directly in terms of the disciplines will thus be composed of the study of at least paradigm examples of all the various forms of knowledge. This study will be sufficiently detailed and sustained to give genuine insight so that pupils come to think in these terms, using the concepts, logic and criteria accurately in the different domains. It will then include generalisation of the particular examples used so as to show the range of understanding in the various forms. It will also include some indication of the relations between the forms where these overlap and their significance in the major fields of knowledge, particularly the practical fields, that have been developed. This is particularly important for moral education, as moral questions can frequently be solved only by calling on the widest possible range of human understanding. As there is in fact no developed discipline of moral knowledge, education in moral understanding must necessarily be approached in a rather different way. For if it is to cover more than everyday personal matters this has to be by the study of issues that occur in certain particular fields of knowledge. The major difficulty this presents will be referred to briefly later. The important point here is that though moral understanding has to be pursued in contexts where it is not the only dominant interest, the aim of its pursuit is precisely the same as for all other elements in a liberal education, the understanding of experience in a unique way. What is wanted (just as in the study of the disciplines *per se*) is, basically, the use of the appropriate concepts, logic, and criteria, and the appreciation of the range of understanding in this form.

It is perhaps important to stress the fact that this education will be one in the forms of knowledge themselves and not merely a self-conscious philosophical treatment of their characteristics. Scientific and historical knowledge are wanted, not knowledge of the philosophy of science and the philosophy of history as substitutes. A liberal education can only be planned if distinctions in the forms of knowledge are clearly understood, and that is a philosophical matter. But the education itself is only partly in philosophy, and that is only possible when pupils have some grasp of the other disciplines themselves.

Precisely what sections of the various disciplines are best suited to the aims of liberal education cannot be gone into here. It is apparent that on philosophical grounds alone some branches of the sciences, for instance, would seem to be much more satisfactory as paradigms of scientific thinking than others. Many sections of physics are probably more comprehensive and clear in logical character, more typical of the well developed physical sciences than, say, botany. If so, they would, all other things being equal, serve better as an introduction to scientific knowledge. Perhaps in literature and the fine arts the paradigm principle is less easy to apply though probably many would favour a course in literature to any one other. But whatever the discipline, in practice all other things are not in fact equal and decisions about the content of courses cannot be taken without careful regard to the abilities and interests of the students for whom they are designed.

Yet hovering round such decisions and questions of syllabus planning there is frequently found the belief that the inherent logical structure of a discipline, or a branch of a discipline necessarily determines exactly what and exactly how the subject is to be taught and learnt. The small amount of truth and the large amount of error in this belief can only be distinguished by clarifying what the logic of a subject is. It is not a series of intellectual steps that must be climbed in strict order. It is not a specific psychological channel along which the mind must travel if there is to be understanding. This is to confuse logical characteristics with psychological processes. The logic of a form of knowledge shows the meaningful and valid ways in which its terms and criteria are used. It constitutes the publicly accepted framework of knowledge. The psychological activities of the individual when concerned with this knowledge are not in general prescribed in any temporal order and the mind, as it were, plays freely within and around the framework. It is simply that the framework lays down the general formal relations of the concepts if there is to be knowledge. The logic as publicly expressed consists of the general and formal principles to which the terms must conform in knowledge. Coming to understand a form of knowledge involves coming to think in relations that satisfy the public criteria. How the mind plays round and within these is not itself being laid down at all, there is no dragooning of psychological processes, only a marking out of the territory in which the mind can wander more or less at will. Indeed understanding a form of knowledge is far more like coming to know a country than climbing a ladder. Some places in a territory may only be get-at-able by a single specified route and some forms of knowledge may have concepts and relations that cannot be understood without first understanding certain others. But that countries are explorable only in one way is in general false, and even in mathematics, the most strictly sequential form of knowledge we have, many ways of coming to know the territory are possible. The logic of a subject is relevant to what is being taught, for its patterns must be accepted as essential to the form of knowledge. But how those patterns are best discerned is a matter for empirical investigation.

School subjects in the disciplines as we at present have them are in no way sacrosanct on either logical or psychological grounds. They are necessarily selections from the forms of knowledge that we have and may or may not be good as introductions for the purposes of liberal education. In most cases they have developed under a number of diverse influences. The historical growth of the subjects has sometimes dominated the programmes. The usefulness of certain elements, the demands of higher specialist education, certain general 'psychological' principles such as progressing from the simple to the complex, from the particular to the general, the concrete to the abstract, all these factors and many others have left their marks. This being so, many well established courses need to be critically re-examined both philosophically and psychologically before they can be accepted as suitable for liberal education. Superficially at least most of them would seem to be quite inappropriate for this purpose.

Though a liberal education is most usually approached directly in the study of various branches of the disciplines, I see no reason to think that this must necessarily be so. It is surely possible to construct programmes that are in the first place organised round certain fields of knowledge either theoretical or practical. The study of aspects of power, natural as well as social and political, might for instance be one element in such a scheme: or a regional study that introduces historical, geographical, industrial and social considerations: or a practical project of design and building involving the sciences, mathematics and visual arts. In this case, however, it must be recognised that the fields are chosen because together they can be used to develop understanding of all the various forms of knowledge, and explicit steps must be taken to see that this end is achieved. There will necessarily be the strongest tendency for liberal education to be lost sight of and for the fields to be pursued in their own right developing the techniques and skills which they need. These may be valuable and useful in many ways, and perhaps essential in many a person's whole education. (Certainly liberal education as is here being understood is only one part of the education a person ought to have, for it omits quite deliberately for instance specialist education, physical education and character training.) But a course in various fields of knowledge will not in fact be a liberal education unless that aim is kept absolutely clear and every opportunity is taken to lead to a fuller grasp of the disciplines. Again some fields of study will be better for this purpose than others but all will demand the highest skill from the teacher, who must be under no misapprehension as to what the object of the exercise really is. Yet it is difficult to see how this kind of approach can be fully adequate if it does not in the end lead to a certain amount of study of the distinct disciplines themselves. For whatever ground may have been covered indirectly, a satisfactory understanding of the characteristically distinct approaches of the different forms is hardly possible without some direct gathering together of the elements of the disciplines that have been implicit in all that has been done.

Whatever the pattern of a liberal education in its later stages, it must not be forgotten that there is being presupposed a broad basic education in the common area of everyday knowledge where the various disciplines can be seen in embryo and from which they branch out as distinct units. In such a basic primary education, the ever growing range of a child's experience and the increasing use of linguistic and symbolic forms lays the foundation for the various

E

modes of understanding, scientific, historical, religious, moral, and so on. Out of this general pool of knowledge the disciplines have slowly become ever more differentiated and it is this that the student must come to understand, not confusing the forms of knowledge but appreciating them for what they are in themselves, and recognising their necessary limitations.

But is then the outcome of a liberal education to be simply the achievement of a series of discreet ways of understanding experience? In a very real sense yes, but in another sense not entirely. For one thing, we have as yet not begun to understand the complex interrelations of the different forms of knowledge themselves, for they do not only have unique features but common features too, and in addition one discipline often makes extensive use of the achievements of another. But we must also not forget that the various forms are firmly rooted in that common world of persons and things which we all share, and into this they take back in subtle as well as simple ways the understanding they have achieved. The outcome of a liberal education must therefore not be thought of as producing ever greater disintegration of the mind but rather the growth of ever clearer and finer distinctions in our experience. If the result is not some quasi-aesthetic unity of the mind neither is it in any sense chaos. Perhaps the most suggestive picture of the outcome is that used by Professor Michael Oakeshott, though for him it has more literal truth than is here intended. In this the various forms of knowledge are seen as voices in a conversation, a conversation to which they each contribute in a distinctive way. If taken figuratively, his words express more succinctly than mine can precisely what it seems to me a liberal education is and what its outcome will be.

> As civilised human beings, we are the inheritors, neither of an inquiry about ourselves and the world, nor of an accumulating body of information, but of a conversation, begun in the primeval forests and extended and made more articulate in the course of centuries. It is a conversation which goes on both in public and within each of ourselves. Of course there is argument and inquiry and information, but wherever these are profitable they are to be recognized as passages in this conversation, and perhaps they are not the most captivating of the passages . . . Conversation is not an enterprise designed to yield an extrinsic profit, a contest where a winner gets a prize, nor is it an activity of exegesis; it is an unrehearsed intellectual adventure . . . Education, properly speaking, is an initiation into the skill and partnership of this converation in which we learn to

recognize the voices, to distinguish the proper occasions of utterance, and in which we acquire the intellectual and moral habits appropriate to conversation And it is this conversation which, in the end, gives place and character to every human activity and utterance.[8]

Notes

1 *General Education in a Free Society:* Report of the Harvard Committee, Oxford University Press, 1946.
2 Ibid., p. 58.
3 Ibid., pp. 64–5.
4 Ibid., pp. 65–73.
5 Ibid., p. 67.
6 Precisely the same criticisms might be made of some remarks by Professor P.H. Nowell-Smith in his inaugural lecture, *Education in a University* (Leicester University Press, 1958), pp. 6–11. In these he suggests that the prime purpose of the study of literature, history and philosophy is that each develops one of the central powers of the mind —creative imagination, practical wisdom, and logical thought. Once more we are up against the question of the definition of these 'powers' and if that problem can be solved, the question of sheer evidence for them and the way they can be developed.
7 *Arts and Science Sides in the Sixth Form:* Gulbenkian Foundation Report, Oxford University Department of Education, 1960, p. 15.
8 Michael Oakeshott, *Rationalism in Politics and Other Essays*, Methuen, 1962, pp. 198–9.

4   Realms of meaning and forms of knowledge

The thesis that human knowledge, meaning and understanding consists of a limited number of quite different kinds, has for many diverse reasons fascinated philosophers from the time of Plato down to the present day. If true, the thesis is of major educational importance as Plato showed, and it is therefore not surprising that it has come to the fore once more in the recent revival of work in philosophy of education. In particular, those interested in articulating a philosophically respectable account of general or liberal education have been drawn into re-examining the thesis. Even in this restricted context, however, it has taken a number of different forms and has been defended in a variety of ways. In this chapter I shall critically discuss a widely known version of this thesis, for it seems to me to go straight for the central questions educationists must ask in this area, starts to answer then in much the right way, but unfortunately takes a number of mistaken turnings which make the final account unsatisfactory. Examining this particular approach will, I hope, throw into clearer relief what is needed in a more acceptable account.

In his book *Realms of Meaning*, Professor Philip Phenix[1] maintains that 'general education is the process of engendering essential meanings',[2] and that there are 'six fundamental patterns of meaning (which) emerge from the analysis of the possible distinctive modes of human understanding'.[3] The six realms listed as symbolics, empirics, esthetics, synnoetics, ethics and synoptics, are seen as providing 'the foundations for all the meanings that enter into human experience. They are the foundations in the sense that they cover the pure and archetypal kinds of meaning that determine the quality of every humanly significant experience'.[4] Though in practice meanings seldom appear in pure and simple form, being almost always compounded of several of the elemental types, these elements give us the basic ingredients in all meaning. What is more, the six realms[5]

may be regarded as comprising the basic competences that general education should develop in every person. A complete person should be skilled in the use of speech, symbol and gesture factually well informed, capable of creating and appreciating objects of esthetic significance, endowed with a rich and disciplined life in relation to self and others, able to make wise decisions and to judge between right and wrong, and possessed of an integral outlook. These are the aims of general education for the development of whole persons.

It is perfectly plain from these introductory parts of his book that for Phenix, general education is concerned not merely with intellectual development. He is explicit that in using the term 'meaning' one must recognise in the life of meaning, which is the essence of the life of man, not the processes of logical thinking only but the life of feeling, conscience, inspiration and other processes not retained in the strict sense.[6] Meaning, he suggests has four dimensions. First that of inner experience, including the quality of reflectiveness, self-awareness, self-transcendence, which all varieties of meaning exemplify. Secondly, there is the dimension of rule, logic and principle, each type of meaning being defined by a particular logic or structural principle. Thirdly, there is the dimension of selective elaboration. Theoretically there is no limit to the varieties of meaning, but not all these are humanly important and selection has occurred leading to the development of those that are significant and have an inherent power of growth and elaboration. These are to be found in the world of disciplined scholarship. One could 'attempt an *a priori* analysis of possible classes of meaning and attempt to forecast which would prove most fertile. It seems far better, however, . . . to regard as most significant the forms that have actually demonstrated their fecundity'. Finally, there is the dimension of expression, for the meanings we are interested in are not private property, but are communicable through symbols. Symbols are objects that stand for meaning.[7]

As the classification of meanings in education is to facilitate learning, Phenix maintains that it is desirable to organise the scholarly disciplines along lines of general similarity of logical structure, for in this way certain basic ways of knowing can be described. By studying the logical patterns of the disciplines, he asserts, they may be divided into nine generic classes.[8]

This can be demonstrated as follows. Every cognitive meaning has two logical aspects, namely *quantity* and *quality*. That is to say, knowledge consists in a relation of the knower to some range of things known, and each such relation is of some kind. Now there are three degrees of quantity: *singular*, *general* and *comprehensive*. That is, knowledge is of either one thing, or a selected plurality or a totality. Furthermore there are three distinct qualities of meaning, which can be designated as *fact*, *form* and *norm*. In other words, the meaning may refer to what

55

actually exists, to imagined possibilities, or to what ought to be.[9]

By pairing the various aspects of quantity and quality, the nine basic or generic classes of meaning are characterised. For the purpose of his book however Phenix reduces these to six realms, treating the two normative classes together under 'ethics' and the three comprehensive classes together under 'synoptics'. The resulting classification of meanings and the disciplines involving them is summarised below:[10]

TABLE I *Logical classification of meanings*

Generic classes		Realms of	
Quantity	Quality	meaning	Disciplines
General	Form	Symbolics	Ordinary language, mathematics, nondiscursive symbolic forms
General	Fact	Empirics	Physical sciences, life sciences, psychology, social sciences
Singular	Form	Esthetics	Music, visual arts, arts of movement, literature
Singular	Fact	Synnoetics	Philosophy, psychology, literature, religion, in their existential aspects
Singular	Norm		The varied special areas
General	Norm	Ethics	of moral and ethical concern
Comprehensive	Fact		History
Comprehensive	Norm	Synoptics	Religion
Comprehensive	Form		Philosophy

In this account Phenix refers little to the concept of 'knowledge', though the term does get used occasionally, and the generic classes are said to be those of 'cognitive' meaning. It is perhaps most significantly used in elucidating the 'quantity' aspect of meanings, where it is said that knowledge is of either one thing or a plurality or a totality. In his paper 'The architectonics of knowledge'[11] however, the same generic classes are described as 'classes of knowledge', 'ways of knowing', 'categories of knowledge', 'species of knowledge', the classification being explicitly said to be one of what people claim to know. 'Quantity' and 'quality' are referred to also under the labels 'extension' and 'intension' being aspects of 'epistemic meaning'. From this evidence, I take it that though Phenix considers meaning to have a number of dimensions, the classification of meanings in the end reduces to, or rests on, the classification of knowledge and that in its turn is accomplished by classifying the objects of knowledge, classifying what is known. With that approach, for reasons which will emerge later, I am in complete agreement. Having said that, however, Phenix's next move is worrying, for his position seems to suffer from a serious lack of clarity about what one is classifying in classifying the 'objects' of knowledge.

In everyday parlance, the objects of knowledge are people, places, physical things, theories, practical skills, feelings, etc. We may know Edward Heath, how a car works, what happens if we break the law, what it feels like to be afraid or to be in love. The objects here are very diverse in kind and presumably could be classified in some way. In a philosophical context, however, the phrase 'objects of knowledge' is in general taken not to cover the objects about which, or of which, we have knowledge, but the logical objects of knowledge when that state of mind is being distinguished from others. In this sense there would seem to be three candidates for the logical objects. First, we know people, places, things—sometimes referred to as 'knowledge with the direct object'. Second, we know what is the case, where what we know is expressed in a true statement or proposition —usually referred to as 'knowledge-that'. Third, we know how or when to do certain things, procedural knowledge in the sense of actually being able to do these things—usually referred to as 'knowledge-how'. Of these, the last is clearly very different in kind from the first two. It may in fact always involve knowledge of both the first two kinds, but it clearly picks out certain capacities over and above the cognitive understanding and mastery of which a person is capable. In seeking to distinguish types of knowledge, these additional aspects are not being denied, but it is not these with which we are concerned. What of 'knowledge with the direct object' however? Clearly much of what this covers is 'knowledge-that' about the persons or objects concerned. To this, however, is usually added a claim to have direct experience of the person or object, and many writers speak here of having existential knowledge, a form of experience which is not itself expressible in statements of propositions. Phenix clearly considers 'knowledge with the direct object' to be a distinct type of knowledge primarily because of these existential aspects. It is, however, very debatable whether it should be so regarded, and particularly so if knowledge is to be kept clear from all other states of mind. If it is indeed types of knowledge one is after, rather than types of experience or feeling, then it seems to me important not to confuse knowledge with other states, particularly states of perception, awareness and feeling.

It helps, I suggest, to remember that in general knowing is not an occurrent, conscious experience or state of awareness at all. One knows all one knows when none of it is before one's mind. Coming to know may be an experience, but the knowledge achieved at that moment is not to be confused with the concomitant awareness. What one knows in the existential form of 'knowledge with the direct object' is thus characterisable as 'knowledge-that' concerning the object on which supervenes an occurrent state of awareness which is of a quite different character. Knowledge of the first kind, I therefore suggest, is reducible to 'knowledge-that'. It is not that existential awareness is being demoted in significance, it is simply that its proper nature needs to be kept clear and it seems to me a mistake to regard the problems it raises as problems for a theory of knowledge as such. In saying this it needs also to be said that the idea of such existential awareness being outside conceptualisation seems to me a contradiction. To have an experience at all is surely for some concepts to be employed under which one becomes aware of the occurrence. It may indeed be true that the experience cannot even in principle be expressed in a proposition or statement, but that is not to say that it is unstructured by concepts of some kind, however primitive or imprecise. Existential experiences then are intelligible and indeed occur only by virtue of the concepts which they involve, but that does not make them states of knowledge. In so far as concepts are involved it may be said that the state involves some element of 'knowledge-that'. But that experience is not equatable with a state of knowing, and the experience itself cannot be indicated simply by expressing that knowledge content.

I conclude that if it is knowledge other than 'knowledge-how' which one wishes to classify, it is 'knowledge-that' which one is concerned with. On the basis of this analysis one can I think produce a classification of concepts which will enable us to classify existential experience if we so wish. Phenix is I think right to hold that types of meaning are classified by first looking at types of knowledge, but he is mistaken in thinking that knowledge must then be taken as a category wide enough to cover existential awareness and other intelligible states. This is all the more unfortunate as the distinction he draws between different dimensions of meaning itself suggests that existential awareness and inner experience are not to be regarded as belonging to the same dimension as that of knowledge. If 'knowledge-that' is taken as characterising one dimension of meaning, it provides categories that then enable us to distinguish different catgories in the dimension of awareness and experience. Phenix has, I suggest, introduced into the dimension of knowledge, where he wishes to distinguish fundamental categories, elements that belong to another dimension, thus confusing the operation. The thesis that the categories of meaning are fundamentally distinguishable as categories of knowledge is only true if it is 'knowledge-that' which is being considered. The categorisation of 'knowledge-that' itself provides the categories adequate for any distinctions in forms of experience or awareness we may then wish to make, for all such experiences must involve concepts that are distinguishable within 'knowledge-that'. What is further confusing is that, as it will now be seen, when he comes to the basis of his categorisation of knowledge Phenix does at first confine himself to 'knowledge-that', only to go back on this later.

If the task of distinguishing types of knowledge is a question of distinguishing different types of the objects of knowledge, it is then in fact a matter of looking for different types of true statements or propositions, for it is in these that the objects of 'knowledge-that' are expressed. But how exactly is this to be done? Although Phenix seems to me mistaken about the objects of knowledge, seeing these as going beyond what is expressed in true propositions, when he comes to the task of classifying the objects, he nevertheless sets about this by examining propositions or statements, seeking to produce a classification of these. All true propositions he sees as having both a quantitative and a qualitative aspect. The first of these, concerned with the number of entities to which a proposition refers, is indeed a feature of all true propositions. There must always be some numerical aspect to what is asserted, and the quantities Phenix gives, singular, general, comprehensive, can be made to cover all the possibilities. The qualitative aspects of fact, form and norm that he distinguishes are, however, another matter. If it is the objects of knowledge we are concerned with, then all the propositions that interest us must be true and all must therefore, in at least one sense of that term, state facts. Yet fact is only one of the qualitative aspects Phenix allows, norm and form being the others. If therefore Phenix takes true statements of norm and form not to be statements of fact but to have other qualities, he is clearly using the term 'fact' in a restricted way. But in what way? Philosophers have debated very thoroughly what this term can mean, but I am far from happy with the idea that it picks out a category of true statements that can be contrasted with true statements of norm and form. If we know that $2 + 3 = 5$, is it not a fact we know? If we know that we ought to tell the truth, is this not again a knowledge of fact? The term is surely much too ambiguous to do the job Phenix wants unless given a very specific characterisation. The notion of form seems to me equally unsatisfactory. It is suggested that this picks out imagined possibilities, thereby distinguishing a feature that characterises the logical or formal truths of language, mathematics and philosophy as well as matters of esthetic form. Similarly, the idea of norm is difficult to tie down. Why is it peculiarly associated with ethics and given no explicit connection with

59

esthetics? From these considerations it seems to me that what is meant by each of the three qualitative aspects is too unclear for them to be used as a classificatory device, and in particular it is not obvious that they are mutually exclusive categories. Nor, unless these three are interpreted widely, am I sure that every true proposition necessarily has one of these qualities, unless, that is, fact is taken to cover any and every proposition that might otherwise cause difficulties.

But even if it is the case that every true proposition has a quantitative and qualitative aspect, why are these two features chosen as the bases for classification? Every true proposition has the characteristic of being tensed, being about the past, the present, or the future. Why has Phenix not chosen that feature? Why not classify propositions into indicative and hypothetical, or into positive and negative? In fact Phenix gives us no reason. He seems to be relying on certain traditional notions of logical differences without any reconsideration in the light of much recent philosophical analysis which shows them to be not only unsatisfactory as logical categories but categorisations not really appropriate to the task in hand.

Manifestly one can classify true propositions in a great variety of ways but if we are to classify them as true propositions and nothing else, we must do this by virtue of their logically necessary features and not by any other characteristics they may happen to have. To take a parallel, if we were seeking a classification of motor vehicles, we might do this by colour if we were concerned with painting them, or by weight for some other purpose. All vehicles are indeed coloured and have weight, even in one sense 'necessarily' so. But to classify them by, say, colour is not in fact to classify them as vehicles but rather as coloured objects. If it is vehicles as such we are to classify we must do this by characteristics that pick out objects under that description and not some other. Such a classification by logically necessary features is in an important sense fundamental, even if it is not in terms of a set of logically primitive and independent categories. It is a classification according to the 'nature' of the 'objects' concerned not according to other non-defining properties.

But what then are the criteria that distinguish the objects of knowledge-that? They are those necessary to there being true propositions, and those I suggest are (a) concepts appropriately related in a logical structure so that propositions can be formed and (b) criteria for judging the propositions to be true. If we are to logically distinguish types of knowledge we must in fact distinguish areas which are different in respect of their conceptual systems and truth criteria. It is not being said that these two features of knowledge are logically independent of each other. Indeed the existence of any concepts that are not in some way logically related to truth criteria is problematic and I am not at this point wishing to make any judgment on that issue. Where the classification of knowledge is concerned, the existence of truth criteria is however certainly necessary and that presupposes the existence of a related structure of concepts.

I have elsewhere sought to work out the implications of such a classification of knowledge.[12] Here I am more concerned with examining, in the light of these comments, the two aspects of true propositions that Phenix uses. The quantitative aspect is, I suggest, no more relevant to a logical classification of the objects of knowledge than a classification by colour would be to a logical classification of vehicles of transport. The qualitative aspect is, however, another matter. This, I suggest, is in fact an unsatisfactory, because confused, classification according to the criteria I have sought to elucidate. Its unsatisfactoriness stems from too restricted a view of possible varieties of truth criteria. The truth criteria of factual, normative and formal claims do indeed differ, but these three types of propositions need careful delineation and on analysis there would seem to be more than three different types of truth. What therefore seems to me to be called for, is simply a more detailed working out of the distinctions made rather dogmatically by Phenix in terms of 'quality', and a rejection of any classification in terms of 'quantity'.

In the light of the criticisms voiced about Phenix's notion of the 'objects' of knowledge, and the criteria he has used to distinguish types of knowledge, certain aspects of his final outline stand out as unacceptable. Only if the objects of knowledge are taken to be 'objects' in the everyday, non-philosophical sense, does it seem to me to be possible to assert that the domain of symbolics is that of a distinct type of knowledge. All knowledge is in fact, at least in principle, expressable in symbols of some sort, for otherwise the public features necessary for judgments of truth would not exist. They are the vehicles of knowledge rather than themselves the basis of one type of knowledge. Knowledge of symbols we do have of course, but of many different kinds, depending on the type of propositions about symbols being considered. It may be grammatical knowledge, knowledge of logical relations or of meaning, of translational equivalents, or simply of one's mother tongue. The logical objects of knowledge in these cases are as varied as the truth criteria that go with them. But symbols as such designate no logically distinct domain of knowledge any more than any other particular 'object', in the non-philosophical sense, does. A knowledge of chairs, say, may be of many different fundamental kinds, scientific, esthetic, even moral or religious. No 'objects' in this sense pick out logically distinct types of knowledge.

A not totally dissimilar problem arises with the area of knowledge

Phenix labels 'synnoetics'. Again a category of 'objects' in the non-philosophical sense is the focus of a type of knowledge, existential experience of these being a second distinctive factor. The focusing on non-propositional 'objects' and the defining concern for experience both seem to me to invalidate the claim to a logically distinct type of knowledge here. A third unsatisfactory aspect of the characterisation of synnoetics arises from the ambiguity of Phenix's use of the quantitative aspects of knowledge. The division of the objects concerned into singular, general and comprehensive is said to be based on the fact that knowledge is of either one thing, a plurality or a totality. If this is taken to mean that true propositions are about one object, a plurality or a totality of objects, singular propositions occur in many areas of knowledge, in the sciences, mathematics, religion and so on. So do statements about pluralities and totalities. Only if the objects of knowledge are not taken as true propositions but as objects in the everyday sense and 'singular' is taken to mean 'unique' or 'not communicable' can the domain of 'singular fact' be equated with what Phenix calls synnoetics.

Trouble with the notion of quantity occurs too in what is said about the comprehensive types of knowledge. It is not at all true to claim that propositions about a totality of objects are characteristic of historical knowledge which is far more likely to be formed of singular statements. Neither religion nor philosophy is to be picked out in this way either, though one can here see why Phenix considers these, in some other sense, comprehensive. Nor do I understand why symbolics should be thought to be concerned with general propositions, if that domain is to cover mathematics and non-discursive symbolic forms.

But all these difficulties with the detail of the classification are surely but the outcome of ambiguity about the objects of knowledge and appropriate classification criteria for them. What it is that the notions of quantity and quality are being applied to, is uncertain, and the resulting meaning of the terms labelling the generic domains is unclear. Why the list is reduced from nine classes to six is left unstated. This is somewhat disconcerting as the resulting six, not the original nine, are regarded as pure, fundamental, archetypal and generic, in spite of the explicitly stated composite character of two of these. This provokes perhaps the most interesting questions one would like Phenix to have answered. What is the status of these six domains? Are they categorically distinct in the Kantian sense of that term? Are they ultimate in some metaphysical sense? Does he consider that the realms he has distinguished are absolute in that they cannot change? Is it conceivable that quite new realms could arise?

It is perfectly clear that the academic disciplines man has developed are in no sense considered by Phenix to be ultimate or absolute, and their composite character is repeatedly emphasised. What strikes one as strange however, is that the disciplines do not reflect more closely the distinct generic types of knowledge, if all knowledge and meaning is to be located in such logically pure domains. Indeed the allocation of traditional disciplines to the generic classes is often unconvincing even idiosyncratic. One can find some reason why each is listed where it is, but these reasons are often uneasily related to the theory that should be their basis. No one could accuse Phenix of producing a theory that turns out to be a vast rationalisation seeking to justify existing disciplines as fundamental categories of knowledge. On the other hand, if the six types are ultimate, it is a little strange that they have not been more extensively developed within their own terms. Indeed one would like to know what exactly Phenix considers the logical features of a discipline to be. Are all established areas of study disciplines, or is that term more appropriate when the area does concern itself with developing one generic type of knowledge within the logical structure peculiar to it? Areas of research and of teaching may be complex, but what of those which are not? Phenix stresses very much the importance of the disciplines in education and gives some valid reasons if these are the areas in which knowledge has progressed. But it is the generic types of knowledge that ultimately justify the range of the curriculum for him and one wonders why those disciplines that express the types of knowledge in the purest forms are not the heart of his concern. Perhaps a tighter logical characterisation of a discipline would help to distinguish those areas of knowledge to which general education ought to pay particular attention. The enterprise is primarily concerned with finding the logical demands a general education ought to respect and may be the notion of a discipline is yet more central to this concept than Phenix implies, if it is seen as tied to the notion of a fundamental type of knowledge.

It has sometimes been maintained that in his analysis Phenix has been concerned with types of meaning rather than knowledge and that his six realms have been distinguished on criteria that pick out varieties of meaning rather than varieties of knowledge. As I was at pains to point out at the beginning of this chapter, this seems to me quite contrary to Phenix's own account of what he has sought to do. What is more it seems to me one of the great strengths of Phenix's work that he, implicitly at least, accepts that the categorisation of meaning is in the end a matter of categorising knowledge or at least knowledge claims. It is quite true that the domain of what is meaningful extends vastly beyond the domain of what is known. For every true proposition that can be the object of knowledge there is an infinite number of false propositions which are meaningful but not the objects of knowledge. Even amongst utterances, meaning extends beyond stating propositions to a myriad of other uses of language in commands, questions, curses, etc. Actions too and events can be said to have meaning. What is more, appreciating the meaning of something may well at times have the kind of dimensions that Phenix outlines. But all aspects of meaning necessitate the use of concepts and it is only by virtue of conceptualisation that there is anything we can call meaning at all. And no concepts can be the basis of shared meaning without criteria for their application. But the criteria for the application of a concept, say 'x', simply are the criteria for the truth of statements that say that something is an 'x'. By this chain of relations, that meaning necessitates concepts, that concepts necessitate criteria of application and that criteria of application are truth criteria for propositions or statements, the notions of meaning and true propositions, and therefore meaning and knowledge, are logically connected. There is a terrible temptation to think that we can understand other people simply by being able to use the same word patterns as they do, relating words in definitions according to agreed rules. But such relations do not themselves give meaning to any of the words employed. At least some words must have meaning other than in relation to yet further words. Nor is it sufficient for meaning that we use the same word patterns in the same circumstances, unless they are being related to these circumstances according to agreed rules. And that means that the words signify in part the application of certain concepts according to agreed criteria, criteria which in their turn constitute the truth criteria for a whole range of propositions.

Professor Hamlyn has expressed this point as follows:

One of Wittgenstein's most important remarks in the *Philosophical Investigations* is the one to the effect that if language is to be a means of communication there must be agreement in judgments as well as agreement in definitions. If people are to understand each other, they must not only understand the words that other people use, in the sense that they could possibly provide a translation of those words into other words; they must also have some appreciation of the circumstances in which these words might properly be given application. To put it another way—an understanding of what men say involves not only an understanding of the individual words that they use (something that might be expressed in definitions) but also the criteria of truth of the statements that they make by means of those words (something that implies agreement on the circum-

stances in which those statements might be said to be true).
There are thus certain conceptual connexions between the
concepts of meaning, truth, and agreement . . . [13]

Of course, none of this means that all concepts must in fact *be*
applicable in the observable world. There is a perfectly good concept
of a mermaid though no mermaids exist and the term is therefore
never in fact applicable. But it is important to notice that we do have
perfectly clear criteria for judging whether it is true that any being
is in fact a mermaid. Meaning and the existence of truth criteria are
clearly tied together here, for if we did not know the criteria for
judging whether or not some being were a mermaid, we could not be
said to know what the term meant. Nor is it at all necessary that the
criteria for application shall always be observable states. That is true
for certain types of concepts. What is important, however, is that the
criteria be publicly agreed and that their satisfaction be matters of
judgment about which there is also public agreement. Varieties of
meaning will thus go with varieties of truth criteria for propositions
involving the application of concepts. Perhaps the importance of the
connection between meaning and truth criteria can best be illus-
trated from the problems that arise in seeking to communicate the
meaning of religious claims. Central here is just the very principle
being defended; that a person understands the meaning of religious
propositions to the extent that he understands the truth criteria for
them. To some, those criteria simply are those used for propositions
about events in the everyday world. God is then understood only in
terms of the concepts we use of everyday occurrences, there being no
others in which religious claims could have meaning. Statements
about God may then be descriptive of a person understood through
strictly human attributes only. To others, religious propositions may
demand translation into moral categories as these are taken to give
us the criteria which can anchor their meaning. To others again
these approaches are dismissed as forms of reductionism. But the
problem then is the character of the truth criteria which are to be
used, criteria which it is insisted are irreducible. Whether there are
such criteria is a matter of very earnest debate. What is however true,
is that there is no distinctive type of meaning to religious propositions unless there are distinctive truth criteria. To think that we
can have a domain of irreducible religious meanings without having
any criteria at all by which to judge any religious propositions to be
true or false, is simply a confusion. Only according to the criteria for
religious knowledge that are available, can we have religious
meaning. Some who regard this approach as too propositional,
might try to seek refuge in meaning that is thought to be non-

65

propositionalisable. All I would wish to say on that is a repetition of a point made earlier: that those forms of meaning or intelligibility which are not themselves propositions must involve the use of concepts and they in turn necessitate the existence of propositions and truth criteria of some kind. There is no escape from the simple claim that we can only talk of meaning in domains where we can talk of knowledge.

I conclude then that if one is to talk of logically distinct realms of meaning, one is in fact necessarily also talking about logically distinct types of truth criteria and therefore of what I have elsewhere called logically distinct forms of knowledge.[14] These forms, I have argued, can only be distinguished by examining the necessary features of true propositions or statements: the conceptual structures and the truth criteria involved. On this basis it seems to me that we must at present acknowledge serious claims to some seven distinct categories of meaning and knowledge. What these are in detail and the educational significance of their being logically distinct, I have dealt with at some length in other chapters. I will not go into these matters further here. On the bearing for curriculum planning of certain similarities and contrasts between the approach of Phenix and that for which I have argued, a concluding comment might, however, be appropriate.

The similarities between the 'realms' of Phenix and the 'forms' which I have proposed are, of course, limited. Three of the 'realms', empirics, esthetics and ethics we can agree about as they are distinguishable propositionally on certain criteria we share. Symbolics, synnoetics and synoptics all seem to me mischaracterised areas, none of which is in fact a fundamental category of meaning and knowledge, all being complex in nature. It has however been suggested[15] that though Phenix's demarcations may be less rigorously formulated, may be less well substantiated and may not all be fundamental categories, his model of six realms is nevertheless more useful for the purpose of planning a total curriculum than a logically more tenable structure. The principal reasons for this claim seem to be the belief that the analysis I have suggested is rigid, logical and academic, being a classification of established truths and knowledge only, whereas Phenix has taken into his purview the wider, evolving human concern of all the dimensions of meaning. Truth, it is considered, should not be put before meaning, for the former only finds expression within a pattern of meaning, and too much concern for known categories of knowledge is liable to make curricula inflexible and backward looking when they ought to be organic and evolving, showing a proper attention to new developments in knowledge.

If the central thesis of this chapter is correct, however, the fundamental realms, or forms, of meaning and those of knowledge are identical. The question is simply which account is correct, for surely that alone can form the basis of defensible curriculum planning. Any total school curriculum must certainly be concerned with more than knowledge, and indeed it must seek to cover all that Phenix includes in his dimensions of meaning. But granted that point, the question remains: what are the fundamental categories of the objectives for a whole curriculum? My contention is that Phenix has failed to work through the truth that the categories for all objectives are mapped out by the categories of the logically basic objectives, those of knowledge. The distinct categories we find in this limited range of cognitive objectives gives us not only the kinds of true statement there are, or the kinds of meaning there are, but also the kinds of experience, feeling, attitudes, symbols, skills, etc. It is because Phenix has not recognised the full implications of the fact that the logical categorisation of all meaning reduces to the categorisation of true propositions, that he seeks to classify at one go a domain of both propositions and existentional experiences, thereby confusing the whole operation. It is therefore not the case that Phenix has produced a set of categories which cover areas of human concern that are not covered by the categories I have outlined. Both are organisations that do in fact cover the same range of educational objectives. The question is simply which is the most defensible.

Where questions of category determination are concerned, I trust it is clear that meaning, truth and knowledge go together, as they are logically divisible by the same criteria. There is in this context no suggestion that truth is being put before meaning, for the criteria for truth are the criteria for meaning. Nor is it in this context significant to say that truth only finds expression within a pattern of meaning, for the pattern of meaning is only established by truth criteria. Whether a particular curriculum emphasises in its objectives a concern for truth rather than a concern for meaning, is a matter of value judgment to be based partly on logical considerations, but the logical categories of the objectives remain the same. Equally, whether a curriculum is designed to be backward or forward looking, rigidly or flexibly constructed, it must be formed with attention to the fundamental categories that necessarily exist within its concerns, whatever they are. Flexibility, comprehensiveness and temporal perspective are irrelevant when seeking to get at the fundamental categories which are what they are because of logically necessary characteristics only. Curriculum patterns, however, can be composed in endless variety and a structure having these features might well be desirable. But neither Phenix's 'realms' nor my forms, are to be regarded as, in the first instance, providing a pattern for curriculum units. A total curriculum pattern can be composed in an infinite variety of ways and needs defending not only in relation to the fundamental categories of objectives, but on psychological, administrative and other grounds as well. A pattern that simply reflects the fundamental categories is possible, and, if one wants that, the accuracy of the determination of those categories is surely vital. A curriculum could be based on Phenix's 'realms', for all their inadequacies as a set of fundamental categories, but why exactly do that when an infinite variety of other schemes are available? Why exactly would one wish to defend this particular non-fundamental structure against all the others that could express the many qualities wanted in a total curriculum pattern? If Phenix's account of the fundamental categories of meaning is, as I have argued, mistaken, it does not provide what it basically sets out to provide. If it is then to be defended as a curriculum model, it needs much more detailed defence than it has so far received. I am sceptical as to whether it can be produced.

Notes

1 P.H. Phenix, *Realms of Meaning*, McGraw-Hill, New York, 1964.
2 Ibid., p. 5.
3 Ibid., p. 6.
4 Ibid., p. 8.
5 Ibid.
6 Ibid., p. 21.
7 Ibid., pp. 21–4.
8 Ibid., p. 25.
9 Ibid., p. 26.
10 Ibid., p. 28.
11 P.H. Phenix, 'The architectonics of knowledge', in S. Elam (ed.),
   Education and the Structure of Knowledge, Rand McNally, Chicago, 1964.
12 See Chapters 3 and 5.
13 D.W. Hamlyn, 'Objectivity', in R.F. Dearden, P.H. Hirst and
   R.S. Peters (eds), *Education and the Development of Reason*, Routledge &
   Kegan Paul, 1972, p. 246.
14 See Chapters 3 and 6.
15 R.C. Whitfield, *Disciplines of the Curriculum*, McGraw-Hill, New York,
   1971, chs 1 and 17.

Language and thought   5

I shall take it for granted in this chapter that one of the central functions, if not the central function, of education is the introduction of pupils to those forms of thought and knowledge which we think peculiarly valuable. I shall also assume it to be obvious that language has been and is of crucial importance in the general development of man's thought and understanding and that it plays a vital role in his transmission of these to succeeding generations. Nevertheless there exists much confusion about the place and function of language in thought and a number of significant educational misconceptions about the nature and development of understanding do, I think, gain support from quite untenable theories in this area. In the first place then I want briefly to discuss two such theories, and then from the general features of what I trust are more tenable positions, I shall say something about what is involved in the development of understanding. It may well be thought that I am trying to tackle far too much for one short chapter even though I am travelling over well trodden ground. But I want to make one or two simple yet key points without which attention to smaller detail lacks perspective. I trust my treatment will not be outrageously superficial. I am also aware that most people in education would deny holding either of the two main theories I shall criticise, but venture to suggest that few are clear enough about these issues to be free from the taint of one or the other of them, and I therefore make no apology for dealing with them quite explicitly.

I

The first theory I am interested in concerns the relationship between language and thought, and its most distinguishing feature is the radical separation it maintains between thought and the words in which thoughts can be expressed. This distinction is taken to be that between the private world of the mind within which thought occurs, and the public world of language. Manifestly there is a world of mental experiences that each of us has that we do not share with others and thought clearly seems to belong to this. On the other hand what is spoken or written is by those very means made public.

Language and thought

Obviously we often think privately without expressing our thoughts publicly and equally we express things publicly in words which in no way reflect our thoughts. Indeed at times we have great difficulty in finding words to express our thoughts and frequently we can hear words which we quite fail to understand.

In the private world of the mind, thinking, it is said, consists of a number of processes, or mental acts, which are behind any intelligent employment of speech. An intelligent person thinks before he speaks. The medium in which thought occurs may be variously described. Sometimes thought is said to be composed of ideas, simple and complex, sometimes it is composed of images, nowadays more often it is composed of concepts or propositions. These units of understanding or thought are formed by abstraction or further operations of the mind on abstractions in relating the ideas or concepts. In these operations the mind is said to abstract, infer, deduce, etc. These activities are carried out by the mind, or the mind is an instrument by which we perform them. As Professor Ayer rather nicely expresssed it once, just as we see with our eyes and we walk with our legs, so we think with our minds.[1] And all this can in principle occur quite independently of any use of language in which thoughts can be expressed. Indeed when expressed in language, the words and sentences have the concepts and propositions of thought for their meaning. In communication, thoughts are coded into words and then decoded by the recipients back into thought. So behind all manifestations of intelligence there goes on this life of thought that may or may not be made public in some appropriate symbolism.

Now in rejecting this account of the relationship between thought and language, I want to make two things clear. First, it seems to me essential to do justice to those distinctions we do draw between thought and language. Second, I am in no way wanting to deny that we do have private mental experiences. Both of these are strong points in the account I have outlined, but in doing more than justice to them it seems to have run into several claims that are surely unacceptable.

First, if thinking can be said to be in anything at all, then at times it would certainly seem to be in words. No matter what else it may be said to be in, for example concepts or images, and even if we want to label as thought many mental experiences of indeterminate content, it seems to me beyond dispute that much of our thought is in symbols rather than in anything else, and that the majority of it is in words and sentences. By this I mean no more than that this thinking involves the use of words and sentences or symbols of some kind. It is not that the thinking is simply the occurrence of a series of words or symbols from which the meaning is determined. It is just that in these cases, nothing is entertained other than the symbols. Intelligible thought is of something, and I take that to imply that being of something, it is symbolic in character.[2]

In saying this I am denying that thought expressible in words is first in some peculiar mental medium whose elements are concepts or propositions—as if what was first in concepts is then translated into words for the sake of communication. That seems to me to be a completely unjustifiable claim. I am denying that thought that is expressible in words need necessarily be in anything other than words. We may have thought which is first in images and which we then put into words. In this case however, it again seems to me that the thought is not first in some peculiar medium unique to thought and then put into words. It is rather that what occurs in visual, tactile or auditory images which function as symbols, is in these cases translated into other symbols, those of language, which are themselves perfectly able to replace the images in thought. This is therefore not to be regarded as a translation from thought to symbols, but as a translation from one set of symbols to another. There may be thought that is not in images or in words, but if the thought is significant, I am suggesting it involves distinctions of some kind, and to that extent must be employing symbols of some kind. I am saying that in these considerations I see no reason to postulate the existence of a peculiar medium in which thought occurs, so that thought is no longer describable as the use of symbols. All intelligible thought involves the use of symbols, and most frequently the use of words.

The objection I am making might perhaps be better expressed by saying that we cannot specify any medium in which the processes of thought can be said to take place. All we have are the achievements of the processes in symbolic occurrences. This is, I think, true. Yet there is also a perfectly good sense in which we can be said to think in words, for we deliberately develop sequences of thought in words and images. In so far then as we can meaningfully be said to think in anything, it seems to me perfectly proper to say that we think in words.

In the second place the denial of a realm of ideas or concepts is, I think, demanded when we consider what is involved in intelligent discourse, in solving problems, etc. For in these circumstances we are surely not aware of a non-linguistic or non-symbolic process of thought that is translated into words. The thought is employed in the making of the statements themselves, or in following accurately the rules of mathematical calculation, not in some prior non-symbolic activity.

Maybe we often think before we speak, but what that phrase indicates is surely no wordless mental process but rather an attempt at a statement or answer in words which we do not speak out loud, though we could do so. We simply inhibit the utterance. That the thinking is not symbolic or not in words, is not at all to be inferred from the fact of silence. Nor when we look for words in which to express what we want to say, is it the case that we have the precise thought in ideas which we cannot adequately code. Rather it is that we have not yet got the appropriate thought because we have not yet formulated it in words. Surely we only have a particular thought if it is formulated in relevant terms, for to have a specific thought is to entertain a set of symbols that have that specific meaning.

And this leads to a third point, that the account endeavours to describe in quite explicit terms the workings of the machinery of the mind, what it is that enables us to have the thoughts that we do. Indeed it postulates a mind as abstracting, deducing, etc., an entity or instrument that registers impressions, acts in quite specific ways and so on. To do this is indeed to go far beyond any evidence we have in our experience. This view regards the term mind as the label of at least a pseudo-object with many different properties; in particular it is something with which we think or which itself does our thinking for us. It is however the case that we can say nothing about mind beyond what we know of thought, feeling, etc. There is in fact nothing over and above these that we know as the source or basis of these experiences. Thinking is not something we find out that minds can do, as if we could track down and identify minds independently of thought and then discover that these minds act in certain ways. To think is part of what it means to have a mind. We cannot therefore give an account of thinking from some prior knowledge of mind, all we know of mind must derive from our understanding of thought, feeling, etc. Of the nature of what underlies these experiences we can necessarily say nothing.

Not only, therefore, can we know nothing of the nature of mind itself, as if this was the label of a directly inspectable object, we can also know nothing of the processes of thought other than by examining the content and sequences of thoughts themselves. This account therefore involves a view of the mind as a kind of entity, it is a theory which is perhaps perpetuated by our tendency to take all nouns as the labels of entities of one sort or another, to commit the most obvious of category mistakes.

Fourth, there are great difficulties in any account which makes thoughts the meanings of words and sentences. How, for instance, is communication even possible? For how can words, the meanings of which are essentially private thoughts, produce the same thoughts in another mind? On this account the meaning of language becomes completely private, for it is composed of symbols for what is neces-

Language and thought

sarily only experienced by the speaker. Given this basis, I fail to see how we could ever learn a common language. Again, if we ask for the meaning of a word or sentence we are surely not in fact asking for some private thought which the word labels. Nor do we clarify what a word or sentence means by introspective inspection of ideas. Rather when we ask for its meaning we ask what function a word or expression has in our public discourse. We want to be told when it would be used and to do what.

Fifth, the account involves a view of concepts as acquired by some process of abstraction that is a thoroughly confused notion. This is far too large a matter to go into here, but a fundamental difficulty is obvious. How is it possible to form a concept by reflection on common features of experience when to recognise those common features is only possible when one already has the concept? To use a hackneyed example, how from a number of red objects can the concept 'red' be formed by picking out the common property of their being red, when to pick out this feature necessitates having the concept 'red' already?

Sixth, the account involves jumping from making a distinction that is necessary to our understanding, that between words and thought or rather between words and their meaning, to asserting the independent existence of words and their meaning. That we must distinguish these two elements in discussions about language, no more justifies asserting the independent existence of these elements than distinguishing the shape of an object from the object itself justifies asserting that the shape is an independent existent.

In the light of difficulties of this kind I suggest that we must maintain:
(a) that in so far as it makes sense to talk about what thought is in, it can occur in words;
(b) that the notion of ideas or concepts as elements of a medium peculiar to thought is redundant;
(c) that what mental processes are we can only know or describe in relation to their achievements as symbolically expressed;
(d) that whatever the meaning of a word or sentence is, it is not a string of related thoughts, ideas, concepts or propositions, if these in any way label mental or psychological elements.

II

What this account now lacks above all else, of course, is a satisfactory positive account of meaning. For if thought is itself in words, then the question of the meaning of words cannot be the thought for which they stand. Immediately, however, a simple alternative answer occurs. The meaning of words and sentences are the objects and events for which the symbols stand. Words and sentences are labels for objects and states of affairs. For a symbol to have meaning is for there to be something which it means. On this view, nothing is said about what goes on in thought. How exactly symbols enter into the processes of thinking is not the point. The question now is: how do those symbols which enter thought, have the significance they do? What is it for a symbol to have meaning? And the answer is that a symbol denotes, or refers. Basically language consists of names.

Now this answer is very neat and simple and if it were true no doubt life and education would be very much easier. But unfortunately it just is not tenable and that this is so can be seen very readily. How on this thesis is one to account for the statements of fiction which are manifestly meaningful? What of the phrase philosophers love so 'the present king of France'? How does this phrase have meaning, as there is no king of France for it to denote? And even when there is an object for a phrase to denote, does the phrase mean what it denotes? Is the meaning of the phrase 'the prime minister' the same as that of the phrase 'Mrs X's husband'? Clearly the phrases may denote the same person but clearly they have different meanings. Again, if words are really names then a sentence is just a string of names or labels. But a string of names does not have meaning as a sentence does. What is more the whole account is in fact in great danger of blurring the distinction between possibility and actuality, for symbolic expressions can surely state meaningfully not only what is the case, but also both what might be the case and even what simply cannot be the case. The theory ties meaning far too closely to sense perception and many of the symbols of language have meaning without any such reference. The content of the world of language and thought is not simply the world as we perceive it. At least the original account I considered, which took thoughts to be the meaning of words, did some justice to this.

If one persists in this theory of meaning, then the only way to cope with phrases like 'the present king of France' or 'a golden mountain' is to say that in some sense these objects or entities subsist as objects of thought, even if they do not exist. But what does this claim? And is it not to start on a quite unjustifiable speculative enterprise when the theory of meaning that made it all necessary ought to be rejected? For after all why should we assume that all words function as proper names? Why should language be conceived as corresponding to the world as a mirror image?

What a phrase denotes is manifestly not the meaning of the phrase in the case of say 'the prime minister'. If we ask the meaning of the phrase, we are asking not who or what it is about, but what it says about whatever it is about. Meaning is concerned with connotation rather than denotation. This is not to say that the referential function of some terms is not important. It is simply to insist that in asking for the meaning of a term or sentence one is not simply asking for its denotation.

The only way to give the meaning of a term is to give an account of what can be done with the term, how it functions as part of a system of symbols which we use in an enormous variety of ways to make assertions about the world, to plot and plan and achieve our purposes, etc. Language is an instrument which we have developed, and do develop, by which we amongst other things, understand the world.

Two well worn analogies might help here.[3] Words, phrases and even sentences are, to some extent, like coins and their meanings are like the values of coins. With the coins one can buy a multitude of different things, get the laundry done, see a film and so on. But the value is none of these particular things nor what is represented say in gold. It is only through its part in the monetary system as a whole, and what that entails, that we can know what its value is. So with the meaning of a word. It is what you can do with it that is the key to its meaning. If a term does denote an object, the meaning is not what it denotes. What can be done with it, recognising its denotative capacity, is the crucial point. We therefore learn to understand words by using them to do things. We certainly learn names, but coming to understand the world in using language is not just naming. A language is not a list of names. The business has not begun until we use the names and do things with their aid. At this point all the other complex elements of language are involved. The terms are employed in an enormous variety of ways and any element's meaning depends on the part it plays. Perhaps it should be said here that the primary unit of meaning is not that of a word, but of a whole sentence or rather statement. A child may first learn to use single words, but they are used as concise symbols for propositions or statements.

In the other analogy, words are like pieces of a game, say chess. In using this picture, Ryle suggests that mere naming is rather like putting a pawn on the board. It is not part of the game as such, it is not using the pawn. The pawn has a use in the game, which can be seen in the game itself, and it fulfils that role by obeying certain rules according to which it can be moved. Similarly the meaning of a term is seen in the part it plays in the whole use of language.

But how, it might be insisted, do words relate to the world? To that question there is surely not one answer. Because of the many uses of language, the relationship is immensely complex. But even to begin to answer the question that way, is to give the impression that the view that has been criticised has some truth in it after all. It is to imply that all that is wrong is that the account is too simple. To take that position however is to perpetuate the assumption that we can understand the world independently of all use of language or symbols, and then to ask how the world so understood, and language, are related. Against this however, I have been insisting that all our understanding, being a form of intelligible thought, involves the use of symbols and much of it the use of our common language. Outside the effective use of symbols of some sort there is no understanding. To understand is to employ symbolic expressions. Maybe these are used to assert something, to call attention, to make moral judgments, to express affection. Whatever it is, the meaning of the symbols is inextricably connected with what language can do in many very different contexts.

If a sentence asserts something about the world, it is only because of the function these symbols have that we understand what they assert. Their use is to indicate something that can be observed which they do not simply name. They say something about what is named. But the crucial point here is that understanding the world in sense-perception itself involves the use of symbols or images of some kind, for only in this way can the elements in perception be identified. When, therefore, a statement whose function it is to pick out something in perception has meaning, its meaning is translatable into the symbolism implicit in sense-perception and thus it is testable in perception. But this is not to say that the symbolic expression is tested against the world which is understood independently of any symbolic structure. It is to test one symbolic expression by an awareness which is itself implicitly symbolic. This being so it is logically impossible to give an account of the relationship between language and the world as if this were an account of how symbols relate to the totally non-symbolic.

In addition then to the conclusions from my criticism of the first theory, that thought can be in language and that thoughts are not the meaning of words, I now want to add that discovering the meanings of words and sentences is a matter of discovering what words and sentences can be used to achieve, not simply a matter of discovering what they denote. I want to make it quite explicit that on this account the words 'concept' and 'proposition' do not in any way label psychological entities in thought or thoughts themselves. The phrase 'To have the concept x' I take to mean just the same as 'To know the meaning of the term x or its equivalent'. 'Concept' and 'proposition' are, I take it, terms for the meanings of words, phrases, sentences. They are, therefore, units of meaning, but only in the sense that they are the meanings of particular terms or phrases which have a distinct function in discourse. I am equating 'having the concept' with 'knowing the meaning of a term', but I am not actually equating 'knowing the meaning of a term' with simply 'being able to use the term correctly'. Being able to use the term correctly is certainly public evidence which we usually regard as sufficient for saying that a person knows the meaning of the term, but the correct use is not itself the meaning, nor is the ability to use the term correctly the meaning either. Moreover although I see no reason to think that a person could not have certain concepts without the use of a common language, those that are expressed in our common language are I think only acquirable by learning the use of that language. I fail to see how we could in general come to have precisely these concepts prior to acquiring the appropriate language. This is because the meaning of a term cannot be grasped without learning how to use the term as part of the whole language structure in which it plays its part. In general, being able to use the term correctly is necessary to having the particular concept associated with that term. There may of course be particular cases, in which special reasons can be given, when a person has the concept without being able to use the appropriate term. But the only way we have in general for introducing others to the concepts we have, is through introducing them to the intricacies of the correct application of our language. If others are to make the conceptual distinctions that we do, then the symbolism necessarily involved in this conceptualisation must be publicly expressed. Only then can others, acquiring the correct rules for an appropriate symbolism, come to make the same conceptual distinctions.

One must of course distinguish between being able to use a term correctly and being able to give an account of its use. If a person can use the term correctly we take this to be evidence for his having the concept and do not usually require that he can also give an account of its use. To be able to use correctly the term 'red' is evidence for a person having the concept 'red'. We do not usually insist that he also be able to explain how the term 'red' is used. That would, I take it, be evidence for having the concept of 'the concept "red"'.

The central thing I am wanting to maintain here, however, is that understanding the meaning of a term cannot be separated from the recognition of the use to which the term is put in our discourse. It follows from this, therefore, (a) that what a teacher is after in the development of understanding can only be got clear by systematically and comprehensively analysing the use of the terms with which he is concerned, (b) that unless he takes care to ensure that these uses of the terms are mastered by his pupils he cannot presume that the related development of understanding has occurred. I will return in a few moments to saying a little more about the implications of this.

III

Between them, the two unacceptable theories that have been looked at, are I think educationally misleading in several important respects.

In so far as the absolutely central function of language in thought is denied, what is involved in the development of understanding is seriously misconceived. On the first theory, the development is held to depend on, or indeed to consist of, the development of certain central mental skills, those of abstraction, inference, etc. The skills are taken to be developable in a great variety of ways, as they relate to no particular thought content, being fundamental to all rational thought. The repudiation of old-style faculty psychology and the rejection of a doctrine of mental discipline as justifiying the teaching of mathematics, language, etc., has not prevented the rise of a great deal of talk about the development of creativity and imagination which comes near to repeating all the old mistakes.

Once this picture of the machinery of the mind is questioned, it becomes clear that terms like inferring, deducing, being creative or imaginative, are not labels for distinctive activities in a private world of the mind. Indeed they are terms we use to express the fact that the public use of language or other symbols has reached certain agreed standards. Of the inner processes of the mind in achieving such standards, we know and can know nothing. To say that a person deduced something, is not to say what processes of mind occurred, it is to say that whatever the sequences of thought were, a chain of propositions that have certain formal relations was set up as a result. How this was achieved is another matter. What is important in this case is not that a uniform pattern of thought processes be established in the mind, but the establishing of sequences of symbolic expressions that come up to agreed standards. There is a great deal of difference between trying to develop or impose a certain number of patterns of psychological functioning and building up the use of a public language to achieve publicly significant things with it. Learning 'how to do things with words' gives a quite different focus to the educational enterprise.

In the second place, the rejected theory falsely pictures learning as beginning with a process of concept formation by abstraction in which isolated units of thought are formed. From these, understanding grows by building, as with bricks, and by forming yet higher level abstractions on them. This is quite different in its practical bearing from a view that holds to no such mental units as ideas or concepts. To acquire the meaning of a term in its use, to learn to employ it correctly and effectively in the complex and subtle ways we recognise, is not at all to set about looking for some way of rigging the situation so that the general can be abstracted from the particulars, and the complex built from simple elements. We learn how to do things with words and other symbols primarily by using them and by discovering what can and cannot be done. That the growth of understanding is by passive registerings and private working on these, is a view that separates thought and language in a quite unjustifiable manner. It denies the connection between being able to use the term and having the concept which must necessarily hold in general. What is more, it is only because there is this neccesary connection that there can be the communication of understanding. Without discovering the rules for the correct use of the terms of public language, how could one learn the rules for the application of the related concept? If one does not discover when the term atom can be used, and when not, I fail to see how one can ever discover the meaning the term has.

It is therefore in general necessary to the growth of understanding to learn to use the appropriate language in which that understanding is expressed and communicated. This is to say that the place of language in education is necessarily central. In so far as teaching methods, be they called discovery methods or anything else, do not meet up to the demands of this necessary relationship between understanding and the correct use of language, they are defective in an absolutely crucial respect. Methods that assume that in general concepts can be formed—and it is the world of public concepts that I have in mind—without developing the use of the relevant language, are doomed before they start.

The theories I have been criticising would seem to be false in another way, for they imply that one either does or does not have a concept according to whether or not one performs the appropriate abstraction. Clearly, however, there is a very real sense in which we may to a greater or lesser extent have any public concept, of the colour red, of the state, etc. In these cases, it is not that a particular psychological process may be incomplete, it is rather that the meaning of a term is only partially understood because its function is only partially grasped. At any stage what the person has achieved in understanding, he has achieved by mastering some function of the term; he then has some concept related to this term. But this is not to have the concept in the sense of the general understanding of the term which abstraction is said to provide. If the facts of experience are to be correctly described, what is wanted is surely an account which sees our coming to understand the meaning of a term as a progressive business. An account which sees this development as related to learning the use of the term according to its complex rules, begins to do just that.

If the place of language in thought for which I am arguing is granted, then there is only one way in which to be clear about what understanding involves. We must discover how in fact we do the things we do with words. If to develop understanding is coming to do just these things with words—to make true empirical statements, pass moral judgments, give historical explanations, etc.—we must discover what these achievements involve. As teachers then, we are forced to ask: What kinds of things do we do with words? i.e. what realms of meaning are there; and how in words are these things achieved? i.e. by what uses of language are these functions fulfilled. It seems to me imperative that we get clear what the structure of language is when fulfilling its various functions. For until we are clear about this, we have no real control over what we are doing in seeking to develop understanding in others. Conceptual analysis, or logical geography as Ryle has called it, is concerned precisely with this, distinguishing those patterns of terms which can be found when we do things with words. This is essentially not the grammatical analysis of language but the analysis of meaning. The distinction between grammatical structure and logical structure must be kept clear. As was mentioned earlier, although children may learn to use individual words before they learn to form sentences, this in no way alters the fact that the words are used to convey a meaning which can only be adequately expressed in complete sentences. What is more, children repeatedly master the correct grammatical structure of sentences and can employ them in appropriate circumstances before they have any very adequate grasp of their meaning.

In emphasising the importance of the logical structure of the terms involved in all we wish pupils to learn, we must however be careful not to assume that the pupils need to be explicitly aware of the formal relations between the terms. They need to be able to use the terms according to the appropriate rules, but there is no need for them to be able to state the rules. It may be helpful at times to teach the rules, to teach formal definitions and so on, but knowing a formal definition is no guarantee that one can apply the term correctly. Just as one can make grammatically correct statements that one doesn't understand, one can equally master definitions without appreciating how the terms are to be used. It is one thing to master a network of abstract terms, it is another to grasp its application. It is the teacher who needs to be explicitly aware of the logical structure involved in what he is teaching. Whether the pupils can state what that structure is, is irrelevant, provided they can work according to it in applying the terms.

There is a further way in which both the theories I have mentioned are educationally significant. However right we may be about the place of language in thought and in the development of understanding, a defective theory of meaning can nevertheless distort our whole approach to the business. If a fundamental position is taken up that words have meaning when they denote objects or events, or if a more sophisticated theory, say that meaning is dependent on being able to verify statements empirically at least in principle, then what counts as meaningful is tightly restricted and the logical geography permitted is limited from the start. But this is in fact to set up arbitrary criteria of meaningfulness in which the only recognised function of language is scientific, and the only meaningful structure of language is that of scientific discourse.

In so far as education conceives itself as restricted to developing only this limited form of understanding it has succumbed to a disastrously narrow concept of its intellectual task. Certainly there is now little backing for any such restriction in contemporary philosophy, for such doctrinaire theories of meaning have given place to a great deal of steady and sober work on the distinctions in language which mark clear distinctions in its uses. That moral discourse has a function and meaning quite distinct from scientific discourse and that both these have a function quite distinct from that of say poetic discourse, is now generally accepted and that without derogatory comments being passed on the function of say moral, poetic or even religious discourse.

Wittgenstein's notion of a language-game is, I think enormously to the point here, for it seems to me one can most profitably think of the different modes of discourse as language-games, each distinct in their rules for the forming of expressions that will carry out the appropriate function. In these terms the mastery of a form of understanding or thought is essentially learning how to play a complex game of terms, and learning to play it so that by sticking to the rules it can fulfil its own peculiar function.

I have argued that the achievement of understanding involves the mastery of a whole range of complex language-games each game having its own peculiar function. And to clarify the matter further, we need

(a) to distinguish the peculiar language games there are, and

(b) to clarify the structure each of these different language games has.

Interest in these questions has recently increased in educational circles. In America in particular, attempts are now being made at the very enterprise I have in mind. Yet work in this area can easily be vitiated by preconceived ideas. In his book, *Realms of Meaning* for instance, Professor P.H. Phenix has much to say of interest on these very questions, but a curious *a priori* theory of meaning seriously distorts his whole approach.[4] There is, I think, no short cut. We simply have to try to distinguish the different language games and their structures in their use.

One can distinguish different uses of language in, for instance, making assertions, asking questions, giving commands, and each of these could be said to involve a different language-game. Certainly the development of understanding demands the mastery of these. There are also distinct uses of language which cut across these distinctions, however, for there are many different types of assertions or questions. One can distinguish between the use of scientific, moral or say religious language, and in each of these domains there can be questions, assertions, etc. In this second sense the distinct languages employ unique concepts according to unique rules that are related to distinctive claims for truth or validity. If one is concerned with different areas of understanding as making different claims to knowledge, then it is with language-games in this second sense that one is concerned. From this point of view, it seems to me that man has achieved some seven or eight distinct forms of discourse that are connected with notions of truth or validity and that each of these language games has distinctive logical features.[5] The development of understanding in that case would seem to involve the mastery of quite a number of different logical structures and their uses. And such mastery is necessary. Failure to master the appropriate game necessarily implies a lack of understanding in say moral, historical or scientific matters. What the structure of each game is, and what has to be learnt in playing the game so that it achieves its appropriate use, is a matter for the logic of moral discourse, historical discourse or scientific discourse.

I take it that it is the structure of discourse in this sense that psychologists like Bruner are concerned with. I am however never quite sure, as the structure of meaning that I am speaking of, is discoverable by the logical analysis of discourse and is not primarily a matter of psychological investigation. Just which questions about the development of understanding are philosophical questions and which are psychological, is far from clear at present. I have been concerned in this matter with *what* is involved in understanding and this is surely a philosophical matter. *How* in fact understanding is developed, how in fact these distinct language-games come to be correctly played and used, is another matter. On the face of it, questions in that area seem empirical, but how far that is true is a complex problem which cannot be tackled here.

Let me conclude by summarising the central points I have tried to make, if not in quite the same order in which I have argued them:

(a) Intelligible thought necessarily involves symbols of some sort and most of it involves the symbols of our common languages.

(b) The analysis of the structure of thought and understanding is possible only through the analysis of the meaning of the terms we use in our langages.

(c) The meaning of language is a matter neither of the thoughts nor the objects to which terms are sometimes said to refer; concepts and propositions are units of meaning and not psychological entities, pseudo-objects or events.

(d) Analysing the meaning of words is a question of analysing what we do with words and how we do it.

(e) Logical analysis does in fact reveal a number of language-games which have different logical structures according to their distinct uses.

(f) Understanding a form of thought necessarily involves mastering the use of the appropriate language-game.

(g) If teachers are to know exactly what they are after in developing their pupils' understanding, they must be aware of the logical structure of the forms of thought concerned.

(h) Teaching the use of any language-game does not necessarily involve teaching the rules of the game explicitly.

(i) Granted all this, there remain the immensely important questions as to how exactly children can be best taught the mastery of these games, and their uses. Although many of these questions appear to be empirical, their precise character remains as yet far from clear.

Notes

1 A.J. Ayer, *Thinking and Experience*, Inaugural Lecture 1947, H.K. Lewis & Co.

2 I do not wish to deny that there may be a level of thought connected with the occurrence of signs rather than symbols. Throughout this chapter, however, I am concerned entirely with thought, meaning and understanding at the symbolic level.

3 See particularly G. Ryle, 'The theory of meaning', in C.A. Mace (ed.), *British Philosophy in the Mid-Century*, Allen & Unwin, 1957.

4 P.H. Phenix, *Realms of Meaning*, McGraw-Hill, New York, 1964.

5 P.H. Hirst, 'Liberal education and the nature of knowledge', in R.D. Archambault (ed.), *Philosophical Analysis and Education*, Routledge & Kegan Paul, 1965. See also Chapter 3.

The forms of knowledge re-visited

In a paper entitled 'Liberal education and the nature of knowledge', first published in 1965,[1] I tried to outline a coherent concept of liberal education concerned simply with the development of the pupil's knowledge and understanding, the diversity of its content being determined by the diversity of the forms that human knowledge and understanding in fact take. An essential part of that argument was the suggestion that within the domain of knowledge a number of forms can be distinguished which are different in their logical character. The account given of those forms was necessarily very brief and its inadequacies have provoked a certain amount of critical comment.[2] Precisely what I was trying to do has been the subject of some debate, as well as the satisfactoriness of some of the arguments I deployed. Since then I have returned to this subject in a number of places, in particular in *The Logic of Education*[3] written in collaboration with Professor R.S. Peters. Over the years, the thesis originally advanced has undergone a number of minor modifications which mark either certain developments in my own thoughts on the subject, or applications of the central ideas to somewhat different educational problems. It is the object of this chapter to outline my present reflections on the original 'forms of knowledge' thesis, elaborating those points which are not discussed more fully in other chapters in this volume.[4]

I

The central element in the original thesis was that the domain of human knowledge can be seen to be differentiated into a number of logically distinct 'forms', none of which is ultimately reducible in character to any of the others, either simply or in combination. For this property of mutual irreducibility I have from time to time used the terms logically 'distinct', 'autonomous', 'independent', 'unique', 'fundamental', and have talked of 'categorial divisions' within knowledge. All these terms carry connotations that make them far from ideal. Some are, no doubt, more misleading than others. But whatever terms are best, the claim I have been concerned with rests on a specific view of the nature of knowledge and the necessary features of knowledge. The domain of knowledge I take to be centrally the domain of true propositions or statements, and the question of their being logically distinct forms of knowledge to be the question of their being logically distinct types of true propositions or statements. Certainly we speak not only of knowing truths but also of knowing people and places and knowing how to do things. Detailed analysis suggests, however, that there are in fact only two distinct types of knowledge here, that in which the objects of knowledge are true propositions and that in which the objects are practical performances of some kind, knowledge of people and places being reducible to complexes of knowledge of these two types based on certain specific forms of experience.[5] Taking this to be so, and not in this context being concerned with practical knowledge, the question of distinguishing autonomous areas of knowledge does reduce to distinguishing types of true propositions.

But what does this involve? Types of propositions can of course be distinguished in many different ways and how are we then to judge which of these, if any, shows the domain of knowledge to consist of a number of fundamentally distinct and irreducible categories? We shall get at the logically fundamental characteristics of true propositions only by looking at those features which are necessary to all such propositions and the question is whether or not within them there exist mutually irreducible categories.[6] On these grounds, the three elements in which the differences are to be found are the concepts and the logical structure propositions employ, and the criteria for truth in terms of which they are assessed.

I do not wish to be interpreted as saying that these three elements within which the distinctions are drawn are logically independent of each other, when manifestly they are not. Nor should it be thought that anything in this approach prejudges the question as to whether in fact the domain of knowledge is logically monolithic or differentiable into a number of distinct forms. That question can be answered only by a detailed analysis of the character of true propositions in the light of these terms and any answer must therefore rest on the results of an extensive range of philosophical work. My original suggestion, that there are at present some seven areas which must be regarded as at least having serious claims to being logically distinct forms of knowledge, rests on my own reading of philosophical work concerned with differences in concepts and logical structures and truth criteria. What I have written therefore must be regarded as disputable at a level where philosophers are indeed not all agreed and subject to revision in the light of new philosophical clarification.

In addition to the three features I have mentioned, I originally suggested a fourth feature in which to distinguish differences between forms of knowledge, that of the methodology employed for amassing true propositions. Forms of knowledge are I think distinguishable in this way, but only in a secondary sense, and in later accounts I have not emphasised this feature. Differences in the methods used to establish true propositions not surprisingly will follow differences in the character of those propositions. These differences in methodology certainly mark out important differences in the pursuit of knowledge in the distinguishable forms, and are therefore most important in education and research. But they do not themselves add anything to the strictly logical distinctions which mark out possible forms of knowledge and I have therefore not referred to them in later writing which has concentrated solely on the logical distinctions.

Over the years, I have modified the terms used to label the forms I consider distinguishable in the light of the three fundamental features, but because of one area of uncertainty only. It has been suggested that I have wavered as to whether moral knowledge constitutes a distinct form. This is however not so. The question that for some while worried me considerably was the character of history and the social sciences, as my original reading of work in philosophy of history and philosophy of the social sciences left me unclear as to their status. It now seems to me that both history and the social sciences as pursued in universities and schools are, like most curriculum areas, logically complex in character. In part they are concerned with truths that are matters of empirical observation and experiment, truths that logically differ not at all from the kind with which the physical or natural sciences are concerned. Large tracts of sociology and psychology, and indeed parts of history, are therefore of the strictly physical science variety. That some of these truths are about the past, or are singular rather than general in character, is irrelevant for the purposes of the fundamental distinctions being made. After all, many of the statements made by biologists, physicists and chemists have these features. On the other hand, history and some of the social sciences are in large measure not concerned simply with an understanding of observable phenomena in terms of physical causation, but with explanations of human behaviour in terms of intentions, will, hopes, beliefs, etc. The concepts, logical structure and truth criteria of propositions of this latter kind are, I would now argue, different from, and not reducible to, those of the former kind. For this reason it now seems to me correct to speak of one form of knowledge as being concerned with the truths of the physical world and another as concerned with truths of a mental or personal kind. Knowledge of one's own states of mind and those of others, sometimes referred to as inter-personal knowledge, is of course here regarded as, in principle at any rate, fully propositionalisable. In these terms, I now think it best not to refer to history or the social sciences in any statement of the forms of knowledge as such. These pursuits like so many other so-called 'subjects' may well be concerned with truths of several different logical kinds and only detailed examination can show to what extent any one example of such a subject is or is not logically complex and in what ways. The labels that I have used for distinct forms of knowledge are to be understood as being strictly labels for different classes of true propositions. In so far as these terms are used for parts of the curricula of universities and schools, they may therefore cover very much more than an interest in one particular type of proposition. Even a term like mathematics, which may appropriately label a great deal of one form of knowledge because of the distinctive features of mathematical propositions, is frequently used in educational institutions to cover a concern not only for propositions of this kind, but also a concern for truths about the physical world and occasionally the history and philosophy of mathematics. I have no desire to legislate on the use of terms. I only wish it to be clear that what I mean by a form of knowledge may have little in common with what elsewhere falls under the same label.

II

The suggestion that in literature and the fine arts and also in religion we have distinct forms of knowledge has not surprisingly provoked opposition. Let me therefore make it clear that they can to my mind only be regarded as such in so far as they involve expressions that have the features of true propositions. We certainly do talk of the arts and religion as being cognitive, as providing distinctive types of knowledge. Whether this is justifiable and there is a form of knowledge in the arts, depends on whether or nor artistic works themselves have features parallel to those of propositions with related objective tests.

It is my concern to take seriously the possibility that we can legitimately refer to knowledge in the arts as well as in mathematics, the sciences and other areas, that has led me to state less clearly than perhaps I should have, the third of my criteria for a form of knowledge: that necessitating unique truth criteria. Wittgenstein's work on meaning and language-games suggests that works of art can well be seen as symbolic expressions having meaning, simply because they have properties logically equivalent to those of propositions. Recent reconsideration of the concept of truth, and the correspondence theory in particular, suggests that the notion of truth is centrally a demand for objective judgment, and there is nothing to be gained by restricting it to one particular form of such judgment.[7] In that case, works of art might well be seen as judgeable in a manner logically equivalent to that appropriate to propositions. It might of course be insisted that terms like 'concept', 'logical structure' and 'truth' are not appropriate in these circumstances, but I fail to see the real force of this objection. Lacking other suitable general terms to draw attention to the features I am interested in, I have therefore used these terms, and that of 'knowledge', as possibly applicable with very good reason to the arts. Whether in fact they are, is a matter of disagreement amongst philosophers. It is however my desire to keep open this possibility that has led me to talk sometimes of 'truth criteria', sometimes of 'validity', sometimes of 'objective tests' and sometimes of 'testable against experience'. Nothing in my purpose turns on using any one of these phrases rather than another. I am in each case simply referring to tests that have the logical function that truth tests have for propositions.[8]

In looking at the arts as possibly propositional, I have not denied for one moment that art may have many other functions that other areas of knowledge may or may not have, say in relation to the expression of emotion or the creation of delight. In considering religion it is also to be recognised that it likewise has concerns beyond the mere pursuit of knowledge. My interest here is simply whether or not it can lay claim, amongst other things, to being a logically unique form of knowledge. On the answer to that question few would dare to pronounce categorically. My own view, as in the case of the arts, is that in the present state of affairs we must at least take the claim to knowledge seriously. Against this, it has been suggested that religious claims may constitute an area of belief or of non-cognitive discourse which does not justify the label 'form of knowledge' in my terms. Certainly, some have sought to give an account of religious meaning which has seen its cognitive core to be totally reducible to knowledge belonging to other forms (usually moral, historical, or esthetic) and the rest to be emotive in character. If such a reduction can be legitimately carried through, then there can here be no distinct form of religious knowledge. But can it? That I doubt. Equally, it seems to me unclear that one can coherently claim that there is a logically unique domain of religious *beliefs* such that none of them can be known to be true, all being matters of faith. The reason for this is just that the meaning of religious propositions, as any others, rests on a grasp of the truth criteria for such propositions. If these propositions belong to a logically unique form, then their truth criteria must be unique. Religious propositions are then only intelligible to those who know these unique truth criteria. But can such unique truth conditions be known without our actually being able to judge any propositions of this kind true or false? Can there be unique truth criteria that are never satisfied? If meaning is

tied to knowing a unique set of truth criteria, is not meaning tied to
our actually satisfying these in judging some propositions true or
false? In so far then as religion is cognitive at all, it seems to me its
claims must be understood as being totally reducible to one or more
of the other forms of knowledge or as being at least in part a unique
form of knowledge itself. The claim to an irreducible, unique form of
propositional meaning, thus seems to necessitate that at last some
proposition of this kind be known to be true. If so, there can only be a
unique form of meaning if there is a unique form of knowledge, and
the claim that religion involves a unique form of belief only, is
incoherent.

III

If my original thesis has appeared to many too strong in claiming the
existence of knowledge in all the seven different forms, it being
doubted whether there are truth criteria in some of these areas, it has
also been considered too strong in claiming unique concepts and
logical structure for each form. Are there not many concepts that are
shared by at least several forms? What about the concepts of 'space'
and 'time' which manifestly pervade not only our knowledge of the
physical world, but also our knowledge of persons, moral knowledge,
artistic knowledge? What about the notion of 'truth' which the thesis
itself suggests is a necessary feature of all the forms? And are there
not certain fundamental logical laws which all forms of knowledge
respect, for example those of identity and non-contradiction?

That there may be such common, even universal elements, I am
perfectly willing to accept. What I do not see is how, if they exist,
they undermine the thesis of the logical uniqueness, mutual irreducibility, call it what you will, of the forms that I have sought to defend.
It was no part of the thesis even in its earliest formulation that the
forms of knowledge are totally independent of each other, sharing no
concepts or logical rules. That the forms are inter-related has been
stressed from the start. Manifestly the concepts of 'space' and 'time'
figure in several forms and are presupposed by concepts in other
areas. Propositions of a moral kind employ concepts for features of
the physical world. Moral argument uses the same deductive rules as
does scientific argument. Religious claims presuppose truths about
the world and about persons. The conceptual and logical elements
shared between forms and the inter-relations they indicate are
considerable. Yet it remains the case that every proposition can be
distinguished by the different kinds of truth criteria it involves, and is
tied to the kind of concept applied in the proposition. Put another
way every concept has criteria for its application which are the truth

criteria for any proposition in which that concept is applied. In this way all concepts can be given a character. There are those that directly or indirectly distinguish features of the physical world. Others distinguish states of mind. Yet others, the moral character of actions. No concept in one of these areas, even if it presupposes concepts from other areas, is entirely analysable into those presupposed concepts. Moral concepts are not reducible to concepts for objects in the physical world, nor vice versa, even though moral concepts presuppose concepts of objects in the physical world. In that sense, every form of knowledge, for all the concepts it may share with other forms, or presuppose from other forms, involves concepts which are distinctive, are unique, to it.

If this is so, it would seem to follow that there is a network of relations between concepts in each case which will in certain respects be distinctive. Moral concepts involve complex relations with each other and with other kinds of concepts that produce a unique structure. If there are different kinds of criteria for truth in the areas concerned, then, for instance, moral argument, being concerned with the application of moral concepts, and not the application of physical world concepts, must have a different logical structure from that of arguments in science. The idea that the relations between concepts and propositions in all forms of knowledge must conform to those of mathematical or scientific knowledge is a matter of pure dogmatism. We must examine these relations for their own structure in each case. Looser forms of relations are not necessarily suspect as these may be of the nature of these concepts. Nevertheless, certain elements within a moral argument may be identical in form with those in a scientific argument. If it can be shown that certain concepts or logical laws are common to all areas of knowledge, that would simply mean no more than that certain elements of knowledge of a specific form are presupposed by elements in all the other forms. This in no way denies any specific determinate character to those concepts or logical laws. In particular I see no reason to think that it implies the existence of an area of common sense knowledge quite distinct from the particular forms of knowledge which is in some sense presupposed by them. In so far as concepts have application, it seems to me they have a specific character, and that goes for all those within common sense as well as for those in more advanced areas of knowledge. Common sense knowledge is to my mind simply that collection of elementary knowledge, or what is claimed to be such, from the different forms, which is largely taken for granted in a given society.

The logical inter-relations between the different forms of knowledge are manifestly many and complex. How far a general map of these can be outlined, I am far from clear. It might be thought that the sharpness of the demarcation lines I have drawn only accentuates the problem of seeing the relations. Certainly the relations of concepts and propositions across the divisions of knowledge are legion. Yet the distinctions I have emphasised, if they are fundamental, must be recognised for what they are, and the inter-relations seen in terms of these. It has been suggested that there might be an over-all hierarchical pattern in which logical and mathematical knowledge is seen as presupposed by knowledge in the physical sciences which in its turn is presupposed by a knowledge of persons. The sequence might be continued to give an order of say moral, religious, artistic and philosophical knowledge. With such a strictly logical hierarchy, not to be seen in any way as a hierarchy of value or metaphysical hierarchy, I have much sympathy. It is, however, a suggestion that would seem to over-simplify the very complex relations there are between elements of the forms, seeing them in too linear a way, particularly where those occurring later in the sequence are concerned. The present state of our detailed conceptual mapping of these areas is, however, such that one can at present do little more than make conjectures about an over-all pattern. The theses for which I have argued is tied to no particular position on this matter.

IV

It will be apparent from various points I have already made that although I was originally concerned simply with distinguishing various fundamentally different forms of knowledge, the approach by means of a classification of true propositions has thereby also provided a classification of the concepts applied in those propositions. From this it follows that if one holds, as I hold, that all forms of experience are intelligible only by virtue of the concepts under which we have them, a classification of forms of knowledge provides also a classification of forms of experience. What is more, the distinctions between the forms that I have been concerned with, are what I understand by categorial distinctions, being matters of the types of concepts, logical structures and truth criteria which are irreducible to each other. I did not use the terminology of categories in the first instance, not wishing to be involved in expressing in detail the fundamental categorial concepts in each case. The examples of concepts applied in propositions within the different forms of knowledge that I have repeatedly given, have therefore not been chosen for their categorial status within each domain. The isolation of the categorial concepts is a technical matter of great difficulty and I am not aware that anything turns on being able to isolate amongst the concepts of a form of knowledge or experience those which have this ultimate status in relation to the rest. Categories can be distinguished within our concepts even when we are uncertain which are the categorial concepts themselves, that fundamentally characterise the different domains uniquely. Indeed I see no reason to assume that we have in fact explicitly isolated all the categorial concepts in our forms of knowledge, some may well occur only implicitly within the more familiar complex concepts we employ. The concepts of 'space', 'time' and 'causality' would seem to be categorial where knowledge of the physical world is concerned and these are closely tied to the kind of truth criteria distinctive of scientific knowledge. Examples of concepts widely regarded as categorial in other domains can readily be given: ought, God, intention. Yet giving these raises a new important question, for one becomes only too readily aware of the shifts these concepts have undergone in the history of human thought. If this is so, what precisely is the status of the distinctions between the forms of knowledge and experience that I have sought to emphasise? How ultimate are they? Are they to be regarded as absolute divisions or expressions of a purely contemporary situation?

V

Although one of the fundamental purposes of the chapter 'Liberal education and the nature of knowledge' was an endeavour to characterise liberal education while rejecting the doctrines of metaphysical and epistemological realism with which it has been historically associated, I have not infrequently been taken to be asserting the existence of a series of absolute domains, having at least the status of Kantian *a priori* categories, if not that of categories of Platonic 'forms'. My use of the terms 'category' and 'form' may give some superficial support to such a view, but superficial it is, and the terms in which I suggest the forms are to be distinguished carry no such implications. The conceptual and logical analysis which indicates the divisions I have stressed is a matter of the logical relations and truth criteria to be found at present in our conceptual schemes. Notions of what is and what is not intelligible are employed, but these are questions of coherent thought and communication in public discourse. As distinct from a Kantian approach, it is not my view that in elucidating the fundamental categories of our under-standing we reach an unchanging structure that is implicit, indeed *a priori*, in all rational thought in all times and places. That there exist any elements in thought that can be known to be immune to change, making transcendental demands on us, I do not accept. I see no grounds for accepting that being rational in any sphere is a matter of adherence to a set of principles that are of their character invariant, nor do I see why formal systems of relations of a mathematical kind should be regarded as providing any necessary ideal of rationality against which all other forms must be assessed. Being rational I see rather as a matter of developing conceptual schemes by means of public language in which words are related to our form of life, so that we make objective judgments in relation to some aspect of that form of life. The precise character of those schemes is a matter of investigation, not something that can be laid down in advance, in terms of some ideal, no matter how successful or attractive one particular scheme may be. How far such schemes do as a matter of fact have an invariant structure, is a question for research. Intelligibility in public language and objectivity of judgment would seem to be the demands of reason. What varied forms these at present take is the question I have been implicitly concerned with.

Looked at this way, reason is a human creation that depends on a whole range of factors all of which we are now prepared to see as variable. The capacity of man for linguistic development, like his sensory apparatus, is an evolutionary product. The environment in which he lives, physical as well as social, is similarly the outcome of change. All of this continues in flux, though the time scale of change for different elements varies hugely. Even the notions of reason, intelligibility and objectivity are within this situation. Nothing can any more be supposed fixed eternally. Yet none of this means that we cannot discern certain necessary features of intelligibility and reason as we have them. Although the nature of man may be changing and we are within a great context of total change, nevertheless we can pick out those concepts and principles which are necessary and fundamental to anything we could at present call understanding, as well as to the understanding we actually have. The ultimacy of these elements is there and they mark out the limits of anything we can intelligibly conceive. What is more, all intelligibility that we can have is tied to the creation of concepts within a setting that being given, we cannot escape, and which is in large measure not of our creating. We are the beings we are with our given capacities and contexts. Even if these are in the process of change, they have now the character they have and not another. Intelligibility is itself a development in this context, and one that is of its nature hedged in and limited by it. To assume that this framework is in any sense necessarily fixed now seems absurd. But to imagine it is not setting limits to what is right now intelligible is equally absurd. Those limits may change, but right now intelligibility is what it is. To ignore 'the bounds of sense' is to produce not a higher sense, but nonsense.

And built into the whole nature of intelligibility and sense, is the

93

notion of objectivity. Whatever conceptual schemes we may in our languages devise for judging what is the case in the physical world, what is indeed the case when we use those concepts, is not of our deciding. Even in our situation of total flux, there is a distinction which is part of our making sense of our experience at all and without which that particular enterprise would itself seem un-intelligible, that is the distinction between thoughts, concepts and propositions on the one hand and that to which they are applied on the other. Nor is this distinction applicable only in science. It is there in all our understanding. The first setting up of words in relation to what is a given in experience is necessary to intelligibility. It is only because we can so establish a relation, because we can agree in the judgments of application it involves, that there is meaning. This is the anchor of reason and sense. Where the principles laid down in the development of such a form of discourse are violated, reason and sense are lost. Not that these principles are simple or all of a piece in any form of discourse. Sense can be retained in part by sticking to some of the principles, or to the principles in general whilst mis-applying them in a particular case. Forms of discourse and types of objectivity may also vary radically in kind because the relationship between words and some element of what is 'given' may vary. Indeed that is again just what the distinction between 'forms of knowledge' is all about.

In terms of this approach, the possibility of objectivity and sense, even if not resting on absolute principles, would seem to rest on a fair degree of stability of judgment and agreement between men. This therefore raises once more the question as to how far as a matter of fact there are universal forms of thought. The concepts of mathe-matics and those of space, time and causality that Kant considered *a priori*, manifestly have enormous stability. Yet these are historical products, and we now recognise that they do not have the unlimited application in our experience that Kant thought. It is hard to believe that any other concepts that might be proposed in their place could come off any better. Yet the generality of certain conceptual schemes and their relatively timeless status are surely worthy of note. They are no doubt a measure of the stability and near universality of very significant features in human nature and the human situation. Social diversity may overlay these features so that more fundamental conceptual similarities are not very apparent. Yet man's universal empirical and social concerns, his own characteristics and those of his context are so alike, no other form of explanation seems necessary for the prevalence of certain categories. What is further, these common features would seem to cast serious doubt on the view that major forms of thought of different communities are mutually incomprehensible. There may be considerable difficulty in understanding the conceptual schemes of another society without comprehensive immersion in its culture. Yet in so far as its purposes and context are shared with one's own, the fundamental basis for understanding would seem to be there. The idea of total lack of communication in many areas of life would seem unlikely. The values and judgments made in one society may not be translatable into the conceptual schemes used by another, but that is of itself no denial of intelligibility. Nor is the fact that the values and judgments of two societies are incompatible.

What is more, the idea that notions of reason are entirely socially relative is also suspect. Reason is expressed in forms of language and thought developing in these circumstances of considerable stability in which many non-social elements are involved. It might then in general be expected to take similar structures in different societies. But, further, if the notion of reason is tied necessarily to that of objectivity, this is for it to be explicitly tied to the 'given', much of which is not a social construction and is common to societies. It is true that what is given can only be judged by means of socially constructed concepts, but what is so judged is not itself a merely conceptual creation. Objectivity may figure in different conceptual schemes in different societies, but in so far as societies share the concern for objectivity in similar human activities, their achievements can here be related and assessed. I see no reason to assume that objectivity is the concern of only a limited number of societies.

In distinguishing forms of knowledge, it is the forms of objective judgment that we now have which I have been seeking to separate. If the thesis is correct, there are some seven types of discourse in which objectivity is at present seriously claimed. In some of these that objectivity might be well articulated, and the agreement in judgments very precise and clear. In others, it might be much less precise and not well characterised. If the ways in which words can be related to experience expressing such judgments can be various and complex, and no one formula can be asserted as the only valid case, there is nothing surprising in that. We can only explore the claims that are made. The seven areas I have suggested are now distinct, have certainly not been so recognised in the past, though their presence in some sense may be discerned by hindsight. Maybe new forms are at present being slowly differentiated out. We can do little but wait and see. What other forms objectivity might come to take in due course is not being prejudged in any sense. Nor is the question of change in the notion of objectivity itself. The thesis is simply about the present state of affairs but that state of affairs is not to be regarded as either a transient articulation of a merely socially relative

95

concept of knowledge, or the latest expression of an absolute and invariant framework implicit in knowledge.[9]

VI

The concept of 'liberal education' I outlined on the basis of the forms of knowledge, was explicitly stipulative, it being suggested that knowledge and understanding alone should be the aim but across the range of the different forms of knowledge we have. The importance of such a concept is I think considerable, but its limitations have to be recognised. As was originally pointed out, such a liberal education can not be regarded as providing a total education. It explicitly excludes all objectives other than intellectual ones, thereby ignoring many of the central concerns of, say physical education and the education of character. Even the intellectual ends it seeks are limited. Linguistic skills, for instance, are included only as tools for the acquisition of knowledge in the different forms, and the skills of a second language are therefore completely excluded. To equate such an education with 'general education', is also unacceptable if that is taken to be everything a total education should cover other than any 'specialist' elements. The lack of concern for moral commitment, as distinct from moral understanding, that it seems to imply, is a particularly significant limitation to this concept's usefulness. Nevertheless, it emphasises, by drawing them together, precisely those elements in a total education that are logically basic, and the exclusion of all logically secondary considerations gives it importance at a time when the ends of education are often looked at purely pragmatically.

The fact that the labels used for the various forms of knowledge are labels that are used too for the various forms of experience that employ the concepts of those categories, can lead to much confusion in discussions of this kind. The classification of the forms of knowledge under various labels such as mathematics, physical sciences, religion, is of course a classification of true propositions which are seen as related by a complex conceptual and logical structure. From this base, the classification can be extended to other areas, to experiences, attitudes or skills and if the same labels are used, what exactly they cover needs careful specification. If the same label is then used for university teaching or research units, what it covers may be very different again, for the concerns of such units may stretch well beyond the confines not only of the forms of knowledge in a strict sense, but all those other areas which use the concepts of that form. In a school curriculum context the same label's significance may be so different again that its connection with the original form of knowledge may be extremely remote. Subjects of infinite variety can be composed under any one banner.

Given this situation, what then is one to make of the frequent use in educational debate of the rather emotive term 'discipline'?[10] Clearly it can be used, and is used, for any of the units of classification I have referred to. In that it suggests a tightly knit conceptual and propositional structure it would seem to apply most readily to a form of knowledge, or a sub-section of a form of knowledge. 'Physics' might in this sense label a conceptual and propositional structure, which is a sub-section of the form of knowledge 'physical sciences'. By extension 'music' might be a discipline within 'literature and the fine arts', or 'Christian theology' a discipline within 'religion'. It is in this sense that I prefer to speak of 'disciplines'. Yet each of these labels could be taken to cover a wider domain, so that the 'discipline' of physics might include not only the conceptual and propositional structure, but the skills and methods, attitudes and values, that go with an understanding and concern for this area of knowledge. This second use of 'discipline' has its limits set in one sense by the elements of a form of knowledge, but its concerns are wider than that knowledge itself. How much wider is a variable matter. Even in these two uses it must, however, be noted that the boundaries are always likely to vary because of the connections of the concepts and propositions of any one form of knowledge with those of others.

The use of the term 'discipline' for university and school units of teaching and research introduces a new range of definitional possibilities. The very diversity of teaching objectives, all of which can be labelled according to some classification based on distinctions in the forms of knowledge, makes the task of saying whether any area of study is or is not a discipline almost always controversial. 'Physics' or 'religion' as a school subject may or may not limit itself to objectives falling within either of the two earlier descriptions. In fact, 'religious studies', as it is now coming to be called, is now usually cross-disciplinary on either of the descriptions. But then so also is the university equivalent. Curriculum units at both university and school level are now so varied in character that to describe them all as 'disciplines' gives the term little significant use. Its use in connection with units of research seems much more satisfactory, though these must not always be assumed to be concerned with elements related to only one form or sub-form of knowledge. There is perhaps a tendency now to use the term in connection with an area of research and university teaching which professionals recognise as focusing on a large enough body of logically inter-related truths, theories and problems to justify its consideration in relative isolation from other

97

matters. Such 'disciplines' however, are not necessarily confined to the concerns of one form or sub-form of knowledge, as the various forms are logically related; nor are they necessarily thought of simply as propositional in character, but as areas of other related elements such as skills, attitudes, or values, as well.

In the light of these comments the question as to how far education should or should not concern itself with the disciplines needs careful handling. If a discipline is equated with a form or sub-form of knowledge in a narrow sense, focusing on the development of knowledge and understanding, then the objectives of a liberal education as I have outlined it are to be found within the disciplines. The objectives of education in a wider or total sense however cannot be found there. If the term is defined as equivalent to a form or sub-form of knowledge in its widest sense, whereby all elements of human consciousness are locatable somewhere within the forms because of the concepts employed, then all education necessarily has objectives taken from the disciplines. If however the term is defined by reference to areas of university teaching and research, the situation is altogether more complex. In this sense, much common-sense knowledge and many forms of experience, attitudes and skills may be regarded as lying outside all the disciplines we have, though not of course outside all the forms of knowledge. Many forms of education, including liberal education in my sense, will have objectives some of which come from within the disciplines and some of which do not. In terms of objectives, then, attention to the disciplines may be on one definition logically necessary for some objectives but very limiting, on another logically necessary for all objectives, on another not necessary for many objectives and a matter that depends on what objectives one chooses. Clearly conceptual sophistication beyond the level of common sense demands objectives from the disciplines in all senses and to this extent a study of the disciplines must form a major goal for education.

But the significance of the disciplines is not only a matter for the objectives of education. What about the formation of curriculum units? Ought these to be organised in terms of the disciplines? Again, it all depends on what is meant by the term. I can see no necessity to have a curriculum structured in terms of the forms or sub-forms of knowledge, whether the objectives pursued are those of the narrowest or widest classification in those terms. The logical relations between the forms are there, if in one sense secondary, and they cannot be forgotten in intelligent curriculum planning. Yet from a purely logical point of view, there are clearly advantages to such form-based units. In the sense of areas of university teaching and research, the structure of disciplines is less relevant, and indeed could be a menace to certain parts of education. This is certainly true of the elementary stages of education, where an apeing of university organisation would be a pretentious fraud, all the objectives being readily available outside those structures. At the later stages too, an organisation of this sort must not mislead educators themselves, for many important school objectives are necessarily excluded from university units of teaching and research which have an explicitly intellectual emphasis. In so far as that emphasis is required in schools, the university structure has much to recommend it, on logical grounds at least; but the range of objectives it serves will need careful re-consideration if much that is important in school education is not to be forgotten. If that structure is used, the danger of apeing university teaching methods must also be carefully watched. No organisation of curriculum units necessarily dictates the methods to be employed. Even if our education needs to maintain a firm hold on the intellectual ends it serves, nothing will be gained if it pursues those by methods totally inappropriate for the majority of pupils.

But the importance of the disciplines, in the various senses distinguished, for school education, must not be minimised. What matters in this discussion is that the logical priority of intellectual objectives be recognised even if in terms of wider human values they are sometimes judged secondary. Equally, their logical structure cannot be denied if they are ever to be attained. The concerns of the universities mean that their organisations of teaching and research necessarily embody these concerns to a high degree. But schools are not universities and their teaching functions are significantly different. These need to be seen in their own right for what they are. And if once that is done, then not only do the disciplines matter, but many other things matter as well, things of major psychological and social concern which must not be overlooked. Education is a complex business and philosophical analysis can contribute to our planning of it in a limited way. What it can do is alert us to the danger of too easy decisions and the issue of the place of the disciplines is more than a philosophical affair. What more there is to it, I must however leave to others.

Notes

1 Reprinted as Chapter 3.
2 See particularly J.H. Gribble, 'Forms of knowledge', *Educational Philosophy and Theory*, vol. 2, no. 1, 1970; D.C. Phillips, 'The distinguishing features of forms of knowledge', *Educational Philosophy and Theory*, vol. 3, no. 2, 1971; E. Hindess, 'Forms of knowledge', *Proceedings of the Philosophy of Education Society of Great Britain*, vol. VI,

no. 2, 1972; J. Wilson, 'The curriculum: justification and taxonomy', *British Journal of Educational Studies*, vol. XVII, no. 1, 1969.

3 P.H. Hirst and R.S. Peters, *The Logic of Education*, Routledge & Kegan Paul, 1970. See also P.H. Hirst, 'Educational theory', in J.W. Tibble (ed.), *The Study of Education*, Routledge & Kegan Paul, 1966.

4 This Chapter should be read in conjunction with the rest of this volume, particularly Chapters 3, 4, 5, 9 and 10. In isolation it does not provide an adequate account of my views.

5 For further comment see Chapter 10.

6 For further comment see Chapter 4.

7 See D.W. Hamlyn, *The Theory of Knowledge*, Macmillan, 1970, ch. 5.

8 For a further discussion of these matters, see Chapter 10.

9 The nature and significance of conceptual and categorial changes have been dealt with at some length in S. Körner, *Categorial Frameworks*, Blackwell, 1970, and S. Toulmin, *Human Understanding*, vol. I, Clarendon Press, 1972. The position outlined here, however, owes more to suggestions to be found in the writings of Professor D.W. Hamlyn, though I have no reason to suppose that he would agree with the particular use I have made of them. See especially D.W. Hamlyn, *The Theory of Knowledge*, Macmillan, 1970.

10 For a very full discussion of some aspects of disciplines, see Toulmin, op. cit.

What is teaching?

7

The question with which this chapter is concerned is simply 'What is teaching?'. How do we distinguish teaching from other activities? This is, I think, a very important question for at least four reasons. First, a lot of new educational methods are now widely canvassed in which the significance of teaching is far from clear. Repeatedly one finds an almost exclusive emphasis on certain activities of the pupils, say those of enquiry, discovery and play, not on the activities of the teacher. In the discussion of such methods it seems to me there is much misunderstanding of what teaching is and therefore of what it involves, and this not infrequently leads to a very distorted view of the whole educational situation. Second, people are now aware of a range of activities, some of them thought to be morally undesirable, whose relation to teaching is by no means clear: activities like indoctrinating, preaching, advertising and propagandising. There are many terms that are as it were in the same logical band as 'teaching', and we are I think rightly getting more sensitive as to whether or not the activities these terms label ought to go on in school. If we can get clearer about the nature of teaching it will surely help us to see the character of these other processes and their inter-connections. Similar problems are raised by the use of teaching machines and other devices, not to mention sleep-teaching.

Third, we are clearly in need of a great deal of carefully controlled empirical research on the effectiveness of different teaching methods. But without the clearest concept of what teaching is, it is impossible to find appropriate behavioural criteria whereby to assess what goes on in the classroom. Most teaching methods new and old are advocated or defended on little more than hunch or personal prejudice. What we need to know are some relevant empirical facts, but these we cannot find if we are uncertain how to identify cases of teaching anyway. And finally, being clear about what teaching is matters vitally because how teachers understand teaching very much affects what they actually do in the classroom. If it is the case that our activities depend on how we ourselves see them, what we believe about them, then if we have crazy, fuzzy ideas about teaching, we will be likely to do crazy and fuzzy things in its name. One of the most important things for a teacher is surely to be clear about the nature of the central activity in which he is professionally involved. And if that is true for teachers in general, it is certainly true for the teachers of teachers in particular.

The question then is how do we characterise the activity of teaching so as to distinguish it from all other activities? How, for instance, on entering a classroom can one tell whether the teacher is in fact teaching? What exactly has to be going on? To begin to answer the problem here we must surely distinguish two obviously different senses in which we talk about teaching. In the first sense we talk about teaching as an *enterprise* in which a person may be engaged for a long period, say all afternoon. In this sense, a teacher spends the afternoon not in shopping, sunbathing or taking the dog for a walk, but in fact in teaching. The term teaching is here functioning at a very general level, labelling a whole enterprise which may be broken down into many more specific activities. And if indeed we look at these more detailed elements of the enterprise, it is perfectly plain that many of them are not activities we would in a more restricted sense of the term wish to call 'teaching' at all. Opening the window to let in more air, sharpening a few pencils, preventing a squabble between two pupils, all these may be legitimate parts of the enter- prise of teaching as a whole. But we do surely use the term teaching in a much more specific sense whereby we can say that these activities are not the activities of teaching. In this second sense then we can speak of specific teaching *activities* which do not include in their number the sharpening of pencils, the opening of windows, and all other such activities which might form a legitimate part of the teaching enterprise as a whole. In the rest of this chapter I am not concerned with the enterprise use of the term and would add only one point about it. Clearly for an enterprise to be that of teaching at all it is necessary that it must contain certain specific teaching activities. If a teacher spent the whole afternoon opening windows, sharpening pencils, cleaning her glasses and so on, she would do no teaching in any sense at all. It is necessary therefore to the teaching enterprise that it include specific teaching activities and all other specific activities are part of that enterprise only because of their relation to these.[1]

But how are specific *teaching* activities to be distinguished from all other specific activities? Why exactly is opening a window or sharpening a pencil not teaching? Manifestly teaching is no one specific activity readily identifiable in general circumstances like say walking or running or riding a bicycle. There are an enormous number of specific activities which may in fact be teaching. One might be describing a historical situation and this could be called teaching. One might on the other hand be saying nothing at all, but be drawing on a blackboard, or doing a chemical experiment in front of the pupils. All these would seem to be teaching activities in a specific sense, so that there is no one immediately recognisable activity which the term teaching picks out. Is there then a limited number of specific activities which constitute teaching, so that to be teaching at all one would have to be carrying out one of these? A teacher would then have to know how to question, how to prove things, how to demonstrate, etc. If this were what teaching involved, it would greatly simplify the business of teacher training and indeed it seems to me that there is a large grain of truth in this idea. Such an approach is however too simple-minded, if only because many, if not all, of the specific activities which occur within teaching, also occur when one is certainly not teaching. One can tell a story to a child who knows it backwards but who just simply enjoys hearing it over once more. One might demonstrate something to entertain a night-club audience. In proving something, one may be actually dis-covering the proof, not teaching someone else. One may be trans-lating something, without teaching anything to anybody. None of these activities implies that teaching is taking place at all. It therefore seems to be the case that we cannot hope to get clear what teaching is simply by producing an exhaustive list of activities of this kind.

Nevertheless, teaching is what is technically known as a poly-morphous activity: it quite literally takes many different forms. Its parallels are thus activities like work and gardening and explicit comparisons with these might help in the process of clarification. What does a person have to be doing to be working? Driving a truck, working a lathe, solving mathematical problems, drawing beer, all these activities constitute somebody's work. Indeed any activity would seem to be in principle a possible form of work. On the other hand, gardening is much more limited in what it embraces. Digging, mowing the lawn, pruning, are activities of gardening, but one cannot be doing *anything* as one might in the case of work. What then about teaching? Is it in this respect more like work or like gardening? Looked at one way teaching can take so many different forms that, like work, there seems pretty well no limit to the activities it can involve. Standing on one's head could in fact be part of teaching something, so could driving, working a lathe, solving a problem. Provided one looks at the whole range of things that can be taught, it would seem that any activity might occur as a teaching activity. Which activities might be involved in any particular instance will depend on exactly *what* is being taught. Yet it might be insisted that though teaching, to say, drive, might *involve* driving, when teaching one must in fact do more than merely drive. One must, say, *demon-strate* driving. This would seem to imply that though any activity might be subsumed under the notion of teaching, for that to be the case it must be carried out in some special way. And this in turn suggests that all the legion activities that can figure in teaching, to figure in that way, must be seen as occurring within a framework of the kind of specific activities mentioned earlier, such as demonstrating, proving, telling, etc. This view is I think correct and the analogy between teaching and other polymorphous activities would seem to be most helpful at the level of say gardening rather than at the level of say work. Yet the parallel with gardening is strictly limited. Activities like pruning and mowing the lawn are necessarily forms of gardening and that concept may be exhaustively analysable in such terms. Yet it was insisted above that demonstrating and proving are not necessarily forms of teaching and it is by no means obvious that, limited though the range of activities of teaching may be, there is an exhaustive list of distinct activities into which the concept of teaching could be even partially analysed. I conclude therefore that we cannot hope to characterise specific teaching activities simply in terms of the activities of proving, demonstrating, telling, etc. Rather, teaching must be characterised some other way which will make it clear to us when these activities are indeed involved in teaching and when involved in say entertaining. It will perhaps also make plain why these activities are peculiarly important in teaching.

How then are we going to characterise specific teaching activities at all? I think the answer to this is that they can only be characterised in the way in which we fundamentally characterise all human activities: by looking at their point or purpose. It is by clarifying the aim, the intention of what is going on, that we can see when standing on one's head to demonstrate something, or any other activity, is in fact teaching and not say simply entertaining. The difference here is in the different, over-riding intentions involved in each case. What a particular activity is, what a person is doing, depends crucially on how he himself sees the activity. To take a standard example, if a person is seen to place a glass of liquid to his lips and slowly drain it, what is he doing? He may be quenching his thirst, committing suicide, or engaging in a religious ritual. Which of these, if any, it is, depends on the point, purpose or intention that lies behind the physical movements. Clearly the physical state of affairs can be described without knowing the person's intention. It can be seen that the glass is moved by a certain force so many inches towards his lips, and so on. But an account of what is observed does not tell us what the activity is. Perhaps in a particular context we may be able to infer very readily the most likely point of the movements and thus what activity is involved; nevertheless it is only by reference to the intention that we can describe the activity, and of course there is no guarantee that our external judgment of the intention, based upon our observation, is in fact correct.

Yet if a 'sufficient' characterisation of an activity can only be given in terms of its intention and not in terms of its observable features, that is not to say that certain observable features are not necessary to many particular activities. Clearly not all observable events could be described as quenching one's thirst or celebrating Mass. Unless liquid of some sort is being consumed, a person cannot be quenching his thirst and on empirical evidence alone we can dismiss such a description of many of his activities. From observation we can rule out many possibilities of what a person is doing even if we cannot from observation say which of the remaining possibilities he is engaged in. The points here are fundamentally quite simple. First, any activity is characterised by its intention, but many intentions cannot, logically cannot, be ascribed unless certain observable conditions hold. Secondly, for a given set of observable conditions a number of quite different intentions may be ascribable. Thirdly, in so far as there are necessary observable conditions for a particular activity, they are necessary conditions for there being the intention concerned in this case. They are not conditions of a logically independent character.

What we want to know then about teaching is first, what is the intention by which its activities are picked out from all others and secondly what necessary observable features are there by which we can judge that some activities could not possibly be teaching, whereas others might well be, though we can never be certain from such external characterisation alone.

A crude answer to the first of these questions is I think simple. The intention of all teaching activities is that of bringing about learning. But simple and banal though this answer might seem, it is I suggest an extremely important answer. It involves the claim that the concept of teaching is in fact totally unintelligible without a grasp of the concept of learning. It asserts that there is no such thing as teaching without the intention to bring about learning and that therefore one cannot characterise teaching independently of characterising learning. Until therefore we know what learning is, it is impossible for us to know what teaching is. The one concept is totally dependent on the other. Because of the tightest conceptual connection then, the characterisation and *raison d'être* of teaching rests on that of learning. If therefore a teacher spends the whole afternoon in activities the concern of which is not that the pupils should learn, but say the inflation of his own ego, then in fact he cannot have been teaching at all. In these terms it could be the case that quite a large number of professional teachers are in fact frauds most of their lives, because their intentions are never clear. Perhaps quite a lot of our work is misdirected because this necessary intention is lost in a welter of secondary intentions, by neglect, if not deliberately. Of course pupils may learn many things when a teacher is not in fact teaching. That is another matter. What would seem to be particularly important here is that in taking a job as a professional teacher one is presumably being paid to carry out this intention whatever else one is paid to do. If one is not going into the classroom to bring about learning, if that is not the intention, then one cannot, logically cannot, be teaching. This is not to say that one may not be doing many other things which are of value. There are many ways of occupying children's time, some of them profitable, but that does not make them teaching. I wish to maintain therefore that the notion of teaching is totally dependent for its characterisation on the concept of learning and that this has important practical consequences for how teachers see their job and therefore for what they do in the classroom.

Before going further, two particular points need commenting on. First, there are two ways in which we talk about teaching activities in the classroom context. The most common relates to the case in which a person may teach in the fullest sense of that word and yet, in spite of the intention and the appropriateness of the activities involved, the pupils may learn absolutely nothing. Here the notion of teaching is simply that of trying to get people to learn and no more. But there is another use of the word, which involves the implication that not only has there been the intention to bring about learning, but that the pupil has in fact learnt what was intended. To say that Mr Brown taught me to ride a bicycle, usually means not merely that Mr Brown tried to get me to learn to ride a bicycle, but that I have in fact succeeded in learning this. There is thus not only a 'task' sense to the verb to teach, where trying or intending alone is implied; there is also a 'success' or 'achievement' sense, where in addition to the intention, there is the implication that learning has in fact occurred. For the rest of this chapter I shall be concerned with teaching in the 'task' sense only, and in this sense it is *not* the case that teaching necessarily implies learning. What teaching implies is merely the intention to bring about learning.[2]

Secondly, if teaching activities are intentional, what are we to say about all the learning that goes on in a classroom, or anywhere else, which is not intended by the teacher? Is there not such a thing as unintentional teaching after all? Certainly, we do sometimes talk in this way, when a particular situation has been the occasion for significant learning. What is important here is surely the recognition that no teacher intended the learning, though significant things might have been picked up in the context. It will be suggested later that it is because of certain important features in the context that make the situation similar to that in which there is the intention to bring about learning, that we use the term teaching here, though in a somewhat different sense. In schools we are not primarily concerned with unintended learning. What we are concerned with is the task of bringing about learning because we believe there is much that we can do towards making learning more than a random business. Of course, taking the education of children as a whole, what they pick up in the context of our unintentional teaching may indeed be important. Still this does not alter the fact that in schools we are centrally concerned with intentional teaching and that as soon as we turn our attention to what has been unintentional teaching, we thereby necessarily change its character.

The characterisation of teaching given thus far makes the concept entirely parasitic on that of learning. That being so, it would seem important in clarifying the notion further to look at what is meant by 'learning'. Even if teaching is not the label of one specific activity, is learning? The answer I think must again be clearly no. One may learn things by trial and error, by discovery or observation, by being told and by many other means. But if there are many different activities of learning, what makes them cases of learning? I suggest the answer is again found, as in the case of teaching, by looking at the intention of the activities concerned. If the intention of teaching involves a concern for learning, what in turn is the intention of learning? Fortunately the answer seems not to be another type of activity whose intention would in turn have to be clarified. The end or aim of learning is, I suggest, always some specific achievement or end state. There are many such end achievements: believing something which one did not believe before, knowing something one did not know before, being able to do something one could not do before, having a habit one had not got before and so on. As a result of learning one may know a scientific theory, know how to ride a bicycle, know how to calculate a square root, know that Henry VIII had six wives, appreciate the symphonies of Beethoven or keep one's engagements punctually. The achievements or end states with which learning is concerned are of enormous variety and not surprisingly therefore the activities of learning are equally varied. Learning like teaching is a polymorphous activity. If then learning is the activity of a person, say B, the intention of which is the attainment of some particular end, we can say that B necessarily learns something, say X, where X may be a belief, a skill, an attitude or some other complex object that characterises this end.

For the purpose of this chapter there is no need to pursue the nature of learning further, though two particular points must be stressed. First, it is I think important to note that the end achievements of learning are new states of the person and that these differ radically from each other. We seem to be under a perpetual temptation to think that all learning results in knowledge. Clearly this is false. Along with this too goes the temptation to think that what we learn, X, is necessarily a truth or fact of some kind. Clearly this is also false. To thoroughly disabuse oneself of these myths is a first step towards getting rid of many common but quite fallacious ideas about the nature of learning and, as a consequence, about the nature of teaching.

Second, it must be noted that I have assumed learning to be an activity on the part of the learner. But just as we have a use of teaching to cover cases when there is in fact no intention to bring about learning, so we have uses of learning where the pupil does not in fact intend to achieve the appropriate end which he nevertheless attains. In this sense we can speak of non-intentional learning, where as the result of a causal process as in hypnotism, conditioning, sleep-teaching or even the unconscious acquisition of something, the intention of the learner is not involved. It is important to recognise here that the term learning is being used for a quite different process, in this case causal and not intentional. Nothing is to be gained by trying to legislate one meaning for the term, cutting across general usage which now covers both these processes. Yet the distinction between them needs to be kept clear. Whether or not causal processes are educationally desirable is a matter with which I am not here concerned.

Putting together what has been said about learning with what was earlier said about teaching, we have the following account of teaching. A teaching activity is the activity of a person, A (the teacher), the intention of which is to bring about an activity (learning), by a person, B (the pupil), the intention of which is to achieve some end-state (e.g. knowing, appreciating) whose object is X (e.g. a belief, attitude, skill). From this it follows that to understand what is involved in teaching, one must start at the other end of a logical chain of relations, with an understanding of the end achievements to which everything is being directed. From this one can proceed to understand what is involved in B's achieving such ends, in learning X, and then proceed to an understanding of what is involved in A teaching B, X. This logical dependence of teaching on learning, and learning on the nature of the achievements to which it is directed, is thus once more no mere academic matter. If teachers are not clear what end achievements their teaching is concerned with, they cannot know what is involved in B's learning X. And until they know what is involved in B's learning X, they cannot know what is involved in A's teaching B, X. Any notion of learning which is not the learning of some particular X, is as vague as the notion of going somewhere but nowhere in particular. Equally some particular person B is necessarily learning this X. Following the logical chain, it is therefore only in a context where both what is to be learnt and who is learning it are clear, that we can begin to be clear about teaching B, X. Just as a pupil B cannot simply learn, but must necessarily be learning X, so A cannot simply teach, he must be teaching B, and he must be teaching B, X. It is as much a logical absurdity to say 'One teaches children not subjects' as it is to say 'One teaches subjects not children'. Both of these phrases might have their slogan use, but the serious discussion of teaching ought surely to reject such slogans in the name of the simple logical truth, that one necessarily teaches somebody something. Not that of course one is necessarily teaching a 'subject' in the traditional sense, but there must always be an end achievement which somebody is learning. A great deal of discussion of modern educational methods seems in danger of going seriously astray because of a refusal to accept the full implications of this simple logically necessary truth.

I have so far argued that in its central use, teaching is the label for those activities of a person A, the intention of which is to bring about in another person B, the intentional learning of X. In addition, there would seem to be uses of the term when the intention on the part of A is missing, but the intentional learning on the part of B remains, and also uses when the intention on the part of A is present, but the intention on the part of B is replaced by a causal process. But even in the central case, the intention on the part of A to bring about the learning of X by B might be thought to leave the characterisation of teaching activities too open. On this account, might not the strangest events count as teaching a pupil say to count, provided this was the intention of the teacher? This would indeed be the case if there were no necessary conditions which an activity must satisfy before it could possibly be described as a teaching activity. Just as not all activities could be gardening surely not all activities could be teaching? What then are the necessary features of a publicly observable kind which all teaching activities must possess? There are I suggest at least two. As it is necessarily the case that A teaches B, X, there is one necessary demand on the activities in relation to the particular X that is being taught, and there is a second necessary demand in relation to the particular person B concerned.

The first of these demands is far from easy to express. But I suggest that in so far as one is necessarily teaching X, the specific teaching activity involved must be what I will call 'indicative' of X. By this I mean that the activity must, either implicitly or explicitly, express or embody the X to be learnt, so that this X is clearly indicated to the pupil as what he is to learn. In this way the teacher makes plain in his activity *what* he intends to be learnt. It is not I think at all the case that what is to be learnt must necessarily be explicitly discernible in the activity, yet it must be so available in some sense that the pupil's learning activity can be directed to this as its object. It is because activities like demonstrating, telling and proving can provide such excellent means for indicating an X that it is intended the pupil will learn, that they play such a central part in teaching. Yet just because these activities are such effective means for expressedly indicating a given X, they can be significant not only in teaching but in such other concerns as entertaining. It is only when such activities are used in a learning context, to indicate what is to be *learnt* that they can become teaching activities. The fact that specific teaching activities must indicatively express what is to be learnt, also helps to make clear why at times we speak of teaching in an unintentional sense. We do this, I suggest, when certain features of a situation can be legitimately interpreted as indicatively expressing something to be learnt, though this in fact may not be anyone's actual intention. The situation is thus interpreted as a teaching situation by the learner, when in fact, from an intentional point of view, it is no such thing. First then specific teaching activities must be indicative of what is to be learnt and it is for this reason that the opening of windows and the sharpening of pencils could never be themselves the teaching of historical facts or of Pythagoras's Theorem.

In the second place, as a specific teaching activity is necessarily concerned with the teaching of X to a particular pupil B, it must be indicatively expressed so that it is possible for this particular pupil B to learn X. One might teach an undergraduate class in philosophy Wittgenstein's criticism of the idea of a private language, by reading to the students sections from the *Philosophical Investigations*. But to carry out such an activity with a class of average six-year-olds would, I suggest, not constitute teaching at all. Indicative though the activity might be, as the six-year-olds could understand practically nothing that was being said, this could surely not constitute teaching *them* Wittgenstein's views on private languages. There is a gap between the knowledge, skills or state of mind of the learner and what it is he is to learn, which it seems to me any teaching activity must seek to bridge if it is to deserve that label. Teaching activities must therefore take place at a level where the pupil *can* take on what it is intended he should learn. It must be possible, and this seems to me a logical point, for learning to take place. This logical demand is for the teacher to have psychological and other knowledge about the learner, and it clearly means that many specific things cannot possibly be taught to a given pupil given his present state of knowledge, skill, etc. I conclude therefore that a specific teaching activity must necessarily indicatively express the X to be learnt by B and be so related to the present state of B that he can learn X.

It might be objected to my second necessary demand for teaching activities, that to misjudge the present state of the pupils does not disqualify a person's activities from properly being described as teaching. Surely he has taught X whether the pupils have learnt X or not. Certainly teaching does not necessarily imply learning, but it does necessarily imply the intention of bringing about learning by someone, and if from one's activities it is impossible for that someone to learn what is intended, it does seem very odd to describe such activities as teaching. One reason why we are inclined to think that there could be teaching even when the present state of the pupils is grossly misjudged, is I think that we spend so much of our time teaching classes not individuals and the condition I am insisting on seems to make almost impossible demands. Must it not be the case that in any class with a wide ability range, what is presented is in fact inappropriate for some of the pupils? If we are to stick to the individualistic model I have used, must we not say that in even the 'task' sense, only some of the class have been taught X, and not others? Strictly I think the answer to that must be yes. But perhaps it would be better simply to recognise that we do use the word teaching both for activities aimed at group learning as well as individual learning. In the case of a group, what a teacher does if he is teaching them all the same X is to work with an appropriate norm for the attainments of that group. What constitutes an appropriate norm cannot I think be generally stated; nevertheless it seems to me that without working to such a norm there could be no activities that could properly be described as teaching the group. It might of course be argued, and with some justice, that properly understood, teaching a group necessarily involves attention to the individual differences of the pupils.

As a final comment on the two criteria which I have suggested are necessary to any teaching activity, it is I think instructive to note that in these terms opposing virtues and defects have tended to characterise both traditional formal teaching methods and more contemporary progressive alternatives. Traditional teaching methods have above all concerned themselves with the indicative features of these activities, often meeting the present learning state of the pupils in an over-generalised and inadequate way. In reaction, more progressive methods have tended to cater extremely well for the present learning state of individual pupils, but at the expense of the necessary indicative features that teaching activities must embody. It is not that either group of methods is of itself necessarily deficient as teaching activities, and each might well have its place according to what exactly is being taught and to whom. What is important is that we come to realise that in all teaching activities both these necessary features need the fullest responsible consideration.

In concluding this paper I would like to return to the problem of clarifying the nature of such activities as indoctrinating, conditioning, preaching, training, instructing and so on, as the characterisation of teaching that I have outlined can I think help in this process. As here considered, teaching activities form a very broad category indeed, one which is in no sense restricted to those activities we think it appropriate for schools to undertake. I have been concerned with teaching and learning in general, whatever the ends concerned, be they bad habits, perversions, concepts, facts, physical skills, etc. In so far then as indoctrination and other activities involve the intention to bring about learning of some kind, they involve teaching and in so far as they are themselves processes for bringing about learning of certain kinds they are themselves forms of teaching. From all that has been said about teaching, different categories of teaching activity can clearly be distinguished in a number of distinct ways. The object or objects to be learnt can be of one particular kind rather than another. The activity of learning may be of a specific sort, or the activity of the teacher might be restricted in some particular way. Clearly there are likely to be labels for certain types of teaching which become important for specific purposes and it is, I suggest, by looking at the particular sub-class of teaching activities involved that we are most likely to distinguish indoctrination, instruction, and so on.

Indoctrination, for example, would certainly seem to be picked out, at least in part, by the distinctive end state of mind of the learner, to which the teaching is directed. An indoctrinated person would seem to hold certain beliefs unshakably.[3] In this case what the person is intended to learn, the X, is distinctive here, though in exactly what way it is important to note. On this criterion, it is nothing about the beliefs themselves that distinguishes indoctrination, but some higher order beliefs about their status, or some attitude to them. But however this characterisation is given, it is expressible in terms of certain distinctive objects for learning. Some have suggested that there is in fact something distinctive about the beliefs themselves in that one can only indoctrinate in matters of opinion or doctrines. Again this is to distinguish the teaching activities of indoctrination in terms of *what* is being taught. It can also be argued that indoctrination is restricted to certain learning processes, or that unintentional indoctrination is a contradiction. My point here is not to decide exactly what is meant by indoctrination or any other of these terms, but rather to indicate how a clarification of them might be helpfully approached.

What is however plain from the work that has already been done on the concept of indoctrination, is that most terms in this area are likely to be in some respects unclear, being used in a number of inter-related ways. What matters then is not what any 'correct' use might be, but rather the conceptual distinctions that arise in this area. If, for instance, the notion of 'believing unshakably' is seen as a distinctive result of some forms of teaching, and we for our purposes call these forms indoctrination, then indoctrination is being sharply distinguished from teaching leading to the holding of beliefs rationally, which many regard as a necessary part of education. Once we know the possible meanings of these very tricky terms we know our way round their relationship much better. We are clearer too about the significance of many of the things we do when engaged in teaching.

The distinctive features of such processes as conditioning and sleep-teaching would seem to be that they involve causal and not intentional learning or if it is intentional, it is intentional in some very particular sense. Whether or not these processes ought to figure within indoctrination or education, will of course depend on one's account of these latter processes. Training and instructing on the other hand would seem to be concepts connected unmistakably with intentional learning, the difference between them being determined by the particular group of end achievements with which each is concerned.

And finally, what of teaching machines: can such machines be properly said to teach? In terms of the analysis I have here given the idea that a piece of hardware can of itself teach is nonsense, for it itself can have no intentions and cannot engage in activities. But taken in the proper context I see no reason why a machine, properly programmed, should not be the instrument of a teaching activity. It is indeed the machine programmed so that it indicatively expresses what is to be learnt, in such a way that the pupil can in fact learn, because it meets his current state of mind, that must be thought of as the teaching agent. The appropriate programming of the machine is of course an essential part of the teaching activity as a whole. What the invention of books, let alone teaching machines, made possible, was a separation in time between the teacher's expression of what is to be learnt and the pupil's encounter with this. Nothing new in principle is introduced into the idea of a teaching activity. What is however available here to the pupil is a programme of indicatively expressive activities, drawn up after expert consideration of the problems involved in pupil's learning, that might be much better for the task than the live activities of the teacher available. As the teaching activities that involve the use of such machines must be completely predetermined, it is of course important that the details of the programme be constructed with the utmost care and that it be appropriate to the learning state of the pupils. It is of course only when these conditions are fulfilled that in using the machine these pupils could be said to be being taught.

Throughout this paper I have been concerned with mapping the features that distinguish teaching activities from all others. It has not been my concern to lay down the criteria for good teaching or even successful teaching. Successful teaching would seem to be simply teaching which does in fact bring about the desired learning. Good teaching is however much more difficult to discern. I am not even sure that successful learning is a criterion for good teaching. Certainly in a given particular case there is no contradiction in saying that a person was successfully yet badly taught. Yet in so far as this account of teaching is correct, it has at least indicated which activities we are concerned to study in a critical comparison of teaching activities. What is more it must have at least some important implications for the methods whereby such comparisons must be made. But what these are, will not be gone into here, if only because such elaboration would be rather premature when the criteria for what teaching is are not yet agreed. It is towards establishing what these criteria are that this paper has been primarily directed.

Further reading

The major philosophical papers which discuss the nature of teaching can be found in three collections of articles:
C.B.J. Macmillan and T.W. Nelson (eds), *Concepts of Teaching*, Rand McNally, Chicago, 1968.
R.S. Peters (ed.), *The Concept of Education*, Routledge & Kegan Paul, 1967.
B.P. Komisar and C.B.J. Macmillan (eds), *Psychological Concepts in Education*, Rand McNally, Chicago, 1967.
There are also important chapters in:
I. Scheffler, *The Language of Education*, Thomas, Illinois, 1960.
G. Langford, *Philosophy and Education*, Macmillan, 1968.

Notes

1 I am here using terminology which is in part the same as that used by
   B. Paul Komisar's, 'Teaching: act and enterprise', in C.B.J. Macmillan
   and T.W. Nelson (eds), *Concepts of Teaching*, Rand McNally, Chicago,

1968. In spite of certain similarities in both terminology and approach however, our accounts are clearly in radical disagreement over the precise relationship between teaching and learning, and the necessary characteristics of at least certain of his 'teaching acts'.

2 The common-place distinction I am here making leaves un-noted a complexity which any full task/achievement analysis of teaching cannot disregard. If teaching is directed towards another activity, that of the pupil's learning, then the task and achievement uses of 'teaching' need to be carefully related to possible task and achievement uses of 'learning'. We are inclined to assume that both uses of 'teaching' are directed to the achievement use of 'learning'. It is, however, far from obvious that this is always the case. Just this problem arises again with activities like demonstrating and proving, as Dr Komisar shows very plainly (see note 1). I am, however, unhappy about his account of these activites, though I am far from certain that I have always understood him.

3 See J.P. White, 'Indoctrination', in R.S. Peters (ed.), *The Concept of Education*, Routledge & Kegan Paul, 1967.

I

8   The logical and psychological aspects of teaching a subject

Most teachers of a form of knowledge or understanding at some time ask themselves the fundamental questions: In what ways and to what extent is the effective teaching of a subject determined by the nature of the subject itself and in what ways and to what extent is the teaching dependent on factors studied in the psychology of learning and teaching? Or putting these questions another way, how are syllabuses and methods determined by the characteristics of what is to be taught and how are they to be determined by our empirical knowledge of teaching methods? Indeed, what sort of questions are questions about how best to teach a subject? This chapter is an attempt to make clear something of what is involved in answering these questions. It will, however, be concerned almost entirely with the teaching of those subjects which are indisputably logically cohesive disciplines. I have argued elsewhere[1] that although the domain of human knowledge can be regarded as composed of a number of logically distinct forms of knowledge, we do in fact for many purposes, deliberately and self-consciously organise knowledge into a large variety of fields which often form the units employed in teaching. The problems that arise in teaching such complex fields as, say geography and educational theory, are much more difficult to analyse than those arising in such forms, as say, mathematics, physics and history. And if the teaching of such fields necessarily involves the teaching of certain areas of more fundamental forms of knowledge, then it is only when questions about the latter have been settled that we can hope to answer questions about the former.

What sort of questions then, are questions about how best to teach a subject? Manifestly these are not questions that belong to the subject itself. How to teach history is not itself a historical question, nor is how to teach chemistry a chemical question. Maybe these questions will never be satisfactorily answered without a knowledge of history or chemistry, but such knowledge is at best a necessary condition for answering the questions, certainly it is not sufficient. Questions about the teaching of history are surely quite different logically from the questions of historical scholarship and where is the evidence that there is any correlation of abilities in these two domains?

If questions about teaching are manifestly not questions within the subject domain itself, are they then simply empirical questions? If so we could hope to discover directly by experiment and observation which activities do in fact lead to pupils learning history or chemistry, and thus which activities are successful as teaching methods. Certainly unless it is the case that activities result in pupils learning history or chemistry, they are useless as teaching methods, whatever the intentions of the teacher may be, and whether or not pupils learn successfully is a matter for empirical test. This answer is, however, too simple. For before any empirical investigation of teaching methods, that has any value, can be carried out, we have to decide what will count as pupils having learnt history. And once we start looking closely at what the learning of history involves, important logical features appear which must necessarily characterise what goes on if the activities we are interested in are even to count as the teaching of history. Here then will be features which on logical grounds must determine the teaching of the subject.

What then are we after in teaching a subject? What does learning it involve? In all subjects surely, we do not just want the learning of a string of propositions. If that were all, we could quickly set out what has to be learnt and find by empirical investigation how best to teach it. But even when handing on information, we want pupils not to become like parrots but to *understand* the information, and, as soon as we say that, difficulties arise as to what exactly we mean by this term and how we would know pupils had understood what was presented to them. Generally speaking we want yet more from our teaching than this, however. What we want is that pupils shall begin, however embryonically, to think historically, scientifically or mathematically; to think in the way distinctive of the particular subject involved and even to achieve some style and imagination in doing so. Thus before we can carry out any empirical investigation of teaching methods we are faced with the difficult task of getting clear what is involved in, say, thinking historically, and thus in learning to think in this way.

At first sight it might be thought that to discover what historical thinking is, we must somehow carry out psychological investigations of the thought processes of historians when doing their job. Certainly these thought sequences could be investigated, but to do that means that we must be able to pick out from all their thinking when they are thinking historically and not say day-dreaming, plotting a family holiday or perhaps thinking mathematically. In fact we are back again on the same kind of question, how can you empirically investigate until you know the criteria of what you are looking for? And it follows from this that the criteria of what constitutes historical thinking must be found independently of such investigation. The only way in which we can successfully distinguish different forms of thought is in fact by reference to the particular set of terms and relations which each of the distinct forms of thought employs. These terms and relations are fully public, and if, therefore, we wish to characterise, say, scientific or historical thought, we must do this in the first place by examining the distinctive features of scientific theories and laws or historical explanations. In science, such an analysis will at the most general level make plain, for example, the particular use of terms in expressing empirical truths, the importance of general laws and the criteria for verifying these. In history, it will involve making plain the features of historical explanation of particular events by colligation, the use of general laws and evidence from sources. Granted an analysis of these public characteristics, it is not impossible to investigate empirically the thought sequences of particular historians. But just what such investigations of historical thought could provide by way of general psychological truths cannot be laid down *a priori*, nor can we know beforehand what bearing they might have on problems of teaching and learning. In general, however, it is surely true to say that when as teachers we seek to develop historical thought, say, we are not aiming at any particular pattern or sequence of thought episodes. Indeed many would wish to rule out of 'coming to think historically' any suggestions that thought sequences are being stereotyped, even if this were practically possible. It would be argued that thinking historically is thinking which, irrespective of the private thought sequence involved, results in propositions which constitute valid historical accounts and explanations. Historical thought necessarily involves the recognition of the rules that govern the meaningful use of concepts and the validity of propositions, but this involves no necessary temporal order to thought. Just as playing chess involves making moves in accordance with the rules of chess, though it involves no one particular order of moves, so thinking historically involves thinking in accordance with historical criteria, though it involves no particular sequences of thought.

Certainly, on this view of historical thinking, what we want pupils to acquire, both in structure and content, can be totally characterised without recourse to any psychological investigation of thought sequences. This does not, however, preclude the possibility that such investigation would enable us to find more effective means of teaching historical thinking, and it might ultimately lead to a reformulation of what we wish to achieve in history teaching. An empirical investigation, not only of the private thought sequences of historians, but also of their more public methods of procedure, for instance in marshalling sources, working from analogy and so on, might be of great value here. Yet whatever possibilities such empirical investigation might open up, it remains true that there must first be clear logical analysis of what criteria distinguish historical thought. This is in fact to say that the effective teaching of a subject necessarily depends on knowing certain features which characterise it, which can be disclosed only by logical analysis of the meaning of 'historical thinking', though once the criteria for this are plain, empirical evidence about thinking based on the use of these criteria becomes important too.

But granted this very rough indication of the boundaries between the logical and the psychological or empirical characterisation of 'historical thinking', we now wish to know further how far the logical analysis of historical thinking determines the teaching of historical thinking. For having got to this point it might be argued that, given a grasp of the criteria of historical thinking, a philosophically self-conscious historian can in fact set out clearly all that is to be aimed at, and that it is then a matter of empirical investigation how far various teaching methods are successful in achieving these aims. Certainly such a historian could set out in detail what had to be mastered, the concepts, the forms of explanation and their criteria, the content, the methods of investigation and so on. But to make all other factors in determining teaching methods an empirical matter, is to take too simple a view of the contribution of logical analysis to determining the teaching of a subject. For though it is quite possible, granted a clear statement of what is to be taught, to investigate different teaching methods, yet a great deal of investigation approached in this way might well turn out to be quite unnecessary. The reason is simply that experiment and observation cannot but confirm matters of logical truth, and all that is necessarily implied by learning to think historically has not yet been made clear. Maybe there are truths about teaching and learning which are rather like that hoary truth beloved of philosophers that all bachelors are unmarried. To prevent irrelevant complications let us take the proposition that all bachelors resident in the London postal area are unmarried. Faced with the question of the truth of this proposition someone might wish to answer the matter by conducting an empirical survey. This would, however, be impossible without clear criteria by which to distinguish bachelors and unmarried people. In the same way it has been maintained that empirical investigation into the teaching of historical thinking is impossible without criteria for distinguishing historical thinking. But granted such criteria, it is a further question whether or not the truth of the proposition depends on empirical investigation. In fact it is immediately clear that empirical investigation cannot but confirm the truth of the proposition as it happens to be logically true. Granted an understanding of the meaning of the terms, it is necessarily the case that the bachelors must be discovered to be unmarried and the empirical investigation is therefore redundant—it cannot but confirm what is logically true. In a similar way there might well be truths about the teaching and learning of historical thinking for which empirical evidence is quite beside the point. We must therefore take a closer look at what is implied logically, not simply in, say, historical thinking, but in coming to think historically.

In the first place such learning involves coming to understand historical propositions, and this in turn involves learning the use of a network of related concepts. It is necessarily the case that any area of knowledge can only be mastered in so far as the use of concepts according to the complex rules that relate them to each other is acquired. Granted this, even the briefest examination of these rules then seems to indicate that it is logically impossible to acquire certain concepts without previously acquiring others; for until the rule-governed use of some terms is achieved, the rule-governed use of others is beyond achievement. In this way the concept of being a bachelor presupposes the concept of marriage, the concept of acceleration presupposes the concept of velocity, the concept of revolution presupposes that of authority. Because of these relations it would seem to be a logical truth that one cannot learn, for instance, about acceleration without first learning about velocity and that therefore any teaching of this area of knowledge must recognise this order of priority in the concepts.

Further it would seem to be a necessary truth about any form of knowledge that there is some ordered sequence to the truths concerned, for the validity of some propositions presupposes the validity of others. If, therefore, the grounds of validity for propositions are to be understood by pupils, the teaching of the area of knowledge must reflect these logical priorities in the order of justification.

But what precisely can we say along these lines about teaching and learning? In the past extravagant claims have often been made to the effect that the problems of teaching a subject are simply problems of logical ordering and that for this, common-sense is all that is necessary beyond a knowledge of the subject itself. Recently there has been a tendency to swing to the opposite extreme with far too much ill-considered appeal to empirical investigation. What is needed is a much more careful examination of what the logically necessary features of areas of knowledge are and, in particular, the extent to which learning a subject involves adherence to what can loosely be called rules of logical order. Once these questions are answered, we can hope to see more useful empirical investigation in this area.

Although there is a strict limit to what can be said in general terms about the logical characteristics of knowledge, it is important to pursue further what is meant by such phrases as logical order, logical method and logical organisation, as these play an important part in the now rapidly growing literature on these questions. John Dewey was the first philosopher to use such terms in an educational context. In a celebrated chapter in *Democracy and Education* he distinguishes two methods of teaching. In one, which is referred to as the logical method:

> Pupils began their study of science with texts in which the subject is organised into topics according to the order of the specialist. Technical concepts, with their definitions, are introduced at the outset. Laws are introduced at a very early stage, with at best a few indications of the way in which they were arrived at. The pupils learn a 'science' instead of learning the scientific way of treating the familiar material of ordinary experience.[2]

Of the logical order which such teaching follows he writes:

> Logical order is not a form imposed on what is known; it is the proper form of knowledge as perfected. For it means that the statement of subject matter is of a nature to exhibit to one who understands it the premises from which it follows and the conclusions to which it points. . . . To the non-expert however this perfected form is a stumbling block. . . . From the standpoint of the learner scientific form is an ideal to be achieved, not a starting point from which to set out.[3]

The other method of teaching which is contrasted with the logical, Dewey refers to as the 'psychological' or chronological method. In this the pupil

> by following in connection with problems selected from the material of ordinary acquaintance, the methods by which scientific men have reached their perfected knowledge, (he) gains independent power to deal with material within his range and avoids the mental confusion and intellectual dictates attendant upon studying matter whose meaning is only symbolic.[4]

Dewey of course made no sharp distinctions between different forms of knowledge, regarding all knowledge as ultimately scientific in character. What he said about the two methods of teaching he therefore thought of very wide application, but so as to avoid complications arising from possible differences between science and other forms of knowledge, I shall here consider these remarks solely in relation to indisputably scientific content. Granted this, there is certainly no doubt which of the two methods of teaching Dewey thought more desirable, and these passages are in fact part of a sustained attack on traditional teaching methods. There have been more extreme attacks which question the existence of a logical order to knowledge at all, but the argument here certainly accepts a logical order of some kind of science. It denies, however, that this is of any significance for the temporal order of events in teaching. Logical order is the end product in scientific understanding. It is a pattern which in teaching is pieced together as one puts together the pattern of a jig-saw. The logical order does not prescribe a series of steps which must be taken. There is a great variety of ways in which the jig-saw can be made up and the same is true in teaching science. The logical order emerges as you go along. The order is not an order of learning or of teaching—it is strictly a logical order not a temporal one. From this it would seem at first sight that the temporal order in teaching, in piecing together the pattern of relations, is for Dewey a matter of the empirical investigation of ways for achieving the pattern. Just what non-logical determination of methods he advocated we will return to later.

The question to be asked first, however, is whether or not the logical features of some form of understanding can simply be regarded as an end product. Is logical order the ideal that Dewey implies? For was it not being suggested earlier that without adherence to the logical characteristics of some form of knowledge even the concepts which that subject uses cannot be grasped? Must not every element of historical knowledge that is taught, necessarily be true to the conceptual structure of that domain? Is it not false therefore to suggest that in developing understanding one can start *anywhere*? And even if logical order is an ideal in some sense, does it not exercise a perpetual control over the method by which it is approached? In a jig-saw the pieces will only fit together one way so as to make up the picture, and the picture has one and only one pattern in the end. Is not knowledge like that?

Obviously if we are to get any further with the problem we must get clearer what is meant by logical order. In doing this, it would seem to be important to recognise that, within any form of knowledge, in, say, a science like physics or in history, at least two separable levels of logical relations can be distinguished, at both of which elements of logical order can arise. There is first the network of relations between particular concepts, relationships by virtue of which meaningful propositions can be formed. In physics the term electron has a certain use. It is only meaningful to say certain things of it, it has to conform to a pattern of relations, and the rules for its use do not permit us to speak of its temperature, its esthetic qualities or moral value. In religious discourse you cannot use the term God in any old way. He is not an object or being in space and time, he has no extension or colour. He does not act as a human being acts. We must, therefore, stick strictly to the rules for the use of the terms or we do not have meaning. At this level, a domain of knowledge can be said to have a logical grammar, which consists of the rules for the meaningful use of the terms it employs.

Second, there is the network of relations between propositions in terms of which valid historical or scientific explanations are formed. The logical analysis of historical or scientific explanations seeks to make plain the criteria for valid explanations in this area. But using these formal criteria in any given case does, of course, presuppose the validity of the propositions in terms of which the explanations are given. Thus the valid explanations in any subject area would seem to depend on the progressive establishment of what I shall call a logical sequence of validated propositions. Any explanation of the repeal of the corn laws in 1846, for instance, must rest on valid propositions about the economic effects of the laws, the famine in Ireland, the political policy of Peel and so on. Similarly, the explanation of the truth that the lengths of the sides of a right-angled triangle satisfy the equation $a^2 = b^2 + c^2$ rests on the truth of a sequence of earlier propositions which, in turn, depend on the axioms of Euclidean geometry.

If then there are two levels at which elements of logical order within a subject can occur, what are the implications of this for teaching? According to the first, any statement to be meaningful must necessarily be true to the logical grammar of the forms of knowledge. Thus the teaching of this form of understanding must always, in all respects, conform to the logical grammar if it is to be intelligible. This logical grammar is therefore no ideal, that might not be attained in some area of understanding. It is implicit in any meaningful statement that belongs to the domain at all, though no one statement will involve more than a very limited number of the rules of such a grammar. Coming to have a new concept involves mastering its often complex logical grammar, and this may involve a long period in which its relation with other concepts and its precise application are being learnt. The concept of a dog is relatively easy to acquire compared with, say, the concept of a matrix or the Christian concept of God. What elements of the logical grammar of a term a person comes to appreciate first may not be important, and many of our very hazy concepts become more refined in time as we acquire the appropriate grammar more thoroughly. In this process of acquiring new concepts a person is heavily dependent on the concepts he has already, but as extremely complex networks of relationships have to be built up in any area of knowledge, it is surely a mistake to think that there is only one order in which all our concepts can be acquired. Certain concepts do undoubtedly depend for their meaning on their relation to certain logically prior concepts. How can one know what a bachelor is unless one can distinguish between men and women, between the married and the unmarried? But how many of our concepts are so clearly and precisely related to others in logical order? In mathematics and the sciences there is frequently such an order, and new concepts are often explicitly composed in this tight way by defining them from other concepts. In many other areas of discourse, in moral and historical matters for instance, such conceptual relations are far from common, the relations are not hierarchical in this way. But in so far as there are elements of conceptual order in any subject the teaching of it must of course fully respect these.

Yet three things must be noted. First, in so far as a child has begun to make the distinctions between men and women and the married and the unmarried, he is, to that extent, able to begin to form the concept of a bachelor. In one sense, learning a concept is not an all or nothing business; for one can know some of the criteria for a concept without knowing them all, and one can begin to build other higher order concepts on this partial knowledge. Secondly, even if this order of conceptual development cannot be intelligibly ignored, yet the teacher does not have to approach the concept of a bachelor by verbal definition. Even if the order of acquisition is logically determined, the means or manner of acquisition is not. Thirdly, developments in those subjects which do involve detailed conceptual order, can at times result in conceptual re-organisation. New mathematical relations or physical properties can lead to a restructuring of a theory, or system, in which the order in which certain concepts enter is changed.

What emerges from this discussion is that it is necessary in teaching a subject that the logical grammar of its key concepts be understood by the teacher; for otherwise vital elements in what he is teaching are not fully clear to him and not adequately under his control. The logical grammar is something given for him; it is not something he can dispense with and yet continue to teach the subject. In so far as the logical grammar reveals elements of logical order, then the teaching must equally respect these too. What they are in any given subject is a matter for the detailed analysis of the concepts of that subject.

When Dewey objected to teaching methods that conformed to a logical order, if he was referring to order in the logical grammar of the subject, he was surely misdirecting his attack. All teaching must be true to this, if it is to be the teaching of the subject. In part he was certainly objecting to the presentation of science as an ordered body of statements developed from definitions, complaining that the pupils then failed to understand. In this case his criticisms were no doubt warranted, but they must be construed as criticisms of the means and manner in which pupils were expected to acquire new concepts, not of the need for adherence to logical order in the learning of new concepts. To learn a new concept is to learn how to use the concept in relation to others and how to apply it. It is not to learn a series of truths about its relations with other concepts. Learning a concept is like learning to play tennis, not like learning to state the rules and principles that govern play. Equally, learning to think scientifically is not learning the formal definitions of terms and a series of true propositions. Indeed such formal learning would seem to be not even a necessary, let alone a sufficient, condition for learning to think scientifically. As far as logical grammar is concerned then, Dewey's criticisms, to be valid, must be regarded as an attack on the manner of adherence to it rather than the necessity for such adherence.

But what of the question of the logical sequence of a subject? If, to be meaningful, the teaching must be true to the logical grammar, must it not, if the validity of the explanations and theories is to be communicated, follow a logical sequence in establishing the appropriate propositions? In so far as it is a body of knowledge one is teaching, and not just a body of beliefs, is there not an order in which its true propositions must be presented?

That there is *one* such logical sequence of the truths in any domain of knowledge must surely be rejected immediately. Even in mathematics the existence of alternative sets of axioms for any given system is now common knowledge. In the sciences equally, alternative ways of demonstrating scientific laws are a common phenomenon, and the discovery of whole new orders of demonstration is not unheard of. There is, therefore, no one logical sequence in which the truths of a subject must be communicated, even in those subjects which seem most strictly sequential. Maybe a great deal of the trouble here has sprung from a confusion between the two forms of logical order that are being distinguished, those elements of order in the logical grammar and those in what is here being called logical sequence. Once a strict distinction is drawn between them it can be seen that,

though adherence to any elements of order within the logical grammar is necessary for intelligibility in teaching, no such adherence to
any one logical sequence is demanded in the same way.

But if the idea of a domain of knowledge having *one* implicit
logical sequence of truths must be rejected, this is not to say that a
subject can be taught without attention to *some* appropriate logical
sequence. In any teaching of a form of knowledge the question
of the justification of the propositions, explanations and theories is
vital, and pupils need to appreciate, not only why these particular
elements are true, but the kind of justification there is in general
within this form of knowledge. Without this one cannot be said to
have taught this subject in any significant sense. The teaching must
therefore involve the development of some logical sequence appropriate to the subject, that is it must involve the development of an
ordered body of truths according to the criteria for validating
historical explanations or mathematical theorems.

From this it is tempting to conclude that the subject must be
taught so as to build up the truths in strict order, following in temporal sequence some particular logical sequence. In reply to this, it
must first be remembered that logical sequence is not an order necessary to the intelligibility of the propositions, as elements of order
within logical grammar are. It is only when one is concerned with
questions of validity and justification that this matter of logical
sequence ever arises. Further, it is surely a mistake to think that
explanations are seen to be valid only when the elements are pieced
together by a temporal following of a logical sequence. To grasp a
valid proof or explanation is to recognise, in the end, an overall
pattern of logical relations between propositions that satisfy certain
criteria. To insist that this sequence of truths can only be grasped as
truths by temporally building on previously adequately established
truths, is to take the characteristics of what is to be achieved as an
end for the characteristics of the process by which the end is achieved.
Maybe the analogy with a jig-saw puzzle is valuable here. In a valid
explanation the elements must fit together as if to establish the
pattern of the puzzle; but there is no one temporal order in which
the pieces must be fitted together to produce the pattern.

A perpetual problem in teaching formal geometry illustrates this
point; for pupils often find it difficult to grasp that the temporal
sequence of the steps by which a geometrical problem is solved is
rarely the logical sequence of steps laid out in the formal proof. To
solve the problem one must somehow complete the vital logical
sequence; the proof simply sets out the established sequence for all
to see. To do a jig-saw puzzle is to somehow complete the picture
which is then clear for all to see; but one does not have to start

piecing together from the bottom left-hand corner or even the edges. Thus, though the significant teaching of a subject must establish at least some logical sequence distinctive of that subject, this is not a demand that the order of teaching temporally follow along logically prescribed lines. The question of temporal sequence is a matter to be decided on empirical grounds, once the logical sequence to be established is clearly determined by the teacher.

Having said this, however, it must not be forgotten that because questions of logical grammar and intelligibility can to some extent be separated from questions of logical sequence and justification, a great deal of so called teaching can, of course, be conducted without much concern for any logical sequence. It is possible to have a great deal of scientific information and little idea of even the kind of justification on which it rests. How far teaching of this kind is defensible is a debatable and a non-philosophical question. To many, such teaching is not in any sense describable as teaching the subject; for the distinctive forms of justification and the criteria for truth in the domain are elements that are necessarily part of the form of knowledge, even if these prescribe no one logical sequence and no one teaching order. But that a great deal of such instruction goes on at present in schools cannot be denied.

In so far, then, as Dewey was objecting to teaching methods conforming to a logical sequence his criticisms are valid; for logical sequence must not be confused with a temporal learning sequence. His comments are, however, misleading in so far as they imply that there is in science, or any other form of knowledge, any one logical sequence. There are, in fact, many such sequences, similar in kind and exemplifying the distinctive logical characteristics of valid explanations in the domain. Further, in so far as his comments suggest that science can be taught without necessarily aiming at any logical sequence, and his views have sometimes been interpreted as implying that the logical 'ideal' of science is only important for would-be professional scientists, they would seem to be dangerously mistaken. Both the method he advocates and the method he rejects must, to be the teaching of science, be true to all the logical features of science, and thus involve the development of some logical sequence.

Some of Dewey's disciples certainly took him to be saying that the outcome of learning can be a personal or 'psychological' organisation of knowledge rather than a logical organisation appropriate for research specialists. Why cannot knowledge be organised round an interest in some practical activity for instance, rather than as a theoretical pursuit? Bode took this distinction between logical and psychological organisations to be worth the argument that the latter are of more limited value than the former.⁵ But what is this a distinction between exactly? If what has been argued earlier is correct there is no non-logical organisation of knowledge; the logical features are those which necessarily characterise knowledge. The contrast cannot, therefore, be between logical organisation and non-logical organisation. What is more, if someone acquires knowledge of any kind, this is necessarily a personal psychological matter. A person cannot have non-psychologically organised knowledge. The contrast can, therefore, only be one between the different organisations of knowledge which we present to children, organisations respecting both the logical features of the knowledge concerned and the necessity for the pupils to individually come to acquire this knowledge. In the end the distinction would seem to come down to whether or not we should teach as school subjects such distinct, logically cohesive disciplines as mathematics, physics and history, or rather teach second-order organisations of knowledge which we compose of elements from these primary divisions, such units as 'the neighbourhood', 'power' or 'the seventeenth-century mind'. Maybe the interest of pupils is more easily aroused when we organise what we teach in such second-order fields and they therefore learn more effectively. But there is here no different *logical* organisation of knowledge as such. The pupils' grasp of the meaning and validity of all the elements in such a second-order organisation depends on their appreciating these elements as logically related to other elements within the primary divisions of knowledge.⁶ The distinction here then is a concern about what is taught but not one that turns on logical questions. Whether or not we should teach according to the primary divisions of knowledge or according to second-order units is a matter that cannot be settled on philosophical grounds.

It might be expected that Dewey's rejection of what he calls the logical teaching method would be complemented by his advocating the empirical investigation of teaching and that his 'psychological' approach would be based squarely on the results of this. In fact this is not what he does; for the method he advocates, though justified to some extent by practical experience with children, rests primarily on assumptions as theoretical and doctrinaire as those behind the method he rejects. Instead of following some logical sequence Dewey suggests that teaching methods should follow the method that lies behind scientific investigation and discovery. This method he elaborates in a series of stages in which from a 'genuine situation of experience', a problem develops 'as a stimulus to thought' about which information and observations are collected, a solution is formulated and tests for validity are carried out.⁷

Dewey advocated this method for reasons connected with his own distinctive views of logic and his pragmatic theory of truth. He considered the methods of enquiry found in science to be the foundation of all knowledge and thus wanted above all that pupils should master, not a subject, but the fundamentals of scientific method as he saw these. This meant that they must learn what is involved in enquiry by conducting enquiries themselves. Certainly *if* we want to teach skill in a methodology, we shall wish pupils to practise such methods; for a skill is necessarily something learnt in this way. This is but to say that the teaching methods employed must be activities designed to produce the relevant learning. But if we take a wider view of what is to be learnt, even within science, we may well question whether the methodology of scientific discovery, assuming there is such a thing, should provide the bases of a general teaching method. Certainly discovery is one way of learning, but it is not the only way, and whether or not it is in general the best way, is an open question that Dewey never seems to consider. Whether or not there is a methodology of scientific discovery and, if there is, whether Dewey is right in his characterisations of it, are also large questions on which there is room for a great divergence of opinion. If, however, we consider other areas of knowledge than science, there would seem little reason to think that scientific methodology can solve our problems of teaching method. And to take in each area the methodology of the subject as a paradigm for the methodology of teaching the subject, is either to confuse methods which are in many ways concerned with achieving different ends, or to prejudge matters which can only be determined on the basis of much empirical evidence. It is, to say the least, ironical that Dewey, in his desire that pupils should acquire a problem-solving outlook, was himself as guilty of pre-judging some of the very empirical questions of teaching method as the advocators of the logical method he so condemned.

In this chapter I have tried to maintain that:

(*a*) A subject like physics or history has a logical grammar which guilty of prejudging some of the very empirical questions of teaching of the subject must necessarily conform to the rules of this grammar or it will not be the teaching of the subject at all.

(*b*) In some cases this logical grammar involves an order of terms such that the meaning of certain terms presupposes the meaning of others. In this case the teaching of the subject must of course respect these elements of logical order.

(*c*) An understanding of the meaning of terms is not to be thought of as necessarily built up in strict order as a wall is built with bricks. Concepts are acquired by learning the complex use of terms in relation to other terms and their application in particular cases. A subject's logical grammar and the order within it must be respected in all teaching methods, but this leaves a vast area in which experimental investigations about the effectiveness of different methods can and must be carried out.

(*d*) Any subject like history or physics or mathematics is based on the use of certain logical principles in terms of which the explanation and theories distinctive of the subject are validated, I refer here to the logic of historical explanations, of scientific explanations, mathematical proofs and so on. These principles, however, do not determine any *one* particular logical sequence for the propositions. Any teaching method for the subject must therefore respect the fundamental logical principles without which no understanding of the distinctive form of validity peculiar to this subject is possible. This means that *some* logical sequence of propositions using these logical principles must emerge in the teaching of the subject. There are alternative logical sequences which may be taken and advances in knowledge often suggest new sequences.

(*e*) To say that some logical sequence must emerge in the teaching of the subject is not to say that the teaching must follow that sequence in temporal order. It is an order that is understood to hold together in the end. It does not have to be built up in any one way.

(*f*) The logical grammar involved and the various possibilities for the logical sequence to be used, are matters for determination by an analysis of the subject to be taught, not for empirical investigation. How far these logical features do determine the teaching of a subject, and areas within the subject, can be worked out in detail only in terms of the specific content that is to be taught.

(*g*) It is only when the fullest logical analysis of what is involved in teaching a subject has been carried out, that the profitable empirical investigation of methods can be conducted. How much further we can get by general philosophical discussion of the kind in this paper is not clear. What is clear, however, is that, if our teaching methods are not to remain the hit and miss business they are at the moment, the careful, detailed analysis of the logical features of exactly what we wish to teach must be pursued far more thoroughly than it has been thus far. More philosophical clarity can, of its own, certainly help us to produce more effective and more rationally defensible teaching methods.

Notes

1 See Chapter 3.
2 J. Dewey, *Democracy and Education*, Macmillan, New York, 1916, p. 257.
3 Ibid., pp. 256–7.

4 Ibid., p. 258.
5 B.H. Bode, *Modern Educational Theories*, Vintage Books, New York, ch. 3.
6 See Chapter 3.
7 Dewey, op. cit., p. 192.

Curriculum integration

Even a cursory glance at contemporary proposals for curriculum reform serves to show that ideas of curriculum integration are immensely popular. Only projects restricted to reform within an existing framework of public examinations seem immune to the appeal of this notion. Yet a second glance at these proposals is enough to convince anyone that what distinguishes an 'integrated' curriculum from any other form of curriculum is far from clear and that the arguments on its behalf are, to say the least, elusive. In this situation, I am not convinced that a piece of standard philosophical analysis, starting with the varied use of the terms concerned, is a particularly profitable procedure in seeking to understand what might be at stake in integrating the curriculum. I shall therefore try instead, to elucidate what seem to me to be some of the major philosophical issues that are involved in forming a coherent notion of curriculum integration and thence some of the issues in arguing for or against reform in this direction.

I

It will perhaps help to focus the issues if I make it plain from the start that I shall in this context take any curriculum, integrated or otherwise, to be a plan of activities deliberately organised so that pupils will attain, by learning, certain educational ends or objectives. This means that I see a curriculum arising only in a teaching situation, where a set of objectives is clearly specifiable. I am therefore not concerned with the planning of discovery or enquiry or research in an open-ended sense. Of course discovery and enquiry methods may be employed as teaching devices whereby pupils learn what is intended, and such approaches are then within the curriculum as I understand it. But if there is such a thing as a completely open-ended enquiry curriculum, it is not a curriculum within my use of the term. Equally the idea of a curriculum in which pupils 'do their own thing', and so cannot learn anything planned for as no learning is planned for, is excluded. A programme in which pupils themselves decide the precise order in which they will learn what is asked of them under the loose control of a teacher would, however, be included. What is more, the definition is broad enough not to restrict either the character of the objectives that might be learnt or the methods of learning that might be employed.

Taking this view of the curriculum, one which clearly embraces at least all that has traditionally fallen under the term, it is far clearer what an integrated curriculum is not than what it *is*. Above all it is not a curriculum organised under a number of quite distinct 'subjects' such as mathematics, history, geography, English, P. E., R.E., reading, writing or arithmetic—where each subject involves a programme of activities for the pursuit, in isolation from all others of a number of very particular and restricted ends. Clearly what each of these subjects does, is take a group of educational objectives as its *raison d'être* and direct itself to the attainment of these and nothing else. In this way the total educational enterprise is made more manageable by being broken down into a number of smaller enterprises. It means that different teachers can be made responsible for different parts of the whole and that teachers can timetable a school day to give appropriate regularity and variety to the pupils' learning activity. Whether manageability of this kind is either necessary or desirable is one of the things now being called in question. Not that existing school 'subjects' have been overtly planned in this way. In fact they have boundaries that are the products of a number of historical factors, primarily the growth of knowledge and the changing social demands placed on schools. But within this historical framework certain logical factors have played a significant, if limited, part, so that the structure of subjects is not entirely a contingent matter. It is these logical aspects of curricula in which I am interested.

The notion of curriculum integration with which I am concerned is therefore, in part at least, an attack on the subject-structured curriculum, the breaking down of the enterprise of education into a number of discreet, limited enterprises of a subject character. But if that is what is being discussed, it must be strongly distinguished from a number of other educational proposals with which it is not infrequently combined and indeed confused. In the present sense, curriculum integration has nothing to do with 'the integrated day' where that means allowing pupils to plan the order of events and the time span they will give to any subject or topic. That pupils plan how long they devote to something and the sequence of things they will do is perfectly compatible with a highly subject structured curriculum. An integrated day may, or equally may not, involve an integrated curriculum; and it is the curriculum structure to which any day's work is devoted that concerns me, not the organisation of the day as such. My concern is with the character of the sub-units of learning from which the total plan of learning is built, not with the particular timing of their use. Equally I am not concerned with integrating, for learning purposes, pupils of different abilities, ages, races, etc. All such forms of grouping are compatible with both an integrated or a subject-based curriculum. Nor is the issue one of teaching methods. Team teaching, enquiry methods, visits, films, work-cards, individual or group projects, are all usable with a subject-structured curriculum, chalk and talk can perfectly well function in an integrated context. Formal and informal approaches, collaboration and competition, none of these picks out a subject or integrated curriculum. What is at stake, is the breaking down of the learning enterprises into a number of sub-enterprises of a particular character, whatever else one does or does not do.

But what then is said to be wrong with organising a curriculum into traditional subjects? There would seem to be three major forms of criticism. First, it is claimed that the traditional organisation is a mere historical anachronism. It has emerged for a number of clearly specifiable historical reasons and is in no sense a logically necessary pattern. Knowledge has no 'subject' structure in itself, it is not pigeon-holed, it is a unity, or perhaps even a chaos, and can be organised for learning in any way that suits our purposes. Knowledge may have been amassed in a number of distinct subjects or disciplines, though in any case these are now breaking down. But be that as it may, one does not have to learn things in the organisational units in which they are discovered and the school curriculum can be planned independently of research or even university teaching structures. Second, it is argued that in much of our education, at secondary as well as primary level, we are no longer concerned with objectives that are part of abstract, theoretical, academic subjects or disciplines. We need a new organisation of the curriculum if we are to begin to develop many qualities of mind we now recognise as important, if we are to educate pupils for the context in which they actually live. Third, if the process of learning is the development of a child's experience or consciousness, whatever divisions academics may see in knowledge, the life and experience of a person ought to be developed as a unity, not in a compartmentalised fashion. A subject-structured curriculum restricts pupils in their thinking, artificialises and limits both the process of learning and their approach to life that results. In fact it hinders the development of an integrated point of view on life which is one of the achievements of a mature adult that education seeks. Each of these criticisms makes a number of important points, but each too is guilty of gross confusions and errors. Their precise force against a subject-structured curriculum is therefore unclear and it is this which I now wish to assess. In the process I hope to draw attention to certain philosophical principles significant for all curriculum planning.

II

That traditional school subjects are the product of many different social and historical forces is perfectly true. Many of them are teaching units which mirror university specialisms and thus the limited range of specialist knowledge that many individual teachers possess. Some subjects have been added to the list simply to bring into the curriculum objectives for which a social demand has arisen but which existing subjects could not readily accommodate. Not that what is taught under long established labels has remained constant. What is now taught under the heading of English or mathematics frequently bears little resemblance to what was taught fifty years ago. Indeed the content of some subjects has changed so much that what the label signifies is far from clear. What goes under one label might well go under several others. The idea that curriculum labels must continue to be those traditionally used has thus come to have little to commend it. Yet, is it true to say either that there is no fundamental logical structure to knowledge, or that knowledge is a unity, so that there are no divisions which curriculum planning must take seriously? Can we intelligibly re-structure the curriculum entirely as we like, or is there some underlying organisation to what we want learnt that cannot be disregarded?

At this point it seems to me important to distinguish a number of different organisations of knowledge that are too often confused. As I have argued elsewhere,[1] all knowledge involves the use of conceptual schemes and related judgments of truth, and for that reason different forms of knowledge can be distinguished according to the character of the conceptual schemes and truth criteria involved. In this sense all our knowledge occurs within some logical structure which is what it is. There simply is no such thing as knowledge which is not locatable within some such organisation, and what that location is, is not a matter of choice or decision. In these terms, knowledge of the physical world, for instance, is logically different from knowledge of minds because of the differences in the kinds of concepts and truth criteria involved. True this diversity of character is in one sense a product of social life, but it is built into the development of knowledge, a classification of the necessary features which make knowledge just what it is, knowledge. If it is already existing knowledge we are concerned with, this has an inescapable, fundamental, necessary organisation.

Such fundamentally different forms of knowledge however must not be confused with even the most long standing university 'subjects' or 'disciplines'. It is simply false to imagine that an area of study, teaching or research must direct itself to knowledge of one fundamental kind. Some university subjects would seem to do just this, but others spread their interest and concern across a wide range of logically very different problems. It is not surprising that areas of *research* tend to follow the logical distinctions in kinds of knowledge, if only because the very features that mark out logically different kinds of knowledge are precisely those that mark out different kinds of questions and even different kinds of methodologies. But strict limitation to one 'form' of knowledge, let alone a sub-form, has never been a necessary feature for demarcating an area of research recognised by a university or any other institution. In so far then as the same labels are used for fundamental forms of knowledge and areas of research, what falls under those labels may well be very different.

A university *teaching* 'subject' or 'discipline' is yet another matter. First, there is again no reason why an area of teaching, any more than an area of research, should necessarily restrict itself to knowledge of one distinctive logical kind. But further, any area of teaching even in the specialised context of a university, may well be concerned with objectives beyond those of one form of knowledge. The relations of one form of knowledge to other forms and its application or use in other areas are frequently considered of significance. What makes a university teaching subject what it is, is the range of objectives it is constructed to serve, whatever those are. They may be primarily associated with one form or sub-form of knowledge as in the case of most courses in pure mathematics, or they may be much wider as in the case of most courses in English. But in no case should it be assumed that a university teaching subject, whatever its label, has objectives limited to those marked out by one fundamental category of true statements.

If one turns to even traditional school subjects, let alone more modern ones, their lack of fit with fundamental categories of knowledge which might legitimately use the same label, is yet more marked. The objectives being pursued in any given subject are usually very varied in character. Yet traditional labels may still sometimes serve the purpose of indicating an area of university research or teaching to which a school subject is related in a major way and perhaps even a particular form of knowledge. Whether or not it is a good thing to preserve subjects with these characteristics remains to be examined. At present I merely want to point out the ambiguity of meaning any subject label has. This sort of ambiguity occurs too in the slogan that schools should 'teach the disciplines'. Whether a discipline is a logically distinct area of knowledge, an established area of research or teaching in universities, or a traditional school subject, is not clear. Nor is it clear whether we are being asked to restrict ourselves to particularly academic objectives, or to a form of traditional curriculum organisation for reaching these, or both.

Behind all these considerations, however, there seems to me to lurk just one simple point. The most fundamental objectives of education are elements within a logical structure of knowledge and there are good reasons for thinking that knowledge consists of a number of distinct, autonomous forms. What exactly follows for the curriculum from that is the question. What does not follow is that the organisation of the curriculum should mirror the fundamental categories of knowledge. Nor is there any immediate reason why the organisation of curriculum units in school should mirror the units of teaching and research in universities. The objectives of the enterprise of school teaching need to be looked at in their own right and the best structure for attaining them developed. Yet nothing is to be gained, indeed much is to be lost, if in attacking traditional curriculum patterns, critics attack the wrong thing. It is nonsense to attack the logical structure of existing knowledge, for that is to attack the very nature of what, presumably, most of us still want to teach. It is the means that need reconsideration, not the necessary character of the ends.

If the logical structure of existing knowledge is one of distinct, unique, irreducible forms, it cannot readily be regarded as a unity, but neither is it a chaos. Within any one domain or form however, there may exist sub-forms, as for example within the domain of the physical sciences, where there exist many different sciences each logically similar, the concepts and truth criteria involved being of the same kind. In such a case it is perfectly possible to conceive of a unification, an integration, of the domain in terms of one set of concepts. At least this would seem logically possible. The idea of the unity of all knowledge is however another matter. The whole thesis of the irreducibility of different forms of knowledge involves the claim that their concepts and truth criteria are of fundamentally different kinds and their unification under concepts of one kind is thereby being denied. The different types of concepts we have have surely arisen precisely because concepts of more limited types have proved inadequate. But the rejection of the unity or integration of knowledge in this sense must not be taken to suggest that there are no logical relationships between distinct forms of knowledge. The concepts of one form may well presuppose the concepts of another. Many moral and religious concepts manifestly presuppose concepts we have for distinguishing features of the observable physical world.

But religious or moral concepts do not thereby become reducible to physical concepts. Truths in one area may presuppose truths in others as, for instance, when truths about a person's state of mind rest necessarily on truths about his physical state. Yet again the types of truths are not mutually reducible. Such inter-relations in our forms of knowledge are no doubt considerable, but they do not constitute an integration of different forms of knowledge. What these signify for the curriculum is that just as the differentiated nature of knowledge must be recognised, so too must the logical inter-relations between the forms. But just as the differentiating characteristics must not be assumed to justify of themselves a curriculum of isolated 'subjects', so the inter-relations must not be assumed to justify an inter-form or topic structure. What we need is a detailed map of the logical relations between objectives and then the best curriculum structure for attaining these, whatever that is.

It may be thought that I have paid too little attention to those advances in knowledge which seem to break down distinctions between kinds of knowledge and thus to discredit old divisions however fundamental. Yet the character of such new areas needs careful examination. Some are indeed breaking down divisions between traditional subjects, but are not in fact bridging the logical distinctions that, I have argued, exist between different forms of knowledge. A new science which bridges areas of physics and chemistry is not breaking down any logical distinctions between two forms of knowledge, for physics and chemistry belong to the same form. Many new organisations for research and teaching are, however, developing new concepts that are significant in more than one distinct form of knowledge. These bring to the fore the inter-relations between the forms of knowledge to which I have already referred. It is, however, not in general the case that even such domains are examples of new, emerging, fundamental forms of knowledge. This may indeed in the odd case be so, though there are considerable difficulties about this idea. The emergence of a new conceptual scheme is itself no guarantee of a new form of knowledge, for new conceptual schemes may simply mark advances within one form of knowledge, for example in the sciences. Even new complex concepts which bridge existing forms of knowledge, by combining concepts from distinct forms, thereby create no new form. Indeed one of the most interesting aspects of advance in knowledge is the fact that concepts and truth criteria of fundamentally new kinds do not seem to be readily forthcoming.

The view that there are no fundamentally distinct categories of knowledge has received considerable superficial support from a simplistic approach to the sociology of knowledge which has been taken by some to vindicate a thesis of the total relativity of all organisations of knowledge. Some of those interested in the sociology of the school curriculum have shown a sympathy for this position.[2] But it must be recognised that the sociology of curriculum is the sociology of certain secondary, non-fundamental organisations of knowledge that have developed in schools. The radical diversity of curricular organisations is thus in no sense evidence for the social variability of fundamental categories of knowledge. Nor is an examination of the organisations of knowledge in other institutions, even universities, of itself going to get at changes in these categories or their diversity between societies. If sociologists are to be able to make any valid comments here, they must surely distinguish those categories from secondary ones by means of careful conceptual analysis. Only then can we see whether, underlying all the diversity of secondary organisations, the fundamental categories of knowledge are as relative as is often implied. When attention to such categories has been distinguished, total relativity seems far from obvious. It is rather the degree to which men share a limited range of these categories that stands out for all the diversity of more particular concepts and forms of thought. I am not suggesting that the fundamental categories of knowledge are anything other than the product of man's form of life and nothing dogmatic is being asserted about their immutability or universality. How far these categories vary between communities and across time is a matter for investigation not dogma. But what evidence there is suggests that only limited variations do occur. Nor is this surprising if one recognises that for all their social diversity, men do as a matter of fact share almost universally many of the elements on which types of conceptualisation must surely rest, such as their apparatus for sense perception and thought, their linguistic capacities and their relatively similar environments.

If, also, one is concerned with categories of knowledge, they are categories in which notions of truth, objectivity and reason are central. To suggest that these are simply matters of conventional agreement and decision that differ from social group to social group, is to mistake their nature and significance. Certainly, like all concepts, these notions are socially constructed, but they arise in contexts, and have a significance in contexts, that are not totally social in character. If, for instance, all the truths of science employ a socially formed conceptual apparatus, nevertheless these concepts, to be the vehicles of knowledge, must be applied in some way to some aspect of our form of life in judgments that we agree about. And these agreements in application must be something given in our experience, not something we decide on. The notions of truth, reason and knowledge are the product of the relations established socially between words and the given form of life we have. Without that given element, and the existence of agreement in judgment as a given, there could be no such things as truth, reason and knowledge. In discussing fundamental forms of knowledge, we are therefore discussing fundamental forms of given agreement in judgment that exist as expressed in socially formed conceptual schemes. Differences in fundamental categories of knowledge, though expressed through different conceptual schemes in different societies and through time, can on this showing hardly be regarded as socially relative in any simple sense.

I have indulged in this somewhat extended diversion from my central theme, in an attempt to put in perspective comments not infrequently made about the relativity of knowledge and the implication that our curricula should be seen in both content and structure as the merely temporary reflection of those forms of thought our society at present happens to 'legitimise'. It is surely time that curricular units be composed to serve the ends we want. They are in this respect socially determined and need constantly to be reconsidered. But in so far as it is truth, reason and knowledge these curricula serve, there is a logically fundamental structure to these objectives that we must recognise. What is more, though this structure is the product of man's capacities in relation to his own nature and environment and is developed in a social context, it is not simply a reflection of social variations but has that stability which comes from being anchored in man's nature and environment. At any given time, conceptual analysis can hope to lay bare the general structure of those categories which in fact characterise contemporary knowledge, and it is this framework with which curriculum planning must work. In so doing, however, education needs not only to communicate to pupils a grasp of the conceptual schemes of contemporary knowledge, it must also communicate that conceptual schemes vary between communities and indeed develop within communities. It is equally important, though, that the next generation be not misinformed as to the fundamental categories there are for such schemes and their relative permanence.

But from none of this does it follow that a curriculum must or ought to be divided into subjects that mirror distinctions between the forms of knowledge. The criticisms of a subject structure that I have been discussing have begun from the premiss that there are fundamentally distinct categories of knowledge, taking this to imply that any logically coherent curriculum most consist of subjects devoted to these distinct categories. They have sought to escape the implication by attacking the premiss. What I have argued is that the premiss is in general sound, it is the implication that is mistaken.

Many subjects have never had this character and there is no reason why a subject should not be concerned with objectives of different logical kinds, provided that fact is recognised at least implicitly.

III

The second set of objections to school subjects that I wish to examine again assumes that the case for them rests on the premiss that there are logically distinct areas of knowledge. This time, however, the claim is that these areas do not contain many of the objectives we now recognise as important in education, for the latter are not theoretical, academic or intellectual in character. Critics are here usually concerned about qualities of mind that seem more general than those associated with traditional subjects, such as an open-ended, enquiring attitude to social and practical problems, or abilities to get on with other people individually and in wider society. They think too of an education that directly illuminates the affairs of life that the vast majority of the population meet every day, rather than the remote, intellectual affairs pupils never meet again once outside the walls of the school. There is no doubt a large measure of justi-fication for the general points such critics are making about many existing curricula, but it is not obvious that they are objections to the subject structure of the curriculum as such, rather than the particular subjects it usually includes and the objectives these subjects serve. The criticisms do, however, have point if subjects are seen as ex-pressions of distinct categories of knowledge which are considered unrelated to these new objectives. It is then thought that by their very nature, these new objectives lie outside those with which subjects based on forms of knowledge can cope. A number of arguments of this kind have been attempted.

Sometimes it is claimed that the division of knowledge into sub-jects or forms is a classification that has significance only in abstract, theoretical or academic knowledge and is not to be found in know-ledge related to every day affairs or in common sense. Much know-ledge that school education is after is not of one particular subject or logical kind and so cannot be allocated to a distinct curriculum unit. In so far as this argument is suggesting that common-sense knowledge is not differentiated into logically distinct forms and that the latter apply only to more developed knowledge, this seems to me quite mistaken. Every element of knowledge, whatever its level of abstrac-tion, involves some conceptual structure and the kind of structure involved, and the truth criteria that go with it, give it a particular character. Common-sense knowledge, like all other knowledge, has these necessary features. It is its general acceptance without question, comment or examination that makes this knowledge common sense, but if its logical character is looked for, it will be seen to be composed of elementary truths of logically different kinds indicated earlier, truths about the physical world, other people, moral situations, etc. What seems to cut this level of knowledge off from more sophisticated knowledge in each form, is just that such common sense is taken for granted. But there is in fact no discontinuity between knowledge at these levels in any particular form. Education which seeks to develop knowledge and understanding at a common-sense level rather than at an academic level, can therefore be just as readily organised into subject or any other curriculum categories. There is no special argument here for or against integration, as the logical issues at stake are identical. Within the sciences, for instance, a much wider range of low-level knowledge about the physical world could be pursued in sciences courses before going on to the more abstract theoretical work of academic syllabuses. Much of this may at present lie outside school and university 'subjects'. That is in no way because of its curious logical character however; it is rather a question of the particular objectives these subjects have set themselves.

A more difficult issue arises in the early years of education. Young pupils may be incapable of acquiring certain forms of knowledge as they lack the necessary prior concepts from some other form of knowledge. In this way a young child might be incapable of acquiring adult religious concepts until certain concepts concerned with the material world or personal relationship, are grasped. It is often said that, to begin with, children have cruder, less refined concepts than adults, failing to make such adult distinctions as that, for instance, between physical and social laws. In the progressive differentiation of consciousness, therefore, certain forms of understanding may appear later than others, and in early years, then, the idea of a curriculum organised into subjects in terms of different fundamental forms of knowledge, would seem inappropriate. This is surely so. The claim that on these grounds young children need a curriculum that can properly be regarded as integrated is, however, more doubtful. If a curriculum not differentiated in terms of the forms is all that the label means, all well and good. But as the aim of this curriculum, whatever its structure, must be the progressive development of the distinct forms of knowledge, with all their differences as well as their inter-relations, differentiation of thought, not integration, is what it is about. There would thus seem to be little more reason here for using this label of integration than there is for a curriculum which can assume that pupils have already acquired some basic elements of the different forms.

But if all the *knowledge* objectives a curriculum may pursue can be located in distinct forms, what of the other objectives many now consider important? If these are not so classifiable, then maybe they offer a basis for curriculum units which will demand some form of genuine integration and thus run counter to the construction of sharp subject divisions. I have said enough elsewhere[3] to suggest that though we have many general terms for activities and qualities of mind, such as enquiry, imagination and critical thought, what we are after in education under these terms is very often a number of distinct achievements. It is not clear that imaginative writing and imaginative scientific investigation have anything in common that suggests we can significantly develop a unitary 'imagination' as such. Equally, enquiry methods are only superficially similar across different forms of knowledge. Indeed they reveal important differences that are not surprising if the conceptual structures and truth criteria they are concerned with are radically different in character. Even where general qualities may indeed exist, must they not be first developed within some specific area of knowledge and then be generalised to apply to other areas? If so, the idea that they are of their nature cutting across the forms of knowledge, and therefore demand a curriculum structure that integrates across the forms, is mistaken. If their character is such that they must always be given an application that is necessarily peculiar to one particular form, then they are not themselves integrating objectives that logically necessitate an integrated curriculum. They have at best a formal character that always needs particular content and therefore cannot integrate the distinct elements they presuppose. What is more, if, as I have also argued elsewhere,[4] the distinction between forms of knowledge is the basis of distinctions which run through all other forms of consciousness, as these necessarily employ the same conceptual schemes, I see every reason to suppose that the argument here being used against these seemingly integrating objectives will have force against any others that might be proposed.

Perhaps the most persuasive case against traditional subjects comes from their lack of explicit attention to the immediate practical and moral problems all pupils do and will face. But again we must ask if this is a necessary weakness of a subject curriculum even if it is structured tightly on the basis of the divisions between forms of knowledge, for if the claim fails there, it must inevitably fail where freer forms of organisation are concerned. Maybe the exclusion of these issues arises for other reasons, perhaps because school subjects mirror university subjects too readily. Certainly there is no obvious reason why a form of knowledge based school subject should not deal with many practical applications of the knowledge falling under that form. Yet some practical problems do not simply involve the direct application of knowledge, of the kind that occurs where, say, scientific knowledge is used to repair a piece of household equipment. Judgments as to what ought to be done can be extremely complex simply because a practical situation may have many different aspects to it. Moral and social issues in particular can involve knowledge that is logically of several different kinds. How best to spend one's weekly earnings is a question that can only be responsibly considered in the light of much knowledge of scientific fact, of people's beliefs and desires, of social responsibilities, even of esthetics. The problems raised by coloured immigration, say, are equally complex in character. What this means is that in the case of moral questions in particular, certain relations between forms of knowledge, rather than their differences, become extremely important. It is of the nature of moral judgments that they presuppose knowledge of other kinds, though they are not unique in this respect. Questions about the states of mind of other people presuppose a knowledge of their behaviour. Questions of the truth of many religious claims rest likewise on much historical and moral understanding. Yet moral and practical issues depend on these inter-relations in a particularly pressing way. As a matter of fact, traditional curriculum subjects do indeed seem to have ignored the important links that exist between different forms of knowledge, and moral questions in particular they have largely left to one side, failing to get to grips with their complex demands. What is therefore at stake here is how a curriculum should do justice not only to the differentiation of knowledge into different forms, but also the inter-relations between those forms. Subjects based on one distinct form only, necessarily emphasise the differences between forms, and many traditional subjects have done just that. Occasionally, as in the case of, say, mathematics and physics, they have made limited efforts to recognise the inter-relations by keeping in step. But where subjects, of which English, geography and religious education are examples, have had a multi-form character, it would be false to pretend that they have usually done full justice to that fact. Many other areas of inter-connection, especially of a moral and practical kind, have traditionally been evaded.

But do such inter-connections, especially in the case of moral and practical understanding, necessitate a new non-subject type of curriculum unit? Not if the term 'subject' is taken as widely as it has traditionally been. Moral education can readily figure as a subject which presupposes the learning of other areas of knowledge, as much physics teaching presupposes a knowledge of mathematics. Or it might figure as a subject that explicitly concerns itself with teaching much of the knowledge that must be presupposed as well as dealing with the moral issues themselves. What matters is not whether we call the units that cope with moral and practical issues 'subjects', but the recognition that such issues do demand an explicit concern for elements of knowledge of different kinds. This knowledge must be acquired somehow and there must be a context in which it is brought together. Subjects, suitably constructed, can do that, though they have only rarely done it satisfactorily. What we need are units, subjects if you like, which do not seek to 'integrate' the forms of knowledge, or cut across them for no real reason, but which are true to the dependence of some elements of knowledge on knowledge of other kinds. These units are needed simply because knowledge is not integrated but differentiated into a complex of distinct but inter-related kinds. However our curriculum units do it, they must come to recognise both the differences and the relations that are necessary features of knowledge.

IV

The third type of objection to a subject curriculum which I want to mention, seeks to undercut all that I have discussed thus far, by making the issue of integration a psychological not a logical matter. In its strongest form the claim is that, whatever the logical structure of the objectives we are after, the mind or consciousness of a person either is, or ought to be, a unity which we distort by the compart-mentalisation of the curriculum. By these means we introduce artificial barriers into thought and feeling, thus inhibiting under-standing and an over-all grasp of what life is all about. The problem with this is the picture of the mind with which it works. True, any person's consciousness is in one sense a unity, in the sense that it is his and no one else's. But that is not what these critics of subjects mean. Rather they wish to assert that the thoughts, emotions, judgments of a person should somehow be inter-related so that no tensions or contradictions occur between these elements. The struc-ture of an individual's consciousness is certainly the structure of the concepts, knowledge, judgments that he has acquired and it has that unity which these elements possess. But the structure that we wish these elements to have as a result of education is precisely that structure which they have as logically organised objectives. I fail to see what unity of consciousness can be sought in education other than that which exists in these elements. In talking of concepts, truth criteria and knowledge, as educational objectives, one is talking about the very elements of consciousness one wants pupils to acquire. To seek to divorce the psychological character of educational achieve-ments from the logical characteristics that make them what they are, is to try to drive a wedge between inseparable elements. There is no

145

formal structure to consciousness of a psychological kind that is not a matter of the logical relations between the elements.

Having said that however, it must be admitted that a subject curriculum, by its rigid compartmentalism, may fail to communicate certain logical relations that concepts have. Equally, it may fail to relate sophisticated abstract concepts to the everyday contexts in which they have application. Such failures are indeed failures to achieve important elements in the structure of consciousness and might well be regarded as a pigeon-holing of the mind. But these are failures to teach adequately the logical relations between objectives that are part of their logical structure. There is no need to invoke some mistaken doctrine of a unity of mind or consciousness independently of logical considerations. What is more, the maximum unity of consciousness a person can ever legitimately hope to have is limited by the unity to be found in the structure of human knowledge and understanding, a domain which, I have argued, is a complex of differentiated yet inter-related forms.

The unity of consciousness thesis is also invoked against subject boundaries in another way. It is the stream of consciousness, the sequence of mental occurrences through time, that some claim ought to be kept free of barriers, so that thought and feeling can range freely, uninhibitedly, at will. The subject curriculum is seen as preventing such freedom, as the mind is conditioned to classify situations in pre-determined ways, to entertain limited considerations about them, to be incapable of wider unrestricted thought, let alone other forms of response and feeling. Such limiting of the mind to restricted, stereotyped, sequential patterns is manifestly undesirable. Yet the ability to think coherently and productively at anything but a superficial level does involve the sustained, persistent use of limited ranges of concepts. The educated person may be capable of a great variety of forms of thought and response, but he is able also to keep distinct, different types of consideration, see differences as well as relations between aspects of any given situation, and sustain thought within some given category at will. Not that these operations are necessarily all self-conscious. It is rather that there is freedom of thought within a rule-governed structure of concepts. Outside such structures freedom is, in general, only freedom to be irrational. The problem is to educate for freedom within these structures, and maybe like all other worthwhile freedoms, it has to be learnt against its background of necessary restrictions. To advocate uncontrolled thought is not to advocate freedom, but being at the mercy of uncontrolled forces of many kinds.

If it is insisted that a pupil's learning should take its pattern from his stream of consciousness, this becomes the principle of following the pupil's felt interests. The limitations of such education have been sufficiently analysed elsewhere.[5] It takes a very naïve view of the source and value of children's interests, but more to the point in this context, is that only in a very modified form can it result in any curriculum in the sense with which I am concerned. If the unity of consciousness is pursued in this sense, it results not in an integrated curriculum, but in no curriculum at all.

One final point on this approach ought perhaps to be added. It is not obvious that the issue of the freedom of thought has anything much to do with any unity of the stream of consciousness. Nor is it clear why any such unity should always be thought valuable. Indeed discontinuities in consciousness would seem to be as much a mark of a sophisticated mind as sustained involvement in any one form of experience. What we would seem to need is both sensitivity and versatility in these matters. But these are complex issues about which we know little and their bearing on the problems of curriculum structure is certainly at present obscure.

V

In discussing objections to the structure of the traditional school curriculum, two particularly important philosophical points have emerged. First, the objectives we are pursuing in education have a complex logical structure which must be accepted for what it is, for to deny it must result in failure to attain the desired ends. Second, this structure of objectives does not of itself determine a curriculum structure. The structure of the means to certain ends is not determined simply by the structure of the ends themselves. Just as the elements in a stage play that are brought together on the first night can be approached in a number of different ways, or the elements of a model plane can be put together in many different sequences, so curriculum objectives can be achieved in many different organisations. Nevertheless some curriculum procedures, like some attempts at model building, will be less effective than others because of the structure of the objectives concerned, and it would be helpful to be clearer about such cases.

In setting out the logical structure of the objectives, we are not only setting out the character of what has to be learnt, but also what, in formal terms, that learning involves. Such a structure will indicate, for instance, that concept A has certain complex relations with concepts B and C such that acquiring concept A is limited by the extent to which concepts B and C are mastered. A particular truth may not be recognisable as such until its logical relationship with some other truth is grasped. An appreciative response to a work of

L

art may necessitate being able to recognise the associations of certain symbols it contains. The point is simply that in these cases, learning necessitates a new element being established in a progressively developing structure of elements. The forging of the formal links is part of what learning entails. The structure of objectives therefore indicates the context of other achievements within which alone the new elements can be mastered. Not that all learning demands the establishment of new formal elements, for some is a matter of applying already learnt structures of concepts and truths in new situations. But the extension of a person's capacities for thought is surely now considered more important than the progressive acquisition of more information of some kind, and the central objectives for the curriculum are therefore those demanding the establishment of new logical relations. What then can we say about curriculum units and the development of learning that necessitates attention to these formal relations?

If we confine ourselves strictly to the development of knowledge, where these formal relations are at present best understood, the significance of certain types of units becomes clear. A curriculum unit concerning itself with objectives that fall within one logically distinct form of knowledge, or a sub-section of such a form, enables systematic attention to be paid to the development of one kind of conceptual structure. The logical complexities to which it must pay attention are thus reduced to a minimum, being those internal to one form of knowledge, and the control over learning can therefore be considerable. In so far as the objectives the unit is concerned with presuppose elements of other forms of knowledge, they will have external relations which can largely be ignored if that knowledge has already been acquired, or must be dealt with at least adequately if it has not. A curriculum unit concerned directly with elementary physics might be an example of such a basically single form unit having external relations with certain areas of mathematical knowledge which are presupposed. To begin to pay attention to these external relations in their own right is, however, to begin to change the character of the unit significantly. Clearly a unit could be composed which, alongside objectives in physics, was concerned equally with objectives in mathematics, the inter-relation of certain of the two groups of objectives being taken as grounds for a composite inter-form unit. The logical complexities involved in the unit would now be much greater, two different kinds of knowledge being its explicit concern as well as certain inter-relations. It is also the case, however, that the internal structure of this unit is likely to be less strong, for it must necessarily tend to fall into two separate if related sections. The learning involved in each section presents its own peculiarities so that the diversity of problems raised by the unit are increased. The external relations that link elements in different forms of knowledge are clearly such that inter-form curriculum units of great variety can be composed; but from the simple example given of a unit concerned with merely two forms of knowledge, one can see the inevitable characteristics of such units and some of their educational strengths and weaknesses. Unless there are significant links between the elements from the different forms of knowledge, there is no clear rationale to such an inter-form unit. It lacks internal cohesion and therefore lacks point if one of the major elements any unit is concerned with is the teaching of formal logical relations. Such an internally weak unit must either degenerate into more cohesive sub-units or be a confusing educational vehicle. If the links between the elements from different forms are significant, their range across the forms is also important. The acquisition of a new scientific notion is only possible if it is grouped in relation to a whole conceptual structure of which it is part. A new notion in our understanding of mathematics can be learnt only in its own distinctive context and so on. But a wide-ranging inter-form unit cannot hope to build-in systematic attention to these necessary formal relations across a whole range of elements from many forms. It is therefore inevitable that the wide-ranging unit cannot do other than content itself with very limited learning that demands the establishment of new links within any one form of knowledge. To this extent establishing inter-form connections must inevitably be at the price of less sophistication of understanding within the different forms. Put another way, attention to forging inter-form links must be at the price of systematic attention to the development of understanding within the separate forms.

Clearly the type of curriculum units one constructs will depend on the objectives one wishes it to serve, and the label it is given is not particularly important. A unit labelled 'man', 'the neighbourhood' or 'ships', might be wide-ranging or surprisingly narrow. If wide-ranging, it could as a 'starter' provoke interests that can be followed up systematically elsewhere. It could equally be allowed to break down into separate studies of a restricted kind. It could equally be used to pull together much that needs inter-relating across different areas of knowledge, where there is no necessity to introduce important new concepts or forms of thought. It is however hard to see how a succession of such wide-ranging topics could lead to the conceptual development within each different form of knowledge which is educationally so central. Not only are individual topic areas not able to attend to such development in any systematic way, a series of such topics has the problem of trying to cope with progressive mastery in each different form from one topic to the next, whilst trying to maintain an inter-form significance. Expressed more directly, it is unlikely that topic work on 'ships' following topic work on 'the neighbourhood' could, even in a school in a sea port, develop in any serious way pupils' understanding not only in, say, matters of social relations, but at the same time in science, mathematics and literature. Of course something of value could be done in all these areas. But necessarily there is a temptation in all such work to settle for learning in some areas which will fit into the project, but which is superficial and secondary in importance.

From a logical point of view, the central problem in designing curriculum units is to cater for the formal structure within the forms of knowledge and the formal structure that links them. I have stressed the fundamental importance of the first of these, as the divisions in kinds of knowledge penetrate all our conceptual development, and it is only in terms of these distinctions that the inter-form relations can be understood. If this is correct, then whilst inter-form relations must be developed as they are necessary to understanding, they must not be allowed to take priority over the logical relations within each form. Let it be said again that this does not imply that a curriculum composed entirely of inter-form units must be unsatisfactory. The detailed logical character of the units proposed and their inter-relations is what matters. A curriculum seemingly composed of units devoted to single forms of knowledge, or even sub-forms, might be equally satisfactory or unsatisfactory dependent on the precise character of these elements and their connections. There is no single and no easy answer to this issue, at least from a philosophical point of view. All there are are the underlying principles which I have sought to elucidate and which can take expression in an endless variety of units and many different combinations of these.

What I have said about the logical demands on the design of curriculum units has arisen from a concern for cognitive objectives. I have earlier stated my belief that a curriculum structure that takes proper care of these objectives can hope to go on to take care of the rest. If all other developments of mind are logically grounded in cognitive developments, these other objectives can be catered for adequately only by elaborating on a curriculum structure that copes with the cognitive. Maybe the character of these further objectives will add to the principles I have sought to express. We can only await the necessary research, meanwhile seeking to adapt progressively our best practice in the light of what understanding we at present have. And what, in summary, am I suggesting that understanding is? Where knowledge is concened: (a) the existence, whether we like it or not, of distinct forms, (b) the existence too of necessary links between them, and (c) the possibility of conceptual integration only between areas that belong to one form. Where the planning of curriculum units themselves is concerned: (a) the primacy of achieving cognitive development in the distinct forms whilst recognising the necessity of achieving a grasp of inter-form relations, (b) the possibility of fully integrated units only if they are devoted to one form, (c) the possibility of constructing under certain conditions units concentrating on the objectives of only a single form, (d) the possibility of inter-form units of immense diversity, from the barely related study of objectives from two forms, to a project or topic study involving related elements from all the forms, (e) the planning of units, and a combination of these, that invariably serves the objectives we want, rather than sets the objectives for us.

Though long, this chapter just must have a brief cautionary coda. I have throughout looked at certain philosophical aspects of curriculum integration only. Of course there are many other considerations that any practical curriculum plan must take into account. To ignore questions of motivation, or the abilities of teachers, or the facilities available, would be absurd. But if the enterprise of education is not to be distorted, it must throughout be true to the demands of the very nature of the elements it involves. It is these demands alone I have tried to elucidate a little. The rest I must leave to others better equipped to comment.

Notes

1 See Chapter 3, 'Liberal education and the nature of knowledge'.
2 See for example G.M. Esland, 'Teaching and learning as the organisation of knowledge', in M.F.D. Young (ed.), *Knowledge and Control*, Collier-Macmillan, 1971.
3 See Chapter 3.
4 See Chapter 4, 'Realms of meaning and forms of knowledge'.
5 See R.F. Dearden, *The Philosophy of Primary Education*, Routledge & Kegan Paul, 1968, ch. 2.

IO

Literature and the fine arts as a unique form of knowledge

I

The arts, like religion, morality or science are significant in human life in many different ways. The thesis I am concerned with is that amongst these, the arts constitute an area in which we have knowledge of a unique form. This may well be the least interesting, indeed the least important or valuable, aspect of the arts. Many who claim that we have religious knowledge also consider the beatific vision or communion with God far more important than that knowledge. In morality, knowing what is one's duty is surely secondary to actually doing it. Knowing what other people think and feel may be less valuable than certain forms of human relationship. In art, enjoyment may be more important than anything else. I am interested in the very limited thesis that amongst the other aspects of art, we do have knowledge in art.

But in what sense do we have artistic knowledge? There are many different senses possible, some of which are mutually compatible, others mutually incompatible, but there is one and only one sense in which I wish to pursue the matter. This is the simple, crude, naïve sense that in art, the physically observable features of shape, colour, sound, etc., have a significance that parallels the shape and sound of the words and sentences we use in making statements about the physical world. In the arts, whether we are talking about painting, poetry, opera, sculpture, the novel or ballet, the observable features are used as symbols, have meaning, can be seen as making artistic statements and judged true or false just as words and sentences can be used to make scientific statements. This is to take 'Guernica', *Middlemarch*, 'Fidelio' or a Haydn symphony, as a statement expressing a truth we can properly be said to know. Certainly we think of these works as symbolic expressions having meaning, which, like sentences making statements about the everyday world, are put up for public assessment. What is expressed in works of art, as in more usual statement forms, can be original or second-hand, profound or trivial, subtle or crude, true or false. This is to suggest that in the fullest sense, art is a language. And before that is rejected out of court, it might be as well to reflect that languages might be as variable as, say, games and nevertheless remain languages for all that.

I am fully aware that there are many differences between words and sentences on the one hand and paintings or musical compositions on the other, and that these have been frequently voiced in criticism of the propositional theory of art which I am outlining. What I am interested in nevertheless, is how far this theory can take us in understanding one aspect of the arts. My view is that it can take us very much further than most people think and that recent work in epistemology lends it new support. Although traditionally this view has been associated with the term 'proposition', I shall in general use the term 'statement' as this emphasises the particularity of the works with which I am concerned.

In seeking to characterise works of art, paintings, poems, symphonies, etc., as artistic statements, parallel to scientific statements or, say, mathematical statements, historical statements or moral statements, I am concerned with the *artistic* knowledge they express and can communicate, not the other elements of knowledge that may well enter into them. Just as an element of scientific knowledge may presuppose elements of mathematical knowledge, or moral knowledge presuppose scientific knowledge, so artistic knowledge may be possible only on the basis of knowledge of other types. A novel may contain much truth about the physical world or of personal and social life. In that I am not interested in this context. It is with those characteristics of works of art that distinguish them as works of art that I am concerned. A novel is not a novel by virtue of the scientific or even moral truths it contains, for these can be expressed in other ways. Representational drawings may express truths of the physical world. But granted all the non-artistic knowledge that these works contain or express, are they also stating something that is distinctly and irreducibly artistic in character? The thesis I am interested in says that works of art are indeed artistic statements, stating truths that cannot be communicated in any other way.

II

There are a number of ways in which works of art may be seen as forms of knowledge, ways in which philosophers have been very interested, some of which may be very illuminating, but which are not my concern. As these can be readily confused with the aspect that interests me, I would like to separate them out from that aspect.

(a) As I am concerned with knowledge, that term is not being used of any form of conscious, occurrent experience. I am not concerned with the experience of coming to know, or of knowing as a form of seeing, thinking, or being acquainted with. In so far as one tries to distinguish 'knowledge by acquaintance' from 'knowledge by description' in Russell's sense, I am interested only in what he calls knowledge by description and therefore in artistic knowledge as falling within this bracket. In my use of the term, 'knowledge' is functioning exactly as when we say that we know that $2 + 2 = 4$ or that water boils at $100°C$. It would seem to be the case that any individual's coming to know whatever is expressed in a work of art, necessitates his direct experience of the work, and 'coming to know' is often taken as the central element in any claim to artistic knowledge. Crucial though this existential element may be in artistic coming to know, and existential elements of some kind may be central to all coming to know, I am not here interested in the character of such personal experiences. It is rather the sense in which there is a content communicated in artistic expressions, and the legitimacy of talking here about knowledge of a propositional or statement kind that I wish to pursue. What is involved in the acquisition of any such knowledge is a further question.

(b) If one distinguishes, as in the 'standard analysis' of knowledge,
  (i) know that—propositional knowledge, or knowledge of what is expressed in true statements,
  (ii) know how—'procedural' knowledge,
  (iii) knowledge with the direct object—as in knowing persons,
then I am not interested in whether artistic knowledge can be construed along the lines of (ii) or (iii). Of course the practice of the arts and their appreciation involve much know-how. I take that for granted. I personally consider that (iii) involves a use of the term 'knowledge' that can either be analysed into uses (i) and (ii) together with other elements of a non-knowledge character, or falls under use (a) above. But I am interested here only in artistic knowledge. Whether or not the parallel between artistic knowledge and our knowledge of persons is illuminating, and I think it might well be, this in no way invalidates my concern here. Indeed, I think my concern is logically more fundamental because our knowledge of persons in any distinctive sense seems to me to presuppose know-that, and in the artistic sphere I see no reason to consider that that logical priority is changed.

III

The thesis I am interested in has, I think, not been pursued as it should be, because of its association with false views about the way in which symbols in everyday discourse have meaning and statements can be judged to be true or false. Only if one gets rid of these has the thesis any mileage. The errors stem from taking the symbols of language in ordinary discourse to have meaning because they either name or refer to objects, or states of affairs which exist independently of the symbols and which are intelligible, are known, quite independently of these symbols. For my purpose many different and very sophisticated philosophical positions on meaning and truth can be put together as sharing the features I think we must vehemently reject. Once these are rejected, it seems to me quite new force accrues to a propositional theory of art. If one holds that the meaning of the word 'cat' is an object, or class of objects, which it names or to which it refers, similarly in the case of 'mat' and what it is for one thing to be 'on' another, then we know what 'the cat is on the mat' means by such referencing and the truth or falsity of the statement comes from looking to see if what is referred to is indeed as it is labelled. If this seems a bit too simple, then 'cat', etc., might be taken to name or refer to ideas or images in the mind. The symbols 'the cat is on the mat' then label a complex image or idea and it is this that we then assess for its truth. The central point on this view is that symbols name or refer either to things outside us or to states of mind. They are the communication-means for what we see, are aware of, or know already. They are logically independent of the knowledge they are used to express.

If one holds any view of this kind, then two quite different views of works of art are possible:

(a) they are linguistic symbols that name or refer either to properties of the external world or to states of mind, or

(b) they are not the symbols of a language at all.

On (a), works of art can be looked at in a number of ways. One can think that as colour words like 'red' refer to colour qualities in the world, an artistic composition can refer to esthetic qualities that exist in the world. Or if the word 'red' is taken to refer to impressions of colour in the mind, then works of art might be considered the language of emotional states of mind: it is emotional states, or the pattern or form of emotions, that are referred to.

Let it be noted that on this approach, works of art are about something that exists quite independently of the works of art themselves. An immediate difficulty of this view is that it is not at all clear that works of art are in this way about something that exists beyond themselves, and immense difficulties have come from trying to identify these existents. There is a huge history in philosophy of people trying to see the meaning of many, more everyday, areas of language in these terms. Mathematical symbols have on this view been seen as referring to objectively existing mathematical entities. Moral terms like 'good' have been thought to be labels for non-natural qualities in situations, such that, if they cannot be said to exist, must subsist—whatever that is. I shall not begin here to go into the inadequacies of looking at meaning in these terms across the whole range of language. Let me just suggest that it is in general quite untenable and an unnecessarily restricted way of looking at the whole issue. A more illuminating and less restricted view will be outlined here. If we can get away from the idea that the meaning of symbols is necessarily tied to reference and look at things another way, then the idea that works of art might have meaning in this way, with all its attendant difficulties, can be left on one side.

But what of the other characterisation of art within the framework of meaning by reference? This concludes that works of art are not *really* symbols and do not *really* have meaning. They are not like words and sentences, they are rather like oohs and aahs, grunts and groans, cries of ecstasy and pain. In other words they are *expressions of* feelings or emotions, not statements *about* anything even about feelings or emotions. They have perhaps emotive meaning, but only in a very extended sense of meaning, for they operate causally, the expressions being caused by emotions or feelings, being effective in communication in so far as they stir or evince emotions in the receiver. The trouble with this account as applied to works of art is that their relationship to emotions and feelings is just not like this, it is in fact much more like that of a language. Indeed those who have endeavoured to build a coherent developed theory of expressionism have been compelled to repeatedly elaborate it more and more by introducing elements that make works of art less like emotive expressions and more like statements. But if an inadequate theory of linguistic meaning is being used, the final account is simply an unsatisfactory blend of two unacceptable approaches, each trying to prop up the weaknesses in the other. What is wrong in this situation is, to my mind, the original theory that the symbols of language have meaning by reference. Reject that and the character of works of art takes on a very different look—they may even turn out to be characterisable as statements after all.

Even when it is explicitly rejected, elements of this mistaken theory of the nature of linguistic symbols seem to me to have unduly influenced many contemporary writers on esthetics in their rejection of a propositional account. Susanne Langer has for such reasons expressed doubts about talking of works of art as symbols and has preferred to speak of their having 'import' rather than 'meaning'.[1] Professor L.A. Reid rejects the idea that works of art are symbols in the ordinary sense, as an ordinary symbol 'refers to a meaning—connotative or denotative—distinguishable from itself, which may be called its referent'. In art, though one must as in ordinary language distinguish the noises and marks from their meaning, that meaning is not separable from those noises and marks. 'The perceptuum does not "symbolize" or "mean" something *else* which is, *aesthetically and in aesthetic experience, distinct* from itself: aesthetic meaning is embodied.'[2] Sonia Greger rejects a propositional account because works of art do not conform to the laws of deductive and inductive logic.[3] But her demand that propositions so conform is that otherwise they would not apply 'in the world' and would thus lose their meaning. She explicitly denies that meaning is a matter of 'reference', but the ghost of that view seems to linger on in her notion of 'application'. Why otherwise should deductive or inductive relations be insisted on? For all these writers, works of art cannot be statements, as they understand statements. If art is a form of knowledge, then it cannot be in the propositional sense. But the trouble seems to me to be traceable to a particular theory of meaning and truth that makes them reject the idea that works of art can indeed be regarded as statements. Get rid of that theory, and we can look at the matter again.

What is wrong, is the central notion of naming and reference and the in-built assumption that the connection between words and their meaning is purely contingent. Instead, I suggest meaning, and intelligibility, are necessarily tied to the employment of symbols in particular rule-governed ways. The thought, the meaning, is not something there in the outside world, understood before language gets off the ground, in some wordless, symbol-less confrontation. Nor is it an idea in the mind formed without symbols or language. Meaning and understanding exist in the *use* of language, are built up in the public use of symbols.

IV

We are better starting our understanding of meaning and truth from the Wittgensteinian slogan 'the meaning is the use'. But what does this mean? Meaning is not a matter of words being pragmatically useful to achieve ends we could obtain in other ways, as in, say, the exercise of physical force. It is rather doing things like commanding, praying, making statements, singing catches, asking questions, i.e. doing things, by the rule-governed use of noises or marks which, used in particular contexts, enable us to achieve what otherwise could not occur. We are able to engage in 'language games', whereby meaning is a matter of a distinctive function that noises and marks can carry out in a given physical and social context. Only under particular conditions can there be noises that command or make statements. If this is so, then works of art can, I suggest, be thought of as constituting a language game or several language games.

In art, as in science or religion, the meaning is tied to the use of the symbols in the context. Meaning exists only with the use to which the marks or noises are put and is not conceivable independently of that. The meaning is separable from the actual marks or noises only to the extent that the use and the marks or noises are separable. The meaning is not a simple direct grasp of a situation or something simply given in experience. Nor is it an object or event. It is rather the role to which the marks or noises can be put in a given context, a context which is always presupposed in any given case of meaning. From this point of view, in which meaning is necessarily contextual, art, like all other symbol systems, has meaning as an essentially human creation, and its meaning is dependent on the contexts in which works of art have point and significance. Art is not a natural given, it is a social product with its own role and function in the life of man. To look at nature artistically is thus to see it as if it were a symbolic expression, in which noises and marks are understood in the conventional rules of works of art.

But why, even granted this, are works of art to be thought of as statements? Do they have the same use as those symbolic expressions we usually label statements? What characterises the 'language game' of stating is surely the notion of truth or falsity. Statements are, in principle, true or false. But if the notion of a statement is tied to that of truth or falsity, the limits on what can be viewed as statements, and whether works of art can be included, turn on the notions of truth or falsity and their applicability to works of art. And before one protests that works of art simply cannot be so assessed, maybe we had better look again at what is meant by saying an expression is true.

On the old theories of meaning and truth I mentioned, it is correspondence with facts, with independently understood states of affairs of some sort, that is labelled truth. This seems plausible enough for statements about the observable world, but even there it is a false account. Certainly it is because of what we observe that a particular statement is true. But it is not the case that the idea of truth comes from the fact that some symbols happen to correspond with what is observed and others do not. This account will not do if only because the very creation of a symbol system presupposes the idea of truth as to when the symbols apply and when they do not. If we could not make judgments of truth, no mere marks or noises could come to have meaning at all. The very notion of meaning presupposes that of truth. What is more, the correspondence theory demands that we can judge what is the case, or what is true, prior to judging any statements to be true. That is clearly a confusion. In fact, the notions of a statement and of truth necessarily go together from the start. They are logically related, the one not being conceivable without the other. Statements simply are expressions that can be judged true or false and vice versa. In addition there are good grounds for thinking that statements are logically the most fundamental form of meaning. It is hard to see how commands, questions, promises or any other language game can operate without presupposing truths of some sort or other. Indeed it would be hard to deny that there is a propositional element in all meaningful linguistic expressions. If this is so then the most basic questions about meaning are questions about the meaning of statements and these are necessarily tied to questions about the nature of truth.

But if one cannot get at the notion of saying a statement is true by its corresponding to independently known facts, what is it for an expression to be true? How do we give an account? To this I think we must answer that the notion of truth cannot be analysed into other notions. It is a fundamental notion whose relationship to other fundamental notions can be indicated, but beyond that we can only say something about the conditions under which it can arise. The notion of truth simply marks out an element within the fact of natural history that, being the sort of beings we are in the sort of context in which we are, marks and noises can be used so that we can agree on their application to do what we call stating the case. This in its simplest form can be seen in our discourse about the observable world, and the paradigm case of stating the case is in our language about the world. But do we not extend the use of discourse of this kind, in language about states of mind, in language about human actions, in mathematical language? The meaning of our symbol systems here comes from the underlying agreement that is possible in judgments about when it is the case that an object is red, or a number is a prime number, or an action wrong. What is needed for there to be mathematical statements is that we can agree about judgments as to when the symbolic expressions are true. We do not have to have precisely the same basis for agreement for mathematical statements as for statements about the observable world. Nor do we have to have the same basis again in the case of moral statements. What we must have in each case is a basis which fulfils the role of judgment for truth that we have in observation where statements about the physical world are concerned. Why should truth be the prerogative of statements judged by observation? There is surely no *a priori* reason, and indeed in mathematics, in matters of states of mind, or morality, we do not so restrict the idea. All that matters is the existence of agreement of judgments. But this agreement is not simply a matter of convention. In setting up a symbol system in which we state what is the case in the physical world, there is a conventional element as to which noises or marks shall be used. But their coming to have a correct use in the context is dependent on the world being what it is.

There must be beyond the noises and marks, a relation to the context in which the correct application of the concepts is objectively determined. It is only by virtue of the relationship that is created between the symbols and, in Wittgenstein's phrase, 'the form of life' that the context presents, that there can be that objectivity of judgment that we call truth. The ways in which noises and marks can be related to 'the form of life' where agreement in judgment is possible, may be many and the kinds of objective judgment may be very diverse. What is needed for meaningful statements is that there be such a symbol system.[4]

V

In the light of these considerations, the question as to whether works of art are statements seems to reduce to the question as to whether or not the use of symbols is here such that in judging works, there is a logical parallel to the judgments made as to whether a mathematical statement is true, or a moral statement is true. Put another way, this is simply the question as to whether or not there are objective judgments of a parallel kind for works of art. If there are, then I see no reason why we should not think of them as statements. But it may be asked, are there not other features that are fundamental to the notion of a statement beyond what is here being claimed—symbolic expressions used with objective tests? I think not. That statements can be broken down into elements that include concepts in logical relations, is surely not a major difficulty. From a logical point of view, if the objective judgment of a statement can equally be regarded as the correct application of the concepts, then works of art can be regarded in this way too. Again, such works are complex units and can certainly be understood as having sub-elements which have meaning in their use. A sequence of notes, a particular metaphor, or particular shape, may have a use in art parallel to that of a word in ordinary discourse. But what of the relations between those elements? Are they the logical relations necessary to statements? Maybe not if one takes as the paradigm certain formal relations sometimes insisted on. But why must one? What I am really suggesting is that recent philosophical work has had to so extend the notions of meaning, statement, truth, concept, logical relation, knowledge, that previous paradigms can no longer be regarded as settling when these terms are to be applied and when withheld. It is inadequacies in past attempts to clarify the meaning of these terms *in accepted paradigm cases*, that has led to a reconsideration of their character. This has itself thrown open the question as to whether or not works of art might not be seen as statements after all. I am not arguing that we should redefine our notions of statement, truth, concept, knowledge, etc. so as to let art into the charmed circle where these terms are used. It is rather that a coherent account of what these notions serve to pick out in the most central cases, itself permits a wider application. If, then, works of art involve the use of symbols in relation to their context, that is in relation to man's own nature and his complex social and physical environment, so that objective judgments of them as works of art are possible, I see no reason why we should not speak of art as a form of knowledge.

VI

The issue of the uniqueness of artistic knowledge, or its autonomy, is a question as to whether or not what can be expressed in art can be expressed in any other way. I am unable to go into this now. The uniqueness is indeed a familiar claim made for art and I shall take that claim as readily defensible. It rests on maintaining for art expressions, as for say moral statements, that they are irreducible to statements of other kinds. As with moral statements there is the perpetual temptation to some form of naturalism, based often on a refusal to accept that meaning need not be tied to reference. In the case of art, as in the case of morals, the fact that the meaning is always parasitic, or supervenient, on other forms of meaning makes reductionism particularly tempting. It seems to me that all arts are arts of some other existing form of knowledge, e.g. art that is based on our knowledge of spatial relations, or on our knowledge of sound relations, or of moral relationships. An art like opera is immensely complex, being a super-art formed out of the arts of music, drama, etc. each of which rests on knowledge of other kinds.

The fact that the arts presuppose other areas of knowledge, as, say, the sciences often presuppose mathematics, does indicate how they can be illuminating about the areas of knowledge they pre-suppose. Many a scientific concern has led people to appreciate new mathematical truths and indeed to the discovery of totally new mathematical truths. So many a novel has led to a new moral under-standing. But none of that justifies that works of art are reducible to other forms of statement any more than that science is reducible to mathematics.

To say that all arts would seem to presuppose a knowledge of the physical world, of persons, or of some other non-artistic kind, is not to suggest that the arts are necessarily concerned simply with formal patterns composed of a content of a non-artistic kind. It is simply to suggest that without these necessary elements of other knowledge artistic knowledge could not arise. A knowledge of the physical world and of persons is presupposed in moral understanding, but this does not make moral knowledge a matter of formal relations only. If artistic meaning always presupposes some other kind of meaning, that is no reason to suppose that it is analysable into meaning of that kind plus formal relations of some sort. Artistic knowledge is autonomous because it involves elements over and above those derived from elsewhere, but no particular character for these elements is being suggested other than that they are essentially artistic.

In discussing the possibility that works of art can be regarded as statements of a unique kind, I deliberately set on one side at the outset questions about the nature of artistic experience. If the thesis is correct however, it suggests that artistic experience, like other forms of experience, can be distinguished only by the artistic concepts it involves. Just as we cannot characterise perceptual experience and distinguish it from say moral experience other than by reference to the concepts applied in perception and those applied in moral experience, so artistic experience will be characterisable only by reference to the artistic concepts it involves. An area of experience arises with the development of the concepts it employs and they in their turn develop in the use of the appropriate public language. Just as our experience of the physical world is determined by and limited by the concepts we have learnt in public discourse about that world, so our artistic experience will be limited by the mastery we have of the language that is art. But what is more, it is an essential part of this thesis that works of art are not conceivable as expressions of essentially non-artistic experience. The type of experience concerned and the type of discourse necessarily go together as they share the same concepts. What experience a work of art expresses, as a work of art, can only be artistic experience. And the same can be said if we are to distinguish forms of artistic judgment or emotion. As with experience, it is the concepts they employ that determine their character and if the arts form a unique domain conceptually, the judgments and emotions with which they are associated are likewise irreducible to those of other kinds. In saying this, however, it must not be forgotten that every art presupposes other areas of understanding and to that extent artistic experience, judgment or emotion will presuppose experience, judgment and emotions of other kinds. But these elements provide simply the occasion for all that is distinctive and irreducible in the arts.

Throughout this discussion, I have made no reference to the nature of art criticism. Again this has been deliberate. It is the character of works of art themselves that has concerned me. Art critics are not, in general, in their criticism creating works of art.

Their statements are thus not themselves artistic satements. Rather, they make statements of many kinds about works of art, that is they make non-artistic statements about artistic statements. Much of what they say is descriptive of the observable physical characteristics of works of art, is about the psychological genesis of works or their location in an historical and social context. All this is understanding of other kinds whose function is to lead one to artistic understanding itself and the development of knowledge, experience and judgment in this distinctive area. That the arts are dependent on other forms of knowledge, experience and judgment is good reason why the domain of criticism looms so large in the arts. But it would be a mistake to think that this critical function does not exist where scientific, moral or other forms of knowledge are concerned, even if the function is not so obviously professionally instituted elsewhere. Much science teaching is concerned precisely with talking *about* the claims of science, aimed at helping pupils to enter into scientific discourse and the meaning it has. Science teachers do not simply mouth the scientific statements they wish their pupils to understand; they are concerned with elucidating how scientists come to say what they do and why. In the discovery of new scientific truths and the teaching of science to others there is a domain of criticism just as there is in the creation and teaching of the arts. But what matters for my purpose is that the character of criticism be distinguished from the character of the expressions with which criticism is concerned. It is the works of art themselves that I have here sought to characterise as artistic statements. What sorts of statements are made in art criticism is another matter. Art criticism may express knowledge, but what it does not and cannot do, on the thesis here discussed, is express the artistic knowledge that works of art themselves state.[5]

VII

All I have done in this paper is outline, with some slight defence, a particular thesis about works of art. Whether or not this claim can be substantiated rests, I think, on the question of the objectivity of judgments of art. But are there such judgments? The confusions of the art world offer no clear answer. Certainly the existence of objective judgments would be perfectly compatible with the present state of affairs. That the man in the street cannot begin to make any significant artistic judgments that could be called objective may just show most men's total lack of understanding of the language that is art. Why should one expect anything else? On most scientific matters the man in the street can make no significant judgments either. That even the specialists in the arts are in dispute over contemporary works is certainly paralleled in the sciences too and once the distancing of time has occurred, specialists in the arts, as in other areas, do show considerable agreement in their assessments. But whether there are objective judgments here, I am not in a position to say. What I do suggest is that the case needs to be carefully considered and not ruled out of court. As I am interested in it, the claim that the arts are a form of knowledge rests on this alone. It may be a false claim, but that seems to me not shown and for educational reasons, if for no other, it matters very much. If we do have artistic knowledge in this propositional, statement, or know-that sense, then this has surely considerable bearing on the significance of the arts in the curriculum, and the way they should be taught. To pursue these implications would however be to follow speculation upon speculation. Whether or not the arts constitute a unique form of knowledge I do not know. Indeed maybe there is no answer to this question because it is misconceived. But then to be clear on that would be a great step forward. It therefore seems to me one can say at least this, that in the light of recent work in epistemology, the parallel between works of art and language needs detailed reexamination and that the outcome can hardly fail to be illuminating.

Notes

1 S.K. Langer, *Problems of Art*, New York, 1957, pp. 126–39.
2 L.A. Reid, *Meaning in the Arts*, Allen & Unwin, London, 1969, pp. 195, 198.
3 S. Greger, 'Aesthetic meaning', in *Proceedings of the Philosophy of Education Society*, Blackwell, vol. VI, no. 2, July 1972.
4 See D.W. Hamlyn, 'Objectivity', and 'The correspondence theory of truth' in R.F. Dearden, P.H. Hirst and R.S. Peters (eds), *Education and the Development of Reason*, Routledge & Kegan Paul, London, 1972. Throughout this section I am much indebted to the writings of Professor Hamlyn. The particular views here expressed are, however, my own.
5 For a further discussion of the nature of criticism, see P.H. Hirst, 'Literature, criticism and the forms of knowledge', in *Educational Philosophy and Theory*, vol. 3, no. 1, 1971.

The two-cultures, science and moral education

Professor G.H. Bantock has put us greatly in his debt by valuable analyses of the issues behind the two-cultures debate; analyses which make explicit problems which neither Lord Snow nor Dr Leavis adequately exposed in their original lectures.[1] In particular we can now clearly see that at the very centre of a conflict between manifestly different forms of understanding, lie vitally important questions about moral values. To Professor Bantock this central issue is pre-eminently a fight between 'two conflicting views of the ends of human existence'. On the one hand there is the Baconian scientific ethic of the extended use of science in industrial development for an escape from the horrors of starvation and deprivation. On the other hand there are the values beyond those of 'bread' and 'jam', values that literary culture has been concerned to preserve and communicate. Snow, certainly in his Rede Lecture, seems to back the former, Leavis for many years now has been the arch-apostle of the latter. That fundamentally Leavis is on the right side and Snow on the wrong, Professor Bantock seems in no doubt. And that not so much because of any straight examination of these sets of values but because he considers Leavis rather than Snow to have the trained capacity that entitles him to make such value judgments. Indeed, in Chapter 5 of *Education in an Industrial Society*, he devotes considerable space to arguing that 'it is pre-eminently to an education in literature that ... training in moral awareness and sensitivity'[2] must be assigned because of the peculiar way in which moral values arise in the making of literary judgments.

To follow Professor Bantock's argument thus far is, however, to reach deeper waters in the two-cultures debate. For what here appears is that behind any straight fight between the values of Baconian minded scientists and those of the writers approved by Leavis, there are rival claims to the right to judge in these matters. Undoubtedly there are imperialistic tendencies in the writings of both Snow and Leavis when it comes to moral judgments. Each of them seems to think the making of such judgments is in some way peculiarly the preserve of either the scientists (Lord Snow) or the students of literature (Dr Leavis).[3] They both seem to think there is something in the pursuits they each advocate that makes them supremely valuable and instructive in moral matters. At this level the rights and wrongs can only be settled by most careful analysis of the relationship between the making of moral judgments and the understanding we have in science and literature. This philosophical work, on which the place of science and literature in moral education turns, has so far not been tackled in sufficient detail. Professor Bantock in his account of Leavis's view of literary-critical judgments has begun the work in one direction, showing more clearly than anyone else, so far, how moral values enter into these judgments. What emerges from this would seem to be the need for caution by advocates of the importance of literary education. For on Leavis's view the peculiarly moral element in literary judgments seems to be some form of intuition for which no rational justification is offered. Unfortunately, moral intuitionism is notoriously unsatisfactory and it is hard to escape the conclusion, though Leavis repudiates any such suggestion, that in this case as in most others, the intuitions are in fact the expression of previously held moral values that are being brought to the critical process. If this is the case then a Leavis-type literary education is most certainly a moral training for it is in part a training in the making of judgments that are in keeping with a pre-determined system of moral values. Unfortunately the moral foundations of all this are going unexamined and the education offered is then, to say the least, dangerously partial and uncritical. However, any such conclusions would at the moment be premature and we must await further philosophical analysis in this area following the valuable lead of Professor Bantock. Meanwhile it is my object in this chapter to make one or two very general comments on the relationship in the other direction, that between moral judgments and the practice and study of science. No detailed analysis of the relationship will be undertaken for the important considerations I am concerned to bring out arise from even the most cursory examination of what that relationship involves.

In considering either the literary or scientific issue it first needs to be recognised clearly that judgments of moral value must be distinguished sharply both from judgments of empirical fact and truth and judgments of literary value. None of these judgments can be equated for certainly we make judgments of fact and truth that are not themselves moral value judgments and we equally make judgments of moral value that are independent of any literary considerations. Granted these distinctions it then becomes important to explore the relationship between moral understanding and either scientific or literary pursuits in at least three ways. In the case of science for instance there is first the question of the moral content of science—what specific moral principles and judgments are used or presupposed in the pursuit and teaching of science? Second, there is the question of the extent to which moral understanding and scientific understanding are similar in formal structure so that the ability to reason in the one area might be of help or hindrance in the other—do they have similar concepts, patterns of reasoning and tests of validity? Third, there is the matter of the scientific content of moral understanding—what specific scientific principles and truths are used or presupposed in the pursuit and teaching of moral understanding? In exactly the same way a three-fold investigation is possible of the relationship between moral and literary understanding, but little further will be said of that here as the former relationship is the one I wish to pursue.

The question of the moral elements in science is one which has attracted increasing attention in recent years. Lord Snow, for instance, suggests that the pursuit of science is necessarily democratic in its human relations, that it recognises a principle of equality between men and even that it promotes a freedom from racial feeling.[4] In *Science and Human Values*, Dr J. Bronowski describes scientists as necessarily committed to truth, to independence in observation and thought recognising no test other than empirical truth to facts. They are committed too to the safeguards of truth, free inquiry, free thought, free speech, tolerance, justice, honour, respect of man for man and democracy.[5]

> Only by these means can science pursue its steadfast object to explore truth. If these values did not exist, then the society of scientists would have to invent them to make the practice of science possible. In societies where these values did not exist, science has had to create them.

Professor F.A. Vick draws attention to many of the same moral principles in his paper 'Science and its standards'.[6]

That at least most of these values are in some way to be found in the pursuit of science is undoubtedly the case. Yet if we are not to misconceive the significance of science as a moral enterprise one or two important comments must be made. In the first place science is of course necessarily committed to a concern for truth. But truth in this case is determined strictly by empirical observation and experiment. Science is focused in its interests and restricted in its sweep by the principles of empirical test. In saying then that the pursuit of science develops a concern and commitment to truth we must insert the term 'empirical'. It is truth under only one of its aspects that is directly involved. Scientists may like to think that a general respect for truth in all its different forms is employed, e.g. literary, historical, moral, philosophical as well as scientific. But the pursuit of science does not presuppose a commitment to these forms of understanding nor is it a training in them and the tests for truth they employ. There is as far as one can see little evidence that scientific training develops a respect for truth in all its aspects and the two-cultures issue is itself strong witness to the fact that frequently the reverse is the case. Further the claim of science to a commitment to truth can be seriously misleading for it all too readily results in truth being equated with scientific truth and other forms of rational knowledge being dismissed. What is here said about truth goes for other values and the many abilities and qualities of mind that science involves. For instance, terms like creativeness and imagination have, as Professor Bantock has pointed out, quite different application in scientific and literary contexts. The tendency to generalise about values and achievements wherever we use general terms for them is a highly dangerous business as I have tried to show elsewhere.[7]

Second, it must be noted that the range of values inherent in science is limited. Although, for instance, Dr Bronowski seems to maintain otherwise, where implicit in science is the respect for men as men when they are scientific fools as well as when they are scientifically expert or useful? It is difficult to see where such a value arises at all. Indeed in the interests of science alone there would seem to be no reason why many experiments we do in fact object to should not be performed on human beings. There is nothing in science that prevents these experiments. It is other values we hold quite independently of the pursuit of science that are the controlling factors. Again, though Dr Bronowski seems to claim otherwise, where is the principle of decision by democratic processes in science? We have these processes in government to decide issues precisely because in certain areas scientific methods are inappropriate.

Third, if there are many moral elements implicit in the scientific pursuit, moral elements are implicit in all other rational pursuits as well and it is misleading to imply that this is not so. Certainly Lord Snow gives this unfortunate impression at times.[8] What is more it must be remembered that the contents of the physical sciences is value free. These studies are not about moral value judgments but about such subjects as magnetic fields and chemical compounds. The human or social sciences do certainly seek to study the empirical facts about the value judgments men make. But here as in the physical sciences the truths with which they are concerned are empirical. No science legitimately contains judgments as to how men ought to live, for by its own canons its pursuit is descriptive and explanatory not prescriptive. This is so even when the descriptions and explanations are about prescriptions. In literary pursuits the content is largely moral and the understanding of moral issues involved is quite different in kind from that in the human sciences. The significance of literature for moral understanding must therefore be important in a way quite distinct from that of the sciences, and particularly the physical sciences.

Finally, whatever is said of the moral content of science it must not be forgotten that very few people are ever educated to a level at which they begin to participate in 'the society of scientists'. Indeed it is doubtful whether our scientific education at school does in fact develop any serious commitment to those moral values and principles that are truly implicit in the pursuit. Maybe our teaching needs reform. Still we should not blind ourselves as to what moral education is in fact being achieved in this way at the moment.

Turning to the question of comparisons between the logical character of reasoning and validation in scientific understanding and those in moral judgments, we very quickly encounter difficult matters of philosophical analysis. One thing that can readily be said however is that contemporary work in ethics has resulted in an almost universal rejection of the view that moral judgments are in character reducible to empirical judgments. Rather there is a thorough-going acceptance of the autonomy or independent character of morals. This means that we must resist any tendency to presume that the pattern of reasoning and justification employed in science can be simply transferred to dealing with moral matters. Scientists have in the past frequently fallen into this naturalistic transference and it is one of the dangers to which an education heavily geared to the sciences gives rise. In this connection it is perhaps unfortunate that we speak of moral 'laws' as well as scientific 'laws' when the two are so different in function and need such different forms of justification.

This leads to the important point that unless we are aware of the differences, there is a danger that particular problems in morals will be solved in the way that we explain particular events in science. In the latter case the explanation rests on some general law. What is happening to this gas is an instance of a general law about the behaviour of gases under these conditions. It is one of the distinctive features of judgments about what ought to be done in particular practical situations that the answer frequently cannot be obtained by an appeal to some general law. For in complex situations several different moral principles may conflict. The principle of truth telling may indicate one line of action, that of concern for minimising unnecessary suffering indicate quite another. Indeed our moral problems are often conflicts of this kind. To make moral judgments crudely by applying some one general rule that is relevant is to distort the whole issue.

Parallel to these dangers of an unjustifiably scientific approach to morals there are the dangers of a form of estheticism produced by too literary an approach. For in that literary judgments are more complex, more clearly related to moral matters, and more radically particular in character than scientific judgments, there is a strong temptation to lose sight of the autonomy of morals in that direction. Only a more developed analysis of literary judgments than we have at present got can help us to respect more adequately the logical differences involved.

But logical differences must not blind us to the possibility of important parallels and thus to recognising how a training in scientific thought can help us in moral understanding. It may be the case, for instance, that the pure scientist's interest in general laws and his facility in handling concepts at this level make him peculiarly able to deal with moral issues at the level of general principles and rules—provided he is aware of important differences between these and scientific laws. Maybe the applied scientist's training makes him peculiarly able to deal with problems of means to ends in less technical matters. The concern for unique, particular human events is not however the characteristic concern of the scientist but that of the writer and the historian. From all this it might be the case that in moral affairs those with different forms of training can best contribute at different levels of understanding. Whether or not there is any significant transfer of reasoning ability in these ways is a matter for empirical investigation on which at the moment we would seem to lack significant evidence. We cannot hope to get further on the value of science or literature as a training in moral reasoning without much more analysis of the logical features involved and much more experimental evidence of what happens in practice.

Finally there is the third question of the significance of scientific knowledge for moral understanding. This has been left until last for on the general answer there is likely to be little disagreement. All the sciences manifestly contribute to the basic factual knowledge of man and his environment on which our moral judgments are made. Both at the level of general principles and of particular judgments we need to draw on all the available empirical evidence that is relevant. In this it is the results of science, its established laws and truths, that are being used. And we use this knowledge not only to determine what we ought to do in practical affairs but also how we ought to do it. No scientific knowledge is in principle irrelevant to moral issues and therefore the results of the pursuit and study of science always have at least potential moral significance. In practice, however, the moral relevance of scientific work can easily be ignored or mistaken and in moral problems we are only too liable to be unaware of the knowledge that is relevant. The domain of science today is so vast that even a scientist is likely to know only a small amount of it and therefore at best to know the moral bearing of very little. Further there is no reason why the scientist, *qua* scientist, should devote his attention to solving related moral problems. After all questions about the moral significance of science are not themselves scientific questions. Yet it is a crucially important matter whether or not, science being so vast and specialised a business, it is not the social responsibility of scientists and teachers of science to make plain to others the moral relevance of their work. But having said that, it cannot also be said too often that moral problems are never merely scientific problems and scientific knowledge is never the sum total of understanding relevant to them.

Educationally we must recognise that in most science teaching scientific understanding itself is what is pursued, not its moral implications. It might well be argued that as well as teaching science itself we should go into its moral significance. To do that however, if the importance of scientific considerations in moral matters is not to be misconceived, school education must get to grips with moral questions directly and explicitly. By their nature these questions are complex and scientific considerations are only part of the story. For instance literary, historical and religious understanding are equally important in their different ways. This being so moral education is a most complicated and difficult matter and it is too important to be mishandled by misleadingly partial treatment. The significance of the pursuit and teaching of science for moral education is not to be ignored but it must not be overestimated either.

Sufficient has been said about science and indeed literature to show that their relationship with moral understanding is far from simple. As moral judgments are distinguishable from other judgments and would seem to be autonomous in character, the presumption must surely be that both literary and scientific studies, and others too, have important but different contributions to make to moral understanding. What precisely those contributions are is a matter for detailed study and it is unfortunate that at times assertion has taken the place of careful analysis. Maybe in the not too distant future any moral opposition there is between the two-cultures will be shown to be the product of misunderstanding becasue we have not seen how to fit the two approaches together when it comes to moral questions. Maybe as a result our education is at present producing what is in fact a totally unnecessary moral antagonism. I should like to think this is so. For in that case at least one of the central issues between the two cultures might prove solvable by changing our educational practice.

Notes

1 G.H. Bantock, 'A scream of horror', *Listener*, 17 September 1959.
   G.H. Bantock, *Education in an Industrial Society*, Faber, 1963, ch. 5.
   G.H. Bantock, 'The two cultures: can the gap be bridged?',
   Education for Teaching, November 1964.
2 *Education in an Industrial Society*, p. 153.
3 See for example: C.P. Snow, *The Two Cultures and the Scientific Revolution*, Cambridge University Press, 1959, p. 45.
4 F.R. Leavis, *Mass Civilization and Minority Culture*, Cambridge University Press, 1930, pp. 3–5. See the passage referred to in the previous note.
5 J. Bronowski, *Science and Human Values*, Hutchinson, 1961. Especially ch. 3 and p. 72.
6 F.A. Vick, 'Science and its standards' in W.R. Niblett (ed.), *Moral Education in a Changing Society*, Faber, 1963.
7 See Chapter 3.
8 See for example: Snow, op. cit., p. 45.

Morals, religion and the maintained school

It is now some thirty years since the 1944 Education Act legislated that in every maintained school there should be religious instruction and a daily act of collective worship. This legislation reflected not only general agreement about the value of religious education itself but also the conviction of many that the moral standards of the nation could best be secured by these means. Thirty years later we are becoming deeply dissatisfied with the moral education our schools give, even amongst Christians there is a growing number who think moral education should be divorced from religious education, and compulsory religious instruction and worship seem to grow yearly less justifiable in a religiously open society.

In this article I want to look briefly at these issues primarily from a philosophical point of view, for they turn in part on two crucially important philosophical questions. First, is man's moral understanding necessarily dependent on his religious knowledge or beliefs? If the answer to that is yes, then any serious moral education must ultimately be religiously based. If the answer is no and moral knowledge is autonomous, then there is a prima facie case for direct specific moral education. Secondly, what is the status of religious propositions? Is there here a domain of knowledge or simply one of beliefs? And if the latter is the case, is it justifiable for state maintained schools to instruct pupils in one particular faith and to conduct worship in accordance with it? In arguing first for the autonomy of morals and moral education, I shall not be denying that moral principles and religious beliefs may be closely connected. Certainly they are in the Christian faith. Similarly in arguing against the provision in maintained schools of religious education, and worship, according to one particular set of beliefs, I shall not be denying the enormous importance of religious education itself. Nor is it my concern to argue either for or from a humanist or religious position in these matters. Rather, I wish to look at them in the light of the philosophical character of moral judgments and religious propositions and I see no reason why both the arguments and conclusions of this discussion should not be acceptable to both say Christians and humanists alike. Throughout I shall be directly concerned with the

Christian faith rather than with any other but much of what I say is applicable more widely.

Of course no adequate educational conclusions can be reached purely on philosophical grounds but one must recognise the general bearings of philosophical considerations on these issues however contentious or unpalatable they may seem. The intention here is to provoke further discussion not to provide final answers.

I

What then of the thesis that moral questions are in fact inseparable from religious questions, that in the last analysis—if you really get down to the business—moral values rest on religious beliefs, for without this foundation there really are no reasons why one should be just, tell the truth, respect other people's property, and so on? In its strongest form this view maintains that for something to be right, is for it to be the command or will of God. 'Right' is 'doing the will or command of God' and thus our knowledge of what is right comes from our knowing what God wills or commands. Without this knowledge of God's will, men can only live according to their personal likes or dislikes for without this foundation moral principles just do not stand up.

Now it is one thing to maintain that whatever is right is also the will of God, it is quite another to maintain, as this thesis does, that for something to be right is just for it to be the will or command of God. On the first view man may have a knowledge of right of a purely natural kind and in addition believe that what he thus knows to be right is also according to God's will. On the other view being right and being the will of God are equated in meaning so that it can be consistently maintained that man only knows what is right because he can know what God wills. Moral terms like ought, right, good are here being so logically tied to religious terms that moral judgments have become essentially judgments of a religious kind, judgments as to the will of God. Because of the equation of meaning it is argued that man's moral knowledge rests entirely on what God reveals as His will in Scripture, the Church or by His indwelling Spirit. This strong thesis really consists of two claims, then. First that to say something is right, good and ought to be done, means that it is willed by God. Second, that we only know what is right or good by coming to know what God wills.

It may, however, be said that few Christians go as far as to make the first claim of the equation of meaning, though more are prepared to accept the second claim as to the source and basis of moral knowledge. To hold simply to the second claim only and not to both is to subscribe to a somewhat weaker thesis. Nevertheless both positions firmly root moral knowledge in religious knowledge. The strong one ties a logical knot making moral knowledge necessarily dependent on religious knowledge. The weaker one, while allowing that other bases for moral knowledge are conceivable, denies that as a matter of fact we have any other. Both theses seem to have an appeal for religious believers but there are, I think, at least three different forms of argument why they must both be rejected by Christians, and among these, reasons for rejection by others.

First, the second claim which is common to both strong and weak theses, that man only knows right from wrong by discovering God's will, is surely quite contrary to the empirical facts. Surely it is plain, unless one is so totally bemused by certain extreme forms of Biblical interpretation, that one cannot see the evidence before one's very eyes, that men *do* know that lying, promiscuous sex-relations, colour bar and war are wrong quite independently of Christian revelation. The terms right and wrong, good and bad have meaning as ordinary everyday terms in human discourse. They are terms used for judgments for which men have perfectly good reasons which have nothing to do with religious beliefs. It is just false to say that there are no reasons for something being good or for my being good, other than that God has willed or revealed this. Certainly it is false to suggest, as Christians who hold on to an exclusive view of revelation must suggest, that outside the Judaeo-Christian tradition men have no genuine moral knowledge because they lack the revelation of God's will. How is it then that one can find the highest moral understanding in other traditions? Not in all, of course, but then all forms of knowledge are known in varying degrees within different traditions. In particular what of the moral understanding of Socrates and Aristotle based on the straight use of reason and observation? Can one honestly maintain that these people had no justifiable moral knowledge? I suggest that it is indisputable that they had a very great deal of it and that they did not derive it from Judaeo-Christian beliefs. Whether or not they lived up to this knowledge is another matter that I am not discussing, nor is it relevant to this argument that we now have more moral knowledge than the Greeks had. What I am interested in is that they *had* moral knowledge and that it rested in fact not on religious revelation but on rational judgment.

Second, it seems to me that the second of the claims is clearly inconsistent with Biblical teaching on the basis of morals. Far from it being the case that the New Testament teaches that man's knowledge of right and wrong comes from revelation, the reverse is explicitly asserted. As Biblical doctrine is not my concern here let me refer to just one clear passage. In Romans 2:14 and 15 the Gentiles are categorically stated to have a knowledge of the moral law quite independently of the law of Moses. They have it by nature we are told. Indeed the essence of the debate in this passage is that *all* men stand condemned before God because they know or can know the moral law and do not in fact live up to it.

Third, both strong and weak theses are I think philosophically quite unsound. The strong thesis rests on the claim that what is meant by 'right' and 'good' is simply 'willed or commanded by God'. To say something is right or ought to be done is just to say that God wills it. Now this can be, of course, a way of winning one's case by definition—a prescriptive definition that legislates that we are only going to count as good or right what we assert is willed by God. But this surely is to be rejected as an attempt to make language do just what one wants when our ordinary understanding of the term just will not allow this. For if we inspect the meaning of right, ought, good, we do not at all find that their meaning is that of willed or commanded by God. There is, in fact, no necessary connection between the meanings of these two groups of concepts at all. If I say something is right I am voicing a judgment on some action. If I say God wills this, then I am saying something quite different. I am describing a state of affairs. The terms have quite distinct uses in our discourse and do not at all mean the same. To draw a parallel I might just as well say that the term 'object' means 'what is created by God'. Of course objects may be created by God, but the meaning of the term 'object' is not at all the meaning of the phrase 'what is created by God'. Similarly what is good and right might, in fact, be willed or commanded by God—but to say that right means willed by God is just simply false.

From this emerges another point that a term like 'right', 'ought', or 'good' has a function which is logically quite different in kind from a phrase like 'what is commanded by God'. The first expresses the moral value of an action, expresses a decision, choice, judgment of value; the second states what is the case. There is a great gulf fixed between knowing any form of facts, knowing what is the case, and knowing what is right or good or what ought to be the case. To confuse the two is just to be guilty of a logical blunder. It is to be guilty of one form of what is known as the naturalistic fallacy, in which two expressions with fundamentally different uses are made to do the same kind of job. It confuses statements or judgments of fact with statements or judgments of value.

But further, to equate good and right with what is commanded by God has disastrous results for Christian doctrine. For if what is good is by definition whatever God wills, then affirmations of the goodness of God, of His moral excellence, become trivial truisms, they are necessarily true by definition. In this way there is no significant content to saying that God's will is good, or even that He is righteous, for by definition things could not be otherwise. This is to make empty truths that Christians hold to be part of a supreme and momentous revelation: that God is righteous, goodness and love rather than a morally indifferent or viciously evil creator. But if God is by definition these things, for Him to be otherwise is made just a formal contradiction in the meaning of terms.

Again this equation destroys the Christian's moral life, for that becomes simply the obedience of will or command, no questions being asked about its moral nature. For to say that certain actions are commanded by God is by definition to say that they are good. The place of moral judgment in life is removed entirely; what remains is simply obedience, indeed supreme might becomes right.

But neither of these consequences is tolerable in Christian doctrine. That God is a supremely excellent being is not a definitional truism. Whether the creator is morally excellent or morally evil is a logically open question that must turn on evidence. Good is not just a label for the character of God's will or commands no matter what their character may be. Nor is the Christian obeying principles that he does not know to be good. In that case good cannot be simply what God wills or commands. Man must have moral knowledge of good and bad, right and wrong independently of any knowledge he has of God's will or of His Nature. It is in fact only if man has such independent moral knowledge that it is logically possible for him to grasp the significant truth that God is good and that His will and commands are righteous.

All the criticisms just made of the strong thesis are in fact also applicable, with only the slightest modification to the weak thesis as well. To say that we will only count as genuine the moral knowledge we can acquire from knowing the will of God, is to win the argument prescriptively once more. To jump straight from what God commands to what it is good or right to do, is to commit the naturalistic fallacy all over again, even where there is no equation of meaning. Though not now true by definition the doctrine of the goodness of God remains empty if the only basis of our knowledge of goodness is our knowledge of His will and the moral life is still reduced to mere obedience. From these criticisms it is surely clear that if Christian doctrine is not to run into serious logical difficulties it must be maintained that man does have moral knowledge which he acquires by some means other than by divine revelation.

Why it has ever seemed important to Christians to think of morals and religion as tied together in these ways it is not easy to understand. For as was said earlier, to hold simply that what is right is indeed willed or commanded by God in no way commits us to saying that we can only learn what is right by knowing the expressed will of God.

An autonomous knowledge of morals is quite compatible with moral principles being also the will or commands of God. Take the parallel of scientific knowledge. A Christian might argue that the laws of the physical world are the laws commanded or willed for it by God. He might then unthinkingly subscribe to the thesis that because the laws are God's commands, the only way to know them is to be told them by God. Indeed he might hold the stronger thesis that for a scientific statement to be true *is* for it to be what God has commanded. As then 'true' means 'commanded by God' the only way to know the laws is to get at the very commands of God themselves. But not even the most fundamental fundamentalist holds that one knows the laws of the physical world by revelation. We know them by scientific investigation. The laws of the physical world may or may not be commanded by God, whether or not they are is quite independent of the fact that the way we know the laws is by scientific experiment and observation.

Similarly with morals. The theses I have criticised maintain that because what is right is willed by God we must come to know what is right by revelation from God. But that moral principles are willed by God in fact tells us nothing about how man gets to know what is right or wrong. Just as man knows the laws of the physical world so man can also know what is right and wrong, by the exercise of reason. Whether or not moral or physical laws are God's commands is another question. There is therefore nothing in my criticisms which is incompatible with maintaining that what is right is also willed by God. Nor is there anything incompatible with holding man's moral knowledge to be gained by the use of God-given abilities. Such general beliefs about moral knowledge are fully consistent with its being attained independently of specifically religious revelation in any form.

II

But if it is agreed that moral knowledge is autonomous, what is the positive relationship between morals and religion in Christian terms, for it would be preposterous to suggest that there is none? Here it is only possible to outline briefly a philosophically more tenable position.

First, the prime significance of the Christian claim to revelation is surely that in it man has an understanding of the nature of God. In this God is understood as a moral being who is righteous and yet love.

From what I have said earlier this is, I think, only meaningful because we first know the meaning of moral terms and know ourselves to be moral beings.

Secondly, it seems to me a mistake to think of the Christian claim as being at all centrally one of having new moral principles. Surely the point is much more that there is in Christianity a crystallisation of man's moral knowledge and the use of this as a basis for understanding the nature of God in moral terms and man's relationship to Him as a moral being.

This is in effect to say that morals are really more than mere morals. Wrong is not a matter of human relationships only, it is a matter of one's relationship to God. Wrong in fact is also sin. The Scriptures contain a great deal of moral teaching of course but surely the emphasis is not that these principles are only known because of divine revelation but rather that man's moral life matters in his relationship to God. I suggest then that to the Christian, man's actions can be known to be right or wrong on rational grounds, but he sees them as not only morally significant, for to him they have a religious bearing as well.

Thirdly, I see no reason to presume that any of the fully general moral principles in the Christian Scriptures are by their very nature unjustifiable on rational grounds. Maybe we cannot at the moment actually justify the Christian sex ethic—maybe we just do not know the facts on which to make such judgments. Maybe many Christians accept the Scriptures on this because on matters where they have independent rational moral justification they find the Scriptures trustworthy. There is nothing irrational about that. Still, we must be clear that such principles would have no justification if man had no basic moral knowledge on some other grounds.

Fourthly, the acceptance of Christian revelation does, however, add to the general moral principles that determine a person's life, certain rules that are specifically related to religious beliefs, e.g. that a Christian ought to worship God, give his time and money to Christian witness, etc. These principles are, of course, quite unjustifiable other than on Christian grounds. They are, however, thoroughly justifiable within such a context.

Fifthly, it is I think, true that Christian teaching, in common with that of other religions, picks out among morally defensible ways of life a particular style of living, in that it sets up certain ideals and gives priority to certain virtues. The justification for these is I think specifically in terms of the religious doctrines. But at this level where I am thinking of the Christian concern to follow in some sense the pattern of the life of Christ and the virtues displayed with an emphasis on self-sacrifice and meekness, we have, I think, left the

N   179 domain of general public moral considerations for something at a logically different level.

What, thus far, I have been concerned to show is that moral knowledge does not in general rest on any religious claims. If that is so, there is no reason why moral education must necessarily be given via religious education. It can, of course, be given as part of religious instruction but it follows from what I have said that unless that is done, fully admitting that man's moral knowledge must ultimately be founded elsewhere in reason, then it is fundamentally misconceived and is a highly dangerous form of miseducation.

Of course a Christian will wish a child's moral education to be given its Christian setting. He will wish to complement what is achieved on a rational basis with instruction in specifically Christian moral principles to teach the religious significance of moral matters and to encourage a Christian style of life. What arises here is whether or not this Christian complement to moral education on a rational basis is the function of the maintained school in our society.

Here I want to argue that this is not an appropriate function for the maintained school but before I can reach that point I must say something about the place of religious education in general.

III

The fundamental philosophical question that arises for religious education in maintained schools is surely whether or not there is in religion a form of publicly accepted knowledge or belief that it is appropriate for these schools in our society to hand on.

In the forms of knowledge which are indisputably accepted in school there is no doubt whatever about the validity of the vast amount of what is taught. What is more there are accepted grounds and criteria in terms of which that validity can be defended. Further we teach as best we can not only the truths and values, but their rational basis. In principle all these school subjects are treated openly so that no questions about the truths are ruled out. What knowledge we teach, we teach because it comes up to publicly accepted rational tests, convinced that all those prepared to investigate the matter to the appropirate extent will agree on the results.

Now religious believers make claims to truth and knowledge. If these claims can be substantiated, then religious knowledge ought not to be denied its place in the school; and if worship is an essential part of such understanding, it too might rightly claim its place. But as a matter of fact not only do people differ radically in their religious beliefs, they differ radically about the basis of them, as to how we are to begin to distinguish between religious truth and religious error.

Such radical difference on what the basis of religious claims is, may or may not be inevitable. Whether or not there is a domain of knowledge and in what sense, needs the most careful investigation. All one can do is look at the attempts there have been and are being made to substantiate these claims to see if they can in fact do the job. In so far as they can, religious knowledge surely must figure in our public education and the possibilities here will be looked at briefly later.

If in fact, as seems to be the case at present, there are no agreed public tests whereby true and false can be distinguished in religious claims, then we can hardly maintain that we have a domain of religious knowledge and truth. All that we can claim there is, is a domain of beliefs and the acceptance of any one set of these must be recognised as a matter of personal decision. If that is the case, as indeed many Christians would hold, what right has the state by legislation, and officially constituted bodies that draw up syllabuses, to lay down the beliefs in which children shall be educated? It is frequently assumed that such a decision by state machinery is perfectly in order provided the process is democratic. But what needs to be asked is whether the state should be involved in the making of any positive decisions in this matter at all. Where no issue of the general public good of the society is at stake is there any ground for the state taking to itself the function of educating children in one religious faith? Is that not a matter in which the freedom of parents and purely voluntary bodies should be fully respected? Ought not the state to refrain most carefully from joining any particular religious cause and rather do all in its power to maintain the fullest freedom for religious education? I personally cannot see why we allow the decision as to which beliefs are to be taught to be taken by public bodies, for it would seem to me to be outside their legitimate province. And from this it would seem to follow that we ought not to permit state institutions to be involved in specific and restricted religious education. It is at least puzzling that the Christian church so readily accepts the principle that the state has a right to make the decisions in this area. Would the church be prepared to accept so readily a democratic decision on this matter if it went against its interests? Would it readily accept the right of the state to decide that all children shall be instructed in Mormonism, Buddhism or atheism? Would it not then wish to contest the very right of the state to make such a decision? If so, then the present position is one in which the church is guilty of opportunism and expediency, not one for which there is real justification. In matters where no public moral issues are at stake the limit of any public concern would seem to me to be preserving genuine religious freedom in every way and therefore in education. This is not to say that in maintained schools there ought not to be factual instruction about the beliefs that have played and do play so large a part in our history, literature and way of life. It is rather that positive instruction in the beliefs and practices of any one religion should be strictly the function of other agencies, the family, the churches and interested voluntary associations.

If, therefore, there is no public rational basis for religious claims, then I see no immediate justification for maintained schools having anything beyond instruction about these beliefs. In this case it would seem appropriate for these schools to be secular, genuinely uncommitted religiously. From this it does not follow that there should not be independent religious schools too for those who might desire them. What I am objecting to is a national system of state maintained schools that is committed to instruction let alone worship in any one particular form of beliefs even when democratically approved. There is, of course, the possibility of having a range of maintained schools giving different forms of religious education and training. It is difficult to see how such a general policy could now be put into practice in England, and to many it would, in any case, be most undesirably socially divisive. It remains however, a consistent possibility though the practical difficulties it would involve cannot be gone into here.[1]

To the position that is being advocated it is sometimes objected that if we do not instruct children in religious beliefs we implicitly declare that they are unimportant. Indeed there is felt to be a danger that what are to many the most ultimately important questions in life might never be discussed in school. But adequate instruction about religious beliefs must surely include treatment of their significance for human life and in our society it is surely imperative that the part played by Christian beliefs in determining our way of life must be taught. This is not, however, to educate children as Christians. The intentions behind these two approaches are quite distinguishable and must not be confused. Further, it is mistaken to suggest that because a school does not instruct its pupils in one particular religion it necessarily suggests that these beliefs are unimportant. What it can quite clearly do is openly declare its recognition of the limits appropriate to its function as a publicly maintained institution. Such limitations are granted where party political beliefs are concerned and surely no one would accuse our educational system of being committed to a suggestion that these beliefs are unimportant.

Against the removal of religious worship the prime objection seems to be that we should then fail to introduce children to a basic experience which they must have if they are to know what religion is about. But is worship a basic experience which beliefs make intelligible? Surely we must distinguish between on the one hand those natural experiences of the ultimate mystery of the existence of things and their contingency and on the other the experience of worship as an intentional act in church or school assembly. The former experiences may well be basic to any understanding of what religion is about. The latter, however, are experiences of a kind that are meaningful only on the basis of commitment to some specific religious beliefs. In this sense one can no more simply worship than one can simply think. One must necessarily worship something or somebody just as one must necessarily think about something. If this is so there is no experience of mere worship, but only the experience of worshipping some particular object or being. For if the activity is to be meaningful at all, it presupposes the acceptance of some beliefs, including the belief that there is point in praising and thanking and asking. But in that case it is quite impossible for a child, no matter how young, to worship unless he already accepts some religious beliefs however vague. Seriously to take part in religious worship is therefore necessarily to be trained in an activity that is part of some quite specific religious way of life that assumes quite specific beliefs. I see no escape from recognising that in so far as school worship is genuinely meaningful it is this kind of training that it gives. If from what has been said earlier it is inappropriate for maintained schools to educate their pupils in one set of beliefs, it must follow that it is equally inappropriate for them to conduct worship in terms of those beliefs. This is not to say that the school should totally ignore the basic experiences earlier distinguished from worship. But it is to say that it should refrain from any activities, like worship, which presuppose commitment to some interpretation of these.

To argue in this way shows that if maintained schools are to be restricted in the range of knowledge and beliefs they instruct in, they must also be restricted in the range of training in the practical conduct of life that they undertake. For worship is not the only form of activity that is dependent for its significance and justification on particular religious beliefs. Earlier in this article attention was drawn to the fact that most religions—certainly Christianity—include some specifically religiously based moral principles. Equally they usually advocate certain particular styles or ways of life. If this is so, then the moral conduct of life in its more detailed positive aspects must depend on a person's beliefs. And if the school is not to teach any such sort of beliefs it seems to me there are strict limits to the practical moral training it can give.

I suggest, therefore, that the most satisfactory position for the maintained school is for the religious education it gives to be confined to instruction about beliefs and for the moral education it gives to be confined both in instruction and training to the common pool of natural moral principles that all share. Beyond these limits we ought to recognise the freedom of the individual and of parents in matters of personal religious beliefs and those principles and practices of a way of life that especially depend on these. The only consistent alternative is, I think, the thorough-going pluralist system mentioned earlier in which maintained schools offering education according to different religious principles are readily available to all children.

IV

In all that has been argued so far about religious education it has been assumed that we can only speak of a domain of religious beliefs and not of a domain of publicly justifiable religious knowledge. At the moment no such domain of agreed knowledge exists and there are no agreed principles of justification. Maybe, by the nature of the case, such justification is impossible. That, however, has not been demonstrated as yet—indeed there are at least some signs of hope for the claim of knowledge in recent work in the philosophy of religion.

It is true that there is now almost universal agreement that the traditional 'proofs' of the existence of God must be rejected.[2] Few are likely to argue today that God's existence can be logically demonstrated in a formal argument from the meaning of the term 'God' or from the characteristics of the finite world. But a number of important attempts have been made at establishing the truth of religious claims in ways immune from the attacks on the 'proofs'. In much Protestant thought a basis for religious knowledge has been sought in personal spiritual insight, in intuition, in private self-justifying encounters with God, or in some commitment or decision.[3] If I have an experience of encounter how am I to know it is an experience of God and not an hallucination? If the core of the matter is simply commitment or decision, what is there in commitment that guarantees the truth of the beliefs? Private beliefs which lack rational justification may be true, but we cannot know that they are true without there being some public justification. And lacking that, we cannot lay claim to a domain of knowledge.

The height of sophistication along these lines is reached in the Barthian claim that God, being 'wholly other', is so beyond our concepts and reason that religious truths can only be known in a revelation which is under no obligation to justify itself to man. Religious reason is beyond reason and 'the very attempt to know God by thought is impiety'.[4] In spite of the plausibility of this language to many religious believers, to reject reason in this radical way is to make religious claims a mixture of the incomprehensible and the purely dogmatic. What is more the thesis presupposes not only the existence of God but also certain quite specific beliefs about His nature and man's relationship to Him. Such assumptions at the outset of the pursuit and investigation of religious knowledge are quite unjustifiable. Indeed, the logically absurd call to reject reason in the name of reason is but an invitation to plunge into a morass of irrationality where again truth cannot possibly be distinguished from error.

In recent philosophy of religion there are, however, two attempts to deal with the meaning and justification of religious statements which seem to offer serious hope of much greater understanding of the nature of the claims. On the one hand a number of neo-Thomists have sought to re-express the traditional metaphysical account of St Thomas in a way that can stand up to contemporary philosophical criticism. In this they have had considerable success. Maritain, Gilson, and others have argued that the proofs of God's existence are to be seen not as tight formal demonstrations but as expressions of a basic intuition or apprehension of the existence of things. This awareness is such that, once it is recognised what it is for finite things to exist, the necessary existence of their ground or source is recognised as well.[5] Mascall writes of the proofs as 'different methods of manifesting the radical dependence of finite being upon God'.[6] Farrer speaks of God being 'apprehended in the cosmological relation'.[7] Closely connected with these careful reinterpretations of the 'proofs' is a renewed emphasis on the analogical nature of all statements about God. Their meaning and validity are therefore to be approached according to the canons appropriate to this particular form of discourse, not those appropriate to the original natural context of the terms used. It is along these lines that Farrer, for instance, has attempted to establish once more a rational theology in which natural analogues afford a basic knowledge of God on which the claim to revealed knowledge can rest.[8]

At the same time a number of philosophers less happy about the traditional categories have sought to characterise afresh the meaning and truth of religious propositions. To them religious statements are attempts to talk intelligibly about certain aspects of man's natural experience, his experience in everyday contexts not simply that in such specifically religious contexts as say church worship. The view is that religious discourse picks out man's awareness that the universe is not self-explanatory, that human experience and knowledge are set in ultimate mystery and that this awareness breaks in on man in a great variety of circumstances. Some such experiences we have come to call numinous, others we regard as more mystical in character.

Religious language is then regarded not as telling us facts about the inner nature of the mystery, but as attempts in parabolic or meta-physical language to relate and make intelligible these experiences. The only language we have is language whose meaning is closely tied to our experience of the finite world. When it comes to understanding this area of mystery and to answering limiting questions about our experience of it, then our language becomes figurative. Most developed religions for instance have come to speak of experiences of mystery as experiences of a 'person' but this is simply an analogy or picture by which to characterise the experiences.

When it comes to tests for the truth of religious statements, the point must be the adequacy of the pictures in making sense of the range and circumstances of the experiences. The tests must therefore necessarily be more on the lines of those appropriate for the 'truth' of literary works rather than those for say scientific theories. Professor Ninian Smart in particular has endeavoured to set out some of these tests in recent writings but the details cannot be gone into further here.[9]

There are, of course, many points of agreement between neo-Thomists and this second group of philosophers and theologians. How far these can be made to extend is not at the moment clear. Along one or both of these lines, however, it does not seem at all impossible that an agreed rational basis for at least some religious claims might be found. In so far as a domain of religious knowledge can be established, the frontiers of the content of education appro-priate to maintained schools must, it seems to me, be moved, so as to include it. The subject would then take its place alongside others in the schools. It would be taught necessarily as a mode of our under-standing of human experience—the pupils' own and others—and the validated knowledge would be set in a context in which the principles and tests on which it rests would be taught as well. The nearest parallel in method of approach might well be that in the teaching of literature.

But perhaps this is just crystal gazing. In the present state of affairs, whatever other considerations might imply, philosophical con-siderations would seem to suggest that the 1944 legislation on religious education is unjustifiable and that thoroughly open instruction about religious beliefs is all that we ought to have. Maybe, however, we live at a time when we can hope for much greater understanding of the nature of morals and religion and their relationship to each other. Certainly in the interests of enlightened educational practice we can-not afford to ignore highly significant developments which at pre-sent are taking place in the study of these domains. For clearly these developments could transform not only our ideas as to what education maintained schools ought to provide but also our ideas on how best to set about those difficult tasks of moral and religious education that do properly fall within their purview.

Additional note

The perspective on religious education which this chapter expresses now seems to me unsatisfactory in two particular respects. First, certain paragraphs can be taken to imply that we have a domain of religious beliefs that may well be autonomous or logically unique in character but for which we have no unique truth criteria. This view I now consider untenable for reasons outlined in chapter 6 in this volume, 'The forms of knowledge re-visited'. If meaningfulness necessitates truth criteria, then religious beliefs can only have that kind of meaning for which we have truth criteria, even if we cannot state what they are. At present, we are, I think, uncertain not only about the truth of religious claims, but about the kind of meaning they have. It is thus an open-endedness about the character of their meaning as much as about their truth that religious education needs to reflect. At its heart religious education is concerned with different claims to both kinds of meaning and truth. It is not concerned simply with one kind of meaning but many conflicting beliefs of that kind amongst which we are unable to say objectively which are true.

This highlights the second unsatisfactory feature. To speak of teaching 'about' religion is open to many different interpretations. In one sense that phrase expresses very well what one wants, for it manifestly excludes all teaching aimed at pupils' coming to hold any particular religious beliefs. Understanding not belief, is what is sought. But 'teaching about religion' is taken by some to mean a study of religion that is always one remove from actually getting to grips with the truth claims religions make. To them it is a matter of studying the psychology, the sociology or history of religion. Whilst there is much that can be said for such studies, and elements of these will no doubt figure in any satisfactory school syllabus, pupils can only understand any religious position if they begin to grasp its concepts and therefore its truth criteria. Indeed any satisfactory study of the psychology or history of religion presuppposes this understanding. But such understanding does not imply belief in or acceptance of, what is understood. My view then is that maintained schools should teach 'about' religion, provided that is interpreted to include a direct study of religions, which means entering as fully as possible into an understanding of what they claim to be true. This will demand a great deal of imaginative involvement in expressions of religious life and even a form of engagement in these activities themselves.

This must not, however, be confused with asking pupils to engage directly in any religious activities for the sake of these activities themselves. To my mind pupils should never be asked to worship, as this is to engage in an activity that presupposes specific commitment. The school should therefore never worship as a community. How far in practice pupils should attend and take part in occasions of worship so as to come to understand what it means to worship, is a difficult matter to which there might be no single answer. What matters is surely that pupils fully recognise that they are not being asked to do anything that either assumes, or is intended to produce, the acceptance of any particular set of beliefs. What pupils are asked to do is not simply a matter of their observable behaviour; so the question is not simply one of the occasions they shall or shall not attend, or what they shall observably do on such occasions. It is as much a matter of how they understand the situation and the point of what they do. That point is always that they shall understand, never that they shall or shall not personally accept the religious beliefs under consideration.

Other issues raised in this chapter have been the subject of published comments and replies. See particularly:

D.Z. Phillips, 'Philosophy and religious education', *British Journal of Educational Studies*, vol. XVIII, no. 1, 1970.
P.H. Hirst, 'Philosophy and religious education: a reply to D.Z. Phillips', *British Journal of Educational Studies*, vol. XVIII, no. 2, 1970.
R. Shone, 'Religion: a form of knowledge?', *Learning for Living*, vol. 12, no. 4, 1973.
P.H. Hirst, 'Religion: a form of knowledge?' A reply', *Learning for Living*, vol. 12, no. 4, 1973.

Notes

1 See A.C.F. Beales, 'The future of voluntary schools' in A.V. Judges (ed.), *Looking Forward in Education*, Faber, 1955. M. Cruickshank, *Church and State in English Education*, Macmillan, 1963.
2 For a discussion of the ontological and cosmological arguments see for instance: Ninian Smart (ed.), *Historical Selections in the Philosophy of Religion*, SCM, 1962; *Philosophers and Religious Truth*, SCM, 1964, chapter IV; E.L. Mascall, *Existence and Analogy*, Longmans, 1949, chapters II and IV.
3 See R.W. Hepburn, *Christianity and Paradox*, Watts, 1958; F. Ferre, *Language, Logic and God*, Eyre & Spottiswoode, 1962; A.C. MacIntyre, 'The logical status of religious belief' in A.C. MacIntyre (ed.), *Metaphysical Beliefs*, SCM, 1957.
4 See B. Blanshard, 'Critical reflections on Karl Barth', in J. Hick (ed.), *Faith and the Philosophers*, Macmillan, 1964. Especially pp. 162–80.

5 See J. Maritain, *The Range of Reason*, Bles, 1953, chapter 7; E. Gilson, *The Christian Philosophy of St Thomas Aquinas*, Gollancz, 1961, Part I.
6 See Mascall, op. cit., p. 71.
7 See A.M. Farrer, *Finite and Infinite*, Dacre Press, 1943, p. 45.
8 Ibid.
9 See Ninian Smart, *Philosophers and Religious Truth; Reasons and Faiths*, Routledge & Kegan Paul, 1958; H.D. Lewis, *Our Experience of God*, Allen & Unwin, 1959.

Index

Peters, R. S., 29, 68, 84, 100, 114,
115, 164
Peterson, A. D. C., 29, 38
Phenix, Philip, 54–63, 66–8, 82, 83
Phillips, D. C., 99
Phillips, D. Z., 188
philosophy
definition of, 1–2
of objectives, 3–9, 11–12, 66–9
of religion, 184–6, 188
Plato, 54, 92
Popper, Karl, 10
problem-solving, 20, 129
progressivism, in education, 6,
111–12
psychology, and teaching, 116–19,
121, 127–8
psycho-motor objectives, 18

rationality, development of, 22,
24–5
reason
concept of, 93, 95
development of, 64
and morals, 169
Reid, L. A., 164
religion
concept of, 87–9, 188
and education, 173, 180–8
and knowledge, 180–1
and language, 185–6
and morals, 173–9, 183–4
philosophy of, 184–6, 188
right, concept of, 174–6, 179
Ryle, G., 75, 80, 83

Scheffler, I., 114
school
concept of, 9
maintained, religion in, 180–4,
187–8
voluntary, 182
see also education
science
and knowledge, 170–1
moral content of, 165–71
teaching, 121, 130
and truth, 167–8, 178

Shone, R., 188
Smart, Ninian, 186, 189
Snow, Lord, 165, 167–8, 172
social science, concept of, 86
socialization, and teaching, 9
specialization, 29
state, and religion, in education, 181
see also school, maintained
Stenhouse, L., 15
subject, school
learning of, 109–10
traditional, 135–7, 141–6
see also disciplines
'subject-mindedness', 29
subject-structured curriculum, 133–
146
symbolics, 54, 56, 61–2, 66
symbolism, 28
symbols, in thought, 71–83
synnoetics, 54, 56, 61–2, 66
synoptics, 54, 56, 66

Taylor, P. H., 15
teaching
and conditioning, 113
and curriculum, 9
as enterprise, 102–4
group, 111
of history, 116–18, 123, 130
and indoctrination, 112–13
intentions of, 104–6
and learning, 105–9, 115
levels, 110–11
logical aspects of, 116, 119–30
machines, 113–14
meaning of, 106, 108, 111, 114–15
methods, 3, 5–7
practical, 6–7
of problem-solving, 129
progressive, 6, 111–12
psychological aspects of, 116–19,
121, 127–8
specific, 102–3, 104–10
and subject, 109–10
traditional, 5–6, 111, 122, 135–7,
141–6
Thomas, St, 185, 189